A TRADING DESK'S VIEW OF MARKET QUALITY

A TRADING DESK'S VIEW OF MARKET QUALITY

edited by

Robert A. Schwartz
Zicklin School of Business, Baruch College, CUNY

John Aidan Byrne

Antoinette Colaninno
Zicklin School of Business, Baruch College, CUNY

KLUWER ACADEMIC PUBLISHERS

Robert A. Schwartz
Zicklin School of Business
Baruch College, CUNY
17 Lexington Avenue
New York NY 10010
robert_chwartz@baruch.cuny.edu

John Aidan Byrne

Antoinette Colaninno
Zicklin School of Business
Baruch College, CUNY
17 Lexington Avenue
New York, NY 10010
antoinette_colaninno@Baruch.cuny.edu

Library of Congress Cataloging-in-Publication Data

A C.I.P. Catalogue record for this book is available
from the Library of Congress.

Schwartz, Robert A.
A trading desk view of market quality
Includes index.

ISBN 1-4020-7510-3 e-ISBN 0-387-23114-5 Printed on acid-free paper.

Printed in the United States of America.

9 8 7 6 5 4 3 2 1 SPIN 11043805

springeronline.com

In memory of my father, Fred J. Schwartz.

Contents

List of Participants

Theodore Aronson	Managing Principal	Aronson+Johnson+Ortiz
Paul Bennett	Senior Vice President and Chief Economist	New York Stock Exchange
George Bodine	Director of Trading	General Motors Investment Management Corporation
Andrew Brooks	Vice President and Head of Equity Trading	T. Rowe Price Associates
Thomas Cardello	Managing Director	Morgan Stanley
Minder Cheng	Global Head of Equity and Currency Trading	Barclays Global Investors
Michael Cormack	President	Archipelago Holdings LLC
Viktoria Dalko	President	RICE Institute
Paul Davis	Senior Managing Director	TIAA-CREF Investment Management LLC
Thomas Doyle	Institutional Sales/Trader	Nutmeg Securities
Fred Federspiel*	Chief Executive Officer	Pipeline Trading Systems

*At the time of the conference, Mr. Federspiel was Chief Executive Officer of e-Xchange Advantage Corporation.

Luca Filippa	Director of Research and Development	Borsa Italiana
William Freund	Director, William C. Freund Center for the Study of Equity Markets	Lubin School of Business, Pace University

Marc Gresack*	Chief Executive Officer	Glen Eagle Securities

*At the time of the conference, Mr. Gresack was a strategic consultant at Brut LLC.

Sanjiv Gupta	Director of Research and Strategy	Bloomberg Tradebook LLC
Nari Jote	Management Consultant and Global Business Coordinator	Jote & Associates
Christopher Killeen	Senior Trader	TIAA-CREF Investment Management
David Krell	President and Chief Executive Officer	International Securities Exchange
Ananth Madhavan*	Global Head of Trading Research	Barclays Global Investors

* At the time of the conference, Ananth Madhavan was Managing Director of Research at ITG, Inc.

Mark Madoff	Director of Listed Trading	Bernard L. Madoff Investment Securities
John Malitzis*	Senior Vice President and Associate General Counsel	Citigroup Global Markets

*At the time of the conference, Mr. Malitzis was Vice President in the Transaction Services Department at the Nasdaq Stock Market.

Seth Merrin	Chief Executive Officer	Liquidnet
Russell Monahan	Director of Strategic Research	American Stock Exchange
Anthony Neuberger	Associate Dean, Full-time Masters in Finance Programme	London Business School
Deniz Ozenbas	Assistant Professor of Finance	Montclair State University
Brett Redfearn	Senior Vice President	American Stock Exchange
Richard Repetto*	Associate Director	Sandler O'Neill & Partners, LP

*At the time of the conference, Mr. Repetto was a Managing Director at Putnam Lovell.

Michael Richter	Chief Executive Officer	Lime Brokerage LLC
Sharon Salamon*	Director of Institutional Equities for Product	Thomson Financial

	Management	

*At the time of the conference, Ms. Salamon was the Senior Sales and Marketing Executive at NeoNet Securities.

Richard Schenkman*	Managing Partner	Elm Tree Group LLC

*At the time of the conference, Mr. Schenkman was Chief Executive Officer of Brut LLC.

Robert Schwartz	Speiser Professor of Finance	Zicklin School of Business, Baruch College, CUNY
Barry Small	Chief Executive Officer	Weeden & Company
George Sofianos	Vice President	Goldman Sachs, Inc.
Holly Stark	Principal and Director of Trading	Kern Capital Management
Joel Steinmetz*		

*At the time of the conference, Mr. Steinmetz was Senior Vice President for Equities, Instinet Corporation.

Natan Tiefenbrun	Senior Vice President	Instinet Corporation
Bruce Turner	Managing Director and Head of U.S. Equity Trading	CIBC
Laura Unger*	Independent Director and Consultant	

*Ms. Unger is a former Commissioner of the U.S. Securities & Exchange Commission.

Wayne Wagner	Chairman	Plexus Group
Avner Wolf	Chairman, Department of Economics and Finance	Zicklin School of Business, Baruch College, CUNY
Robert Wood	Distinguished Professor of Finance	The University of Memphis
Steven Wunsch	Partner	Exchange Lab

Conference Sponsors

The American Stock Exchange
Archipelago, Inc.
Brut, LLC
Instinet Corporation
International Securities Exchange
Liquidnet, Inc.
Bernard L. Madoff Investment Securities
The Nasdaq Stock Market, Inc.
New York Stock Exchange
Plexus Group
Security Traders Association
Weeden & Company

Preface

This book is based on A *Trading Desk's View of Market Quality*, a conference hosted by the Zicklin School of Business on April 30, 2002. The text includes the edited transcripts of each panel as well as separate presentations by two distinguished industry officials, Joel Steinmetz, who at the time was Senior Vice President, Equities, Instinet Corporation, and Laura Unger, formerly Acting Chairperson and Commissioner of the U.S. Securities and Exchange Commission.

This book is not simply a historical record of the conference. It is also an exposition of the complex issues raised by the industry experts and speakers in attendance. Therefore, we introduced new material from follow-up interviews with many of the panelists so that the final result would be a more valuable document. Our intention was to examine the discussions with a critical eye, then modify or expand various sections to reflect contemporary conditions. In addition, we have included a paper by Ozenbas, Schwartz and Wood (see Chapter 8, page 151) that provides further analysis on the connection between market quality and intra-day volatility that was noted several times during the conference.[1]

During the production process, we worked with the panelists, and took pains not to put words in their mouths. They have all approved the final draft of the manuscript, and we thank them for their assistance and patience. We also express our heartfelt thanks to the sponsors who made this

[1] Chapter 8 was reprinted, with permission, from D. Ozenbas, R. Schwartz, and R. Wood, "Volatility in U.S. and European Equity Markets: An Assessment of Market Quality," International Finance, Blackwell Publishers, Volume 5 Number 3, Winter 2002, pp. 437-461.

conference possible (see page xiii). Their funding and, more importantly, endorsement of our mission, are deeply appreciated. In addition, a number of people have been helpful in preparing this manuscript. In particular, we thank Dror Parnes and Faisal Aslam for their help, and Avner Wolf, chairman of Baruch's Economics and Finance Department, for his constant support and encouragement.

The Baruch conference focused on market quality, right from the firing line, at the desks where trades are made and the costs of trading are incurred. After we turned to 'market quality' for the focus of the conference, a surprising number of people asked, 'What is market quality?' as if we had coined a new term. This was surprising, in part because 'market quality' is the name of a major Nasdaq committee. That is where we got the term. It is an excellent term, but what does it mean?

'Market quality' is a broad concept. How efficient are our markets? How tight, or narrow, are spreads? Is liquidity deep? How low are trading costs? Is there connectivity between liquidity pools? How accurate is price discovery? These are only some of the important questions. Another thought that I have been focusing on – and I hear that others are focusing on – is quantity discovery: getting orders out of traders' pockets, onto the table, and making the trades.

'Market quality' also relates to the magnitude of price volatility that we see in the course of a trading day. I have said at some of our previous conferences that I think too much attention is paid to the size of bid-ask spreads, and that not enough attention is paid to the level of intra-day price volatility. I would like to suggest that the accentuation of intra-day volatility is a comprehensive, inverse indication of market quality. Whether the term has been used widely or not, we have been debating issues about market quality since at least the 1975 Securities Act amendments. What is the objective of the debate? What are we trying to accomplish? We have talked about tight spreads, acceptable transparency, consolidation, connectivity and competition. Market quality encompasses all of these issues and more. At the heart of these discussions are questions about market structure and the ability of participants to obtain best execution. Best execution has typically been viewed as a responsibility placed on individual traders who handle orders in an agency capacity. Market centers share a best execution obligation. If we want participants as a group to get better executions, we must offer them better market structure.

Our hope with the conference and this volume is to shed new light on some old issues. The issues do not change, but the light that we see them in does. Perhaps a fresh perspective will help us to obtain more answers and, ultimately, to achieve a more efficient market structure.

Robert A. Schwartz

CHAPTER 1: RECENT EVIDENCE ON MARKET QUALITY

Moderator – Paul Bennett, *Senior Vice President and Chief Economist, New York Stock Exchange*
Anthony Neuberger, *Associate Dean, Full-time Masters in Finance Programme, London Business School*
Deniz Ozenbas, *Assistant Professor of Finance, Montclair State University*
Robert Schwartz, *Speiser Professor of Finance, Zicklin School of Business, Baruch College, CUNY*
Robert Wood, *Distinguished Professor of Finance, The University of Memphis*

PAUL BENNETT: Like many of you, I have been wrestling with the concept of market quality. It is a complicated and difficult topic. Even if you narrow the perspective to just the trader's viewpoint, it is hard to assess market quality. Part of the difficulty is that various markets offer different qualities. Some trading systems offer blinding speed. Others offer traders the ability to negotiate anonymously. Some offer face-to-face trading. For different types of transactions and strategies, each of these features can be an important characteristic.

You have to figure out what you want. My daughters used to love a kind of toothpaste that tastes like bubble gum. That is quality for them. Now I am trying to figure out whether or not to get the kind that makes your teeth really white - does it have sand in it? The bottom line is, quality is in the eye of the beholder. You have to figure out what your objective is.

If you do settle on a quality measure, you must make sure that you are truly measuring what you think you are measuring. I have cooked up a little example of this. Suppose you have two markets, A and B. Market A offers speed, and basically what you see in the quotes is what you get. Market B is a little more complicated; it has some reserve orders. With reserve orders allowed for, you do not know what orders might be in the market but not displayed. If you hit market A with a relatively large order, or if somebody else gets there first, you will walk up the book. In market B, you might get more of your order filled at a better price than you expected. So, what do people do?

Some will avoid market A, especially those participants with large orders. Consequently, posted spreads, a common measure of market quality, might be small on market A, but market A may not offer much depth. On market B, on the other hand, posted spreads may be wider, but market B may offer more depth and liquidity. This is an identification problem. You are not really looking at the difference in market quality; you are looking at the difference in the types of orders that each market attracts. This is part of why it is so hard to assess market quality.

The Securities and Exchange Commission has weighed in on this topic. The Commission is having various dealers and stock exchanges publish something called, in Washingtonese, 11Ac1-5.[2] This is a huge data set that I am sure a lot of people will try to do research on. It measures things like effective spreads, and price improvement in different market centers. It is an excellent initiative that the New York Stock Exchange has always been very supportive of. With it, we should be able to compare market quality.

Most of us can tell if our own market is getting better. But this does not mean that we are able to contrast one market with another. The problem I see with any comparison is making sure that it is an apples-to-apples contrast. For example, in the research department of the New York Stock Exchange, we compute data on behalf of all the specialist firms. It is a big job. There are a lot of uncertainties. You want to make sure that you are doing it right. Sometimes we hire an outside data processor to do the numbers. They always come up with different results, and sometimes the difference is sizable.

So, when I look at the various market websites that are out there, I wonder if the markets are really comparable. That is something the SEC is going to have to reconcile. All of those market quality measures should be audited, or something should be done, to make sure that they really are comparable. The moral is that, even under the best of circumstances, effectively assessing market quality requires a lot of sustained effort, and some critical thinking.

With that, let me turn the floor over to Anthony Neuberger who is going to discuss his new study.

2 The Securities and Exchange Commission Final Rule: Disclosure of Order Execution and Routing Practices, 17 C.F.R. pt. 240, Release No. 34-43590; File No. S7-16-00. Under Rule 11Ac1-5, market centers that trade national market system securities will be required to make available to the public monthly electronic reports that include uniform statistical measures of execution quality.

ANTHONY NEUBERGER: I want to talk about the precursors to market quality, the economic forces that drive market quality. The quality of a market is driven to a large extent by the economic pressures on traders to minimize transaction costs. To understand market quality, we need to understand the incentives and structures that encourage the trading desk to minimize costs. Are these effective, or are they defective in some way?

The incentives on fund managers have been fiercely debated in the U.K. following the publication of the Myners Report.[3] But this is not a specifically British preoccupation, and the debate in the U.K. may usefully illuminate some issues here in the U.S. Indeed, this would not be the first time that discussion on one side of the Atlantic illumined debate on the other side.

First, some background on the U.K. debate. In 2000 the U.K. Government launched an inquiry to investigate the factors impeding financial institutions from investing more heavily in venture capital. It was essentially a one-man inquiry carried out by Paul Myners, with some support from civil servants. Paul Myners is the chairman of one of the major U.K. fund management firms. He was asked in particular whether the U.K. could learn from the much more successful U.S. experience.

The report was wide-ranging, and many of its conclusions were generally accepted. But Myners came up with one recommendation that caused great controversy. That recommendation was unexpected, given the terms of reference of the study. He said that the traditional fund management contract did not give managers adequate incentives to control and minimize transaction costs. He recommended that broking commissions and other charges should be borne not by the plan sponsor, as is standard practice in the U.K. and elsewhere, but by the fund manager.

This recommendation sparked a huge controversy. The Government, while accepting the report in full on publication, put it out for consultation. The fund management industry commissioned a study by myself and my colleague Professor Dick Brealey,[4] on the impact of the Myners recommendation.

3 In 2000 Gordon Brown, the Chancellor of the Exchequer of the United Kingdom, asked Paul Myners, Chairman of Gartmore Investment Management, to investigate possible distortions in institutional investment decision-making. Mr. Myners published his report titled "Myners Review of Institutional Investment: Final Report," on March 6, 2001 (www.hmtreasury.gov.uk/mediastore/otherfiles/31.pdf).

4 See Richard A. Brealey and Anthony Neuberger, "The Treatment of Investment Management Fees and Commission Payments: An Examination of the Recommendations Contained in the Myners Report," available at http://www.investmentfunds.org.uk/investmentuk/about_ima/reports/brealey.pdf.

In the face of industry opposition, the Government did retreat somewhat from the Myners proposal, and asked the industry to come up with alternative proposals to meet Paul Myners' criticisms. In response, the fund management industry has drawn up a code of conduct on transparency.

I want to draw on the work that Dick Brealey and I did to look at the pressures on fund managers to manage transaction costs in the best interests of their client. I will start by showing evidence on the size of transaction costs in the U.K. before examining the way that fund managers are rewarded for managing funds.

In our study, we surveyed fund managers about the way they manage funds, the costs and other areas. Figures vary hugely from fund manager to fund manager. To give some idea of what is typical, I will quote median numbers (see Exhibit 1).

Assume a £200m actively managed UK equity portfolio, turnover 40%

Annual costs (bp/yr)

Management fee	30
Brokerage	12
Execution (impact)	62
Tax (stamp, VAT)	25
TOTAL	**129**

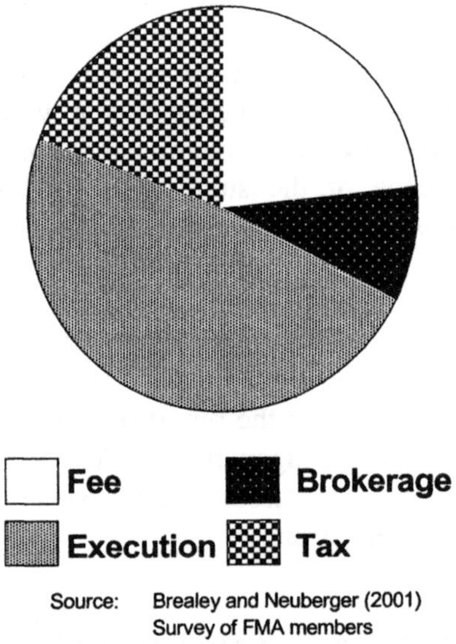

Exhibit 1. How Large Are the Costs?

We focused our survey on U.K. actively managed equity portfolios so that we could standardize across fund managers. The median fund size is $300m. The median level of total transaction costs is 1.3% per year (130 basis points). Of this, the broking commissions that had so exercised Myners amount to 12 basis points (about 10% of the total). Management fees are 30 basis points. The government itself accounts for a further 25 basis points, largely in the form of stamp duty, which is a tax on turnover.

The remainder, half the total cost, is market impact cost. The figures on market impact come from a survey by the consultants Plexus Group. I am going to talk some more about the measurement of market impact costs at the end of this presentation but, for the moment, I want to note that direct costs are only one component of total transaction costs. I want to emphasize that measures to cut explicit costs will not be useful if they are offset by an increase in implicit costs.

- fee levels for £200m UK actively managed portfolio ranged between 17 and 50 basis points
- interquartile range of 25-35 basis points
- wide spread also in commission rates and annual cost of commission charges
- possibly reflects differences in service levels

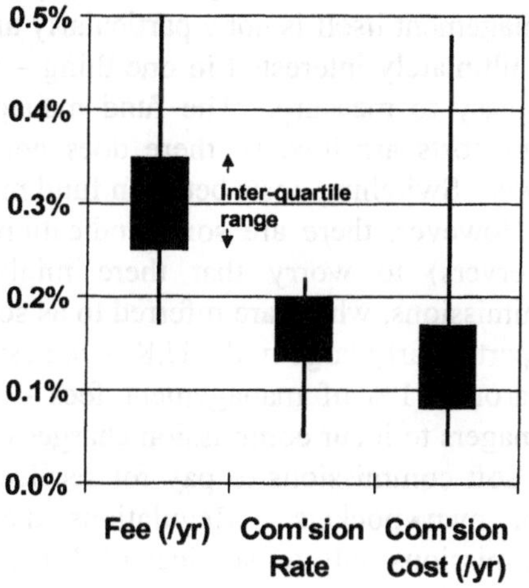

Exhibit 2. There Are Substantial Variations

As I said, these are median figures, and the range across portfolio managers is wide (see Exhibit 2). Management fees in our sample range from 17 basis points to 50 basis points. This is not the result of just one or two outliers. The inter-quartile range is also wide, being 25-35 basis points. Commission rates for active management vary widely too, with the inter-quartile range being 13-20 basis points. I had assumed that competition would lead to them being reasonably standardized, but I presume that this reflects the different levels of service being expected by different managers – it does not reflect the size of funds.

For commission costs per dollar of assets under management per year (rather than per dollar transacted), the inter-quartile range is even wider at 4-17 basis points. This reflects the enormous variations in turnover across managers. We can conclude that transaction costs, both explicit and implicit, are large compared with fund management fees, and they also vary widely across broadly similar funds.

The size of transaction costs and their variation are interesting, but they do not in themselves clearly indicate that there are any problems in the relationship between fund managers and their clients. Indeed, on the face of it, this seems to be an industry where competition would be expected to do a pretty effective job at arriving at an optimal contract. Clients are not private individuals who may be easily misled, but trustees with some degree of sophistication. In many cases they are advised by consultants. Fund management itself is not a particularly arcane or difficult subject. All clients are ultimately interested in one thing – the return on the fund – and returns are easy to measure. The fund management industry is fragmented, and entry costs are low, so there does not seem to be an issue of monopoly power. Switching costs between fund managers are pretty low.

However, there are some indications that have led Myners (and other observers) to worry that there might be real problems. While soft commissions, which are referred to as soft dollars in the U.S., do not seem to be particularly large in the U.K. – we estimate them in our report as equating to around 1% of management fees – they do give an incentive to fund managers to incur commission charges on behalf of the fund, and then to use the soft commissions to pay for services they would otherwise fund out of their own pockets. Regulations that force the manager to use soft commissions only on services of direct benefit to the client do not mitigate this problem. Soft commissions do not appear to be in the best interests of the ultimate clients.

The existence of commission recapture arrangements is another cause for concern. It is hard to see how the practice of paying a commission and then rebating it or channeling it to some other party is consistent with there being an open, transparent market for fund management, brokerage and execution services.

It was also clear to Myners, and my investigations with Dick Brealey confirmed this, that plan sponsors have very little awareness of the level of transaction costs incurred by their funds. The sponsors were very much aware of what they paid in management fees, but not of the costs of commission or the costs of market impact, which were incurred on their behalf. They lack crucial information to judge these costs. Very few sponsors, for example, get any consolidated information about the commission charges which are paid on their trades.

Others have pointed to the large amount of research of questionable quality released by brokers, which does not seem to be greatly valued by their clients, as a sign that there is some form of market failure. Others have noted that low cost transaction systems have failed to get a large market share despite substantial apparent cost advantage (particularly true in Europe, but also to some extent in the U.S.). This suggests, they argue, that the investment managers may not have strong incentives to minimize trading costs.

There are some indications that managers are not transacting as efficiently as they could. What are the defects in the market for fund management services that prevent clients from forcing managers to trade efficiently?

I believe the answer is that it is hard for the client to distinguish a manager who trades efficiently from his less efficient competitor. That may sound implausible. There are a number of consulting firms that analyze transaction costs. They sell their services to both sponsors and fund managers. But the measurement of transaction costs, particularly of market impact costs, is not easy. It is even more difficult to interpret the measures and to decide whether the costs are excessive.

Faced with this problem, the client may well decide just to monitor the number that is of ultimate interest – the net return after all costs. It is easy to measure. The client may well reason that if incentives are in place to encourage the manager to maximize net returns, these same incentives will encourage the manager to trade efficiently.

This argument suggests that we should look at the relationship between the client and the manager to see what incentives it creates. If the incentives are too weak, one could investigate whether alternative structures might lead to better results.

We assume that managers are motivated entirely by their economic self-interest. This is a simplification. Managers are constrained by regulation, and by their own ethical and professional standards, and these doubtless do encourage managers to trade efficiently whatever the formal contractual arrangements. But both sides in the argument on the Myners Report implicitly accepted that it would not be enough to rely on the professionalism and goodwill of the manager. The contract needs to be designed to encourage appropriate behavior.

We can analyze the situation using the classical economic framework of the principal agent problem. The client has engaged the manager to manage the portfolio on his behalf. The client can readily monitor the outputs – net returns – and can also monitor the inputs -- what the fund manager is actually doing. But it is hard for the client to tell whether the manager is exerting maximum effort and using all possible skill.

Let us start by looking at the incentives relating to output. These seem rather weak. The ideal contract would make the manager manage the fund with as much care and effort as if it were his own money. The manager would then be prepared to spend up to $1 in effort, or out of his own pocket, if it could increase the size of the fund by $1. Now, the median fee for active fund management in our survey is 30 basis points. This does give the fund manager some incentive to make the fund grow because the manager receives 30 basis points on any growth in the fund. But the incentive is very weak. It would not be worth spending more than one dollar of one's own money as a fund manager unless it is likely to make the size of the fund grow by at least $300.

But the argument is incomplete. The main economic incentive on the fund manager to work hard is not the fee on the increased size of the portfolio, but the fact that he is liable to be fired if the fund under-performs. To quantify this incentive, we built a simple model. We assumed that managers get sacked if they under-perform their peer group over a period of seven years. They then lose the profit element of future fees on that portfolio, which we estimate at 10 basis points per year. But performance depends only partly on skill. Chance is also a factor. The manager therefore has to decide whether to exert additional effort to improve the expected out-turn, knowing that he may still be unlucky and lose the mandate.

Putting in plausible parameters, we concluded that the threat of losing the mandate does sharpen the incentive to exert effort. It is now worth the manager spending a dollar if the fund value increases by 17 dollars. This is a great improvement on the 1:300 ratio we estimated before, but a long way from the 1:1 ratio that is optimal.

Could changes to the management contract do more to improve incentives? One obvious improvement is to tie fees to performance. This certainly sharpens the incentives, but also shifts risk from the client to the manager. The client is highly capitalized and has a high tolerance for risk. The fund manager has capital that is a small percentage of funds under management and is highly risk averse. It becomes very inefficient to shift much risk to the manager.

An alternative is to base the manager's fee much more heavily on those components of the return that are more directly under the manager's control. For example, you could, as Paul Myners proposes, give the manager a higher fee, but require him to pay all commissions on the grounds that these are more fully under the manager's control. This removes the incentive that currently exists to get research done by the broker rather than in-house. (In a standard contract the costs of broker research are met out of commission, and that is paid out of the fund rather than out of the manager's pocket). But it creates new perverse incentives. If the fund has to trade a large block of stock, then, under a traditional fund management contract, the agent's incentives are to trade in such a way as to minimize the costs to the fund. If it is advantageous to the client to pay a broker commission to work the order over a long period rather than to do it as a single block trade with a market maker, the agent will do so. If the agent has to pay the broker's commission however, the agent will have an incentive to trade in a way that minimizes commission payments.

No contractual form is perfect. All contracts involve trade-offs. We examined the empirical evidence to see whether it provides a guide towards a better contract structure, but it is not possible to draw any strong conclusions. The standard fund management contract – commissions borne by the fund, fee as a proportion of funds under management – is near universal. This makes it difficult to compare the effects of different contractual regimes. It also suggests that the contract is unlikely to be severely sub-optimal. Hedge funds, where managers tend to have much stronger incentives to maximize net returns, spend more on commissions. Our survey provides weak statistical evidence that funds that are managed in-house spend more on commissions.

We concluded that the traditional contractual form provides rather weak incentives to manage transaction costs efficiently, that alternative contract designs could remove some of the undesirable incentive effects of the current system, but that they would do so only by creating new incentive problems. We found little evidence to suggest that one particular contractual form is preferable. Indeed it seems unlikely that there is a single form of contract that is optimal for all funds.

The incentive problem cannot be solved purely by concentrating on the outputs – the net returns. To mitigate the incentive problems, clients need to look at the inputs. In particular, they must monitor the activities and performance of their fund managers. Understanding the managers' policies towards commission payments is an essential part of this task. According to our survey, few plan sponsors receive information from their managers on these payments. We argue that this is unsatisfactory.

The U.K. fund management industry has now developed a code of practice on transparency. Clients will be regularly informed on managers' policies on commissions and other explicit charges, and will be told how much has been paid out of the fund. But monitoring the trading efficiency of a manager goes beyond the measurement and comparison of explicit costs.

As we have seen, implicit costs, notably market impact costs, are generally larger than direct costs, and they are hard to measure. To give some idea of the problem, consider the following. Two well-respected consulting firms put out regular figures on transaction costs in different markets using their own definitions of transaction costs.

Country	Average Commission (bp)	Price – VWAP (bp)	Price – $close_{-1}$ (bp)
Australia	27.6	3.4	38
France	18.7	8.9	60
Germany	17.7	17.8	75
Hong Kong	23.8	4.1	68
Japan	11.7	7.4	66
Netherlands	19.5	3.4	51
Sweden	19.4	11.5	68
Switzerland	18.8	6.9	51
UK	15.5	7.0	78

Source: GSCS Survey 2000, Plexus Q1 2001

Exhibit 3. Execution Costs in Various Countries

As shown by Exhibit 3 above, there is reasonable agreement about commission levels, but the two sets of figures on implicit costs differ enormously both in their absolute level and in their ranking of countries. These differences are due to the way in which they define transaction costs.

But even if there were a general agreement on the appropriate way of defining transaction costs, it is difficult to use it as a measure of the manager's skill. A manager who is following a momentum strategy is bound to experience higher transaction costs than a value trader, whatever the relative trading skill of the two managers.

I conclude that market quality does depend, at least in part, on the pressures on fund managers to trade efficiently. The conventional fund management contract does not give the manager very strong incentives to do this. Changing the contractual relationship between the client and the fund manager will not solve the problem, because you cannot improve the incentives in one area without reducing them in another. Improvements will therefore depend on sponsors understanding transaction costs far better than they currently do.

We are still a long way from getting a form of reporting on transaction costs which sponsors can understand, and which would enable them to compare effectively across managers. This represents a major challenge, which the industry – managers, clients, consultants and academics – needs to address.

BENNETT: Thank you very much Anthony. We have a lot of ground to cover this morning, so I suggest we hold questions until the end. If you want a copy of this report, is it available on the net?

NEUBERGER: It is available on the Internet.[5]

BENNETT: The report is well worth reading. I recommend it to you. Our next set of speakers will be a relay between Bob Schwartz, Deniz Ozenbas, and Bob Wood. They will talk about their study, *Volatility in US and European Equity Markets: An Assessment of Market Quality*.[6]

ROBERT SCHWARTZ: My job this morning is to set the foundation. Deniz Ozenbas will talk about the empirical results on volatility, and Bob Wood will summarize the results of two surveys of people's opinions about market quality. We will suggest that trading costs, which Anthony Neuberger was talking about, and which we all know and care about, have an impact that we can see in the full array of trades that are made and prices that are set.

Our primary window to trading costs and, hence, to market quality, is the volatility of intra-day transaction prices. In a moment, Deniz will present our evidence that intra-day volatility is accentuated. I believe that this finding would not surprise many practitioners. And other academic researchers have also found this to be the case. Nevertheless, it is important to capture the accentuation in the data.

Before turning to the data, I would like to clarify the link between trading costs and accentuated short-period price volatility. I will do so with the aid of some charts. This will be a very simplified, stylized representation. First, let's define some terms (see the legend in Exhibits 4).

[5] See Richard A. Brealey and Anthony Neuberger, "The Treatment of Investment Management Fees and Commission Payments: An Examination of the Recommendations Contained in the Myners Report," available at http://www.investmentfunds.org.uk/investmentuk/about_ima/reports/brealey.pdf.

[6] Reprinted, with permission, from D. Ozenbas, R. Schwartz, and R. Wood, "Volatility in U.S. and European Equity Markets: An Assessment of Market Quality," International Finance, Blackwell Publishers, Volume 5 Number 3, Winter 2002, pp. 437-461.

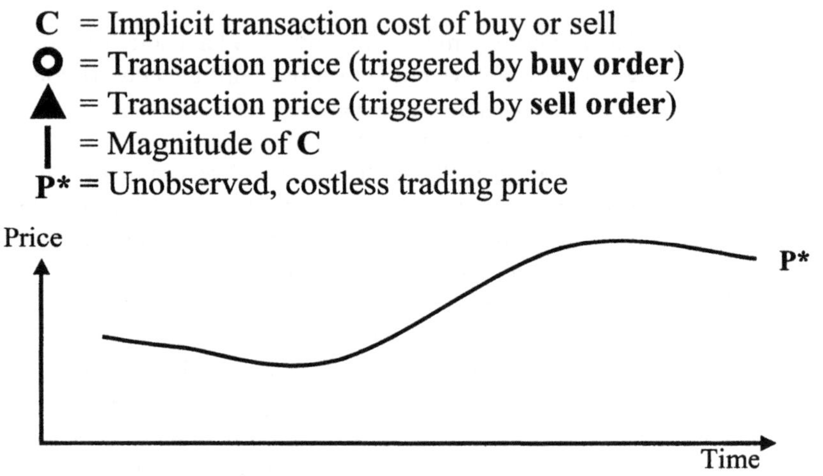

Exhibit 4. Trading Costs and Price Volatility

C is the implicit transaction cost, per share, of buying or selling a stock. The implicit cost is imbedded in the price of a transaction. It includes the bid-ask spread and market impact. It does not include commissions.

In our diagrammatic presentation, a donut represents a transaction price that we observe when the transaction has been triggered by a buy order. A buy-triggered transaction price can reflect the bid-ask spread (that is, an offer price that is higher then the bid), market impact, or whatever else might be pushing price up.

A triangle represents a transaction price that we observe when the transaction has been triggered by a sell order. A sell-triggered transaction price can reflect the bid-ask spread (that is, a bid price that is lower then the offer), market impact, or whatever else might be pushing price down.

A straight, vertical line represents the magnitude of C. As we all know, implicit transaction costs are very difficult to measure. Anthony, you certainly reflected that in your talk. And, as I say this, I am watching Wayne Wagner of Plexus Group. I see him nodding his head in a positive direction.

P* represents a value that we cannot see but can, nevertheless, conceptualize. It is the unobserved, costless trading price that is only talked about by academicians. You might think of P* as a frictionless market, consensus value (or equilibrium value).

Let's start with P*. There it is, in Exhibit 4. Exhibit 4 shows how P* may evolve over the course of a trading day. What causes P* to change? The consensus value changes because the fundamental desire of investors to hold shares of the stock in their portfolios changes. Informational change (news) is the simplest factor to point to.

Exhibit 5 replicates Exhibit 4 and adds the transaction prices.

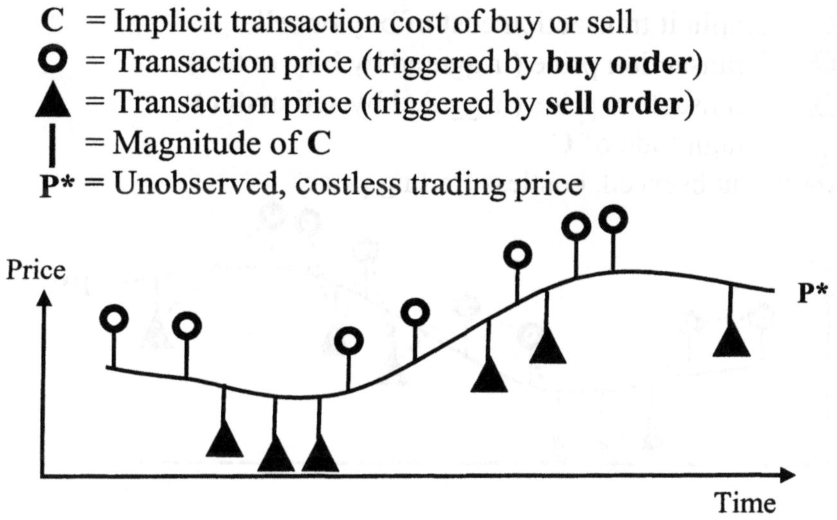

Exhibit 5. Transaction Prices Added

In Exhibit 5, each transaction price is P* plus C for a buy-triggered trade, or P* minus C for a sell-triggered trade. The first trade of the day was triggered by a buy order that arrived early in the morning. The first transaction price that we see is represented by the first donut. Next, another buy order came in, triggered another trade, and we see a second donut. The third trade of the day was triggered by a sell order, and the first triangle identifies the price of that trade.

Let's keep the presentation simple. All of the vertical straight lines are the same length. That is because this is an academic environment and we academicians like to keep complex things simple.

The trading day continues. There are more trades and transaction prices. More donuts and triangles. Let's next consider the volatility implied by this set of transaction prices. Volatility refers to how much these prices jump around. The price changes we observe from jump-to-jump are returns. Alternatively stated, a return is any price change. So let's see what the returns look like. In Exhibit 6, I have added dotted lines to help identify the returns.

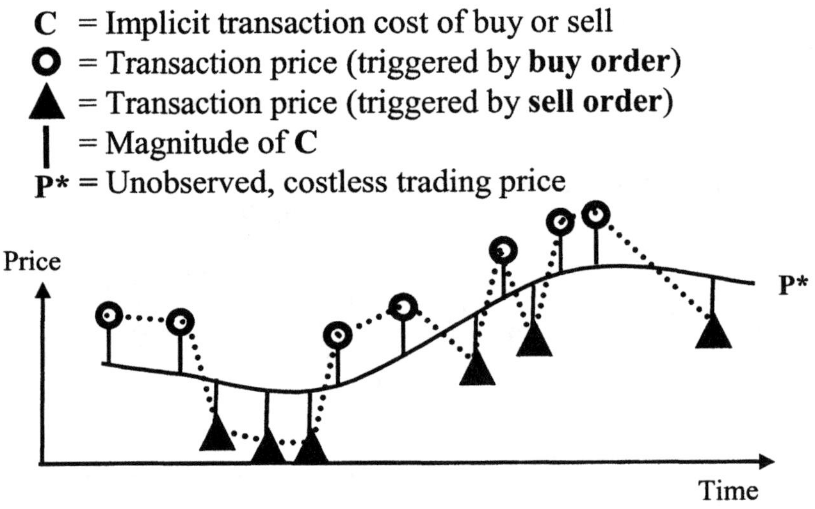

Exhibit 6. Returns Added

The returns are the slopes of the dotted lines. Sometimes the dotted lines slope up, sometimes they slope down. Sometimes they are relatively flat.

Exhibit 7 is the same as Exhibit 6 with the donuts, triangles, and vertical lines removed.

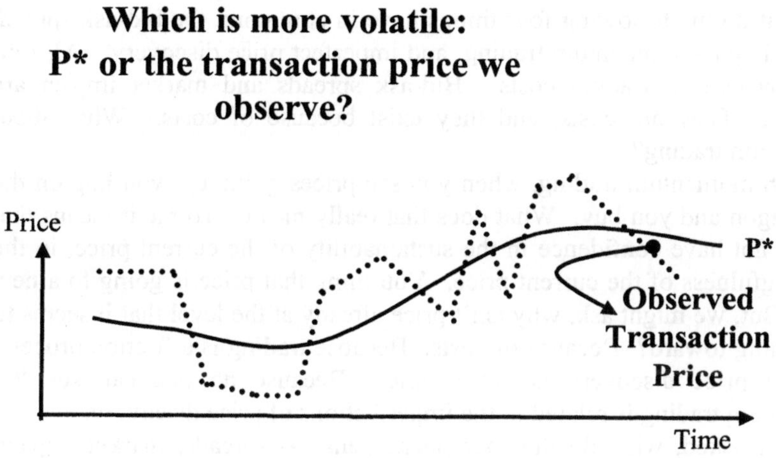

Exhibit 7. Donuts, Triangles, and Vertical Lines Removed

Exhibit 7 shows the dotted lines more clearly. I want to ask you all a question. Which is more volatile, P* or the transaction prices that we observe? Can we have a vote on this? How many of you say P*? Thank you. How many say the transaction prices that we observe? Come on, raise your hands, and don't be shy. Thank you. More of you are saying that it is the observed transaction prices that are more volatile. Yes, I agree. The observed transaction prices do jump around more. Why? Because of implicit transaction costs. It is in this context that I would next like to talk about the *accentuation* of intra-day volatility.

Why *intra-day* volatility? If I were to extend the price charts out over far longer periods of time, the changes in P* would become very appreciable relative to the magnitude of the implicit trading costs. This is because the collective importance of informational change cumulates over time.

Let's look at it this way. How important would the straight, vertical lines be if the value of P* changed a lot over time? Relatively speaking, they would be a lot less important. As they become relatively less important, an interesting thing happens – the volatility of observed transaction prices converges with the volatility of P*. Because these two volatilities converge for longer period returns, we are able to infer P*'s intra-day volatility. It is this inference, in turn, that enables us to assess the intra-day volatility accentuation. Hence we can assess market quality and the magnitude of the implicit trading costs. This, in essence, is what we have done. Deniz will explain further in a few moments. First, I have another question.

What do the following four things have in common: the bid-ask spread, market impact, momentum trading, and imperfect price discovery? All four exist because of trading costs. Bid-ask spreads and market impact are obvious. They are costs, and they exist because of costs. What about momentum trading?

With momentum trading, when you see prices going up, you hop on the bandwagon and you buy. What does that really mean? To me it means that you do not have confidence in the sustainability of the current price, in the meaningfulness of the current price. You think that price is going to a new level. But, we might ask, why isn't price already at the level that it seems to be heading toward? Because of costs. Because trading is a friction process. Because price discovery is not simple. Because no one can see P*. Momentum trading is related to the imperfections of price discovery.

I just asked, what do the four phenomena -- spreads, market impact, momentum trading, and imperfect price discovery -- have in common? I pointed out that they all exist because of trading costs. There is a second thing, and it is important. The four things all result in prices bouncing between two values, one high and the other low. Whenever you have price bouncing between two values, it translates into accentuated volatility.

Think again about the donuts and the triangles. Visualize price bouncing between the higher donuts and the lower triangles. With a bid-ask spread, you are bouncing between the higher offer and the lower bid. With market impact, you have the same thing. With market impact, price is effectively bouncing back and forth across a larger spread. If it is momentum, price went down too low or it rose up too high. Either way, price is swinging too far. And the last momentum trader always gets killed. You never want to be the last momentum trader.

Price discovery can be viewed in this context. Some of my frictionless world, random walk colleagues will not like me for this, but I will say it anyway. I am not anti-technical analysis. There is good theoretical support for technical analysis. One of the clearest patterns it looks for is support and resistance levels. Let's further extend the notion of the bounce to include price swinging between a lower support level and a higher resistance level. All of these bounces give you accentuated volatility.

The question is can the accentuation in short-period volatility that is attributable to these bounces be measured? Deniz will tell you what we found.

DENIZ OZENBAS: The volatility accentuation can indeed be measured.[7] Our study took the following perspective. In academic circles, the length of time over which returns are measured is referred to as the "differencing interval." In a perfectly frictionless, random walk world, all differencing intervals will give the same measure of volatility, if the volatility measure is adjusted to reflect the length of the differencing interval. That is, if we look at half-hour returns, hourly returns, daily returns, weekly returns, or whatever, the volatility for all of these adjusted for the length of the differencing interval, should be the same. And the adjustment is simple. To normalize all measures to a one-day volatility, for instance, divide a two-day measure by two, a one-week measure by five, etc. In other words, simply divide by the relative length of the differencing interval.[8]

On the other hand, in a world where prices do not follow a random walk, the scaled volatility may be observed to be higher when a short differencing interval is used to measure returns. In other words, short-period returns may exhibit accentuated volatility.

We analyzed the short-period volatility accentuation for five markets – The New York Stock Exchange and Nasdaq in the U.S., and The London Stock Exchange, Euronext Paris, and Deutsche Börse in Europe. Transaction prices for the year 2000 were used. We looked at the largest stocks in each market, and assessed each stock individually.

Let us first look at half-hour volatilities. Average values for the stocks in each of the five country samples are shown in Exhibit 8.

[7] "Volatility in U.S. and European Equity Markets: An Assessment of Market Quality," Deniz Ozenbas, Robert Schwartz and Robert Wood, *International Finance,* Volume 5 Number 3, Winter 2002, pp. 437-461.

[8] The procedure of dividing by the relative length of the differencing interval holds when logarithmic returns are used to compute a variance. If the standard deviation of logarithmic returns is being taken to measure volatility, then the square root of the differencing interval should be used.

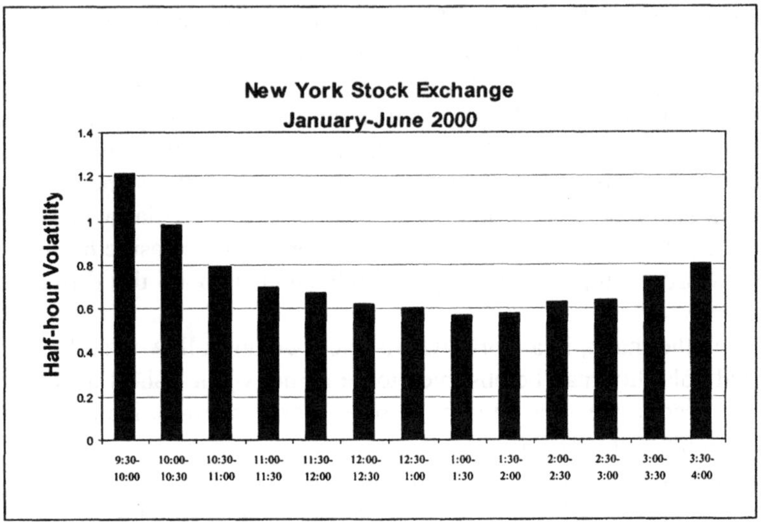

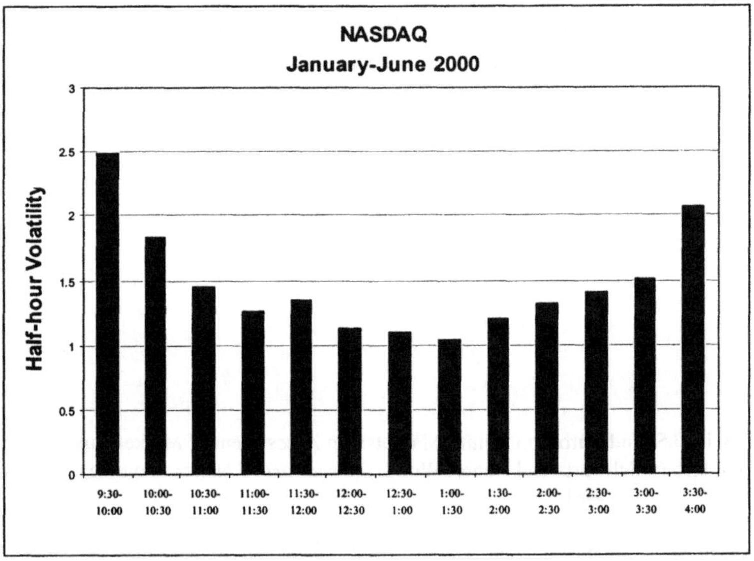

Exhibit 8. Half-Hour Volatilities for Five Markets

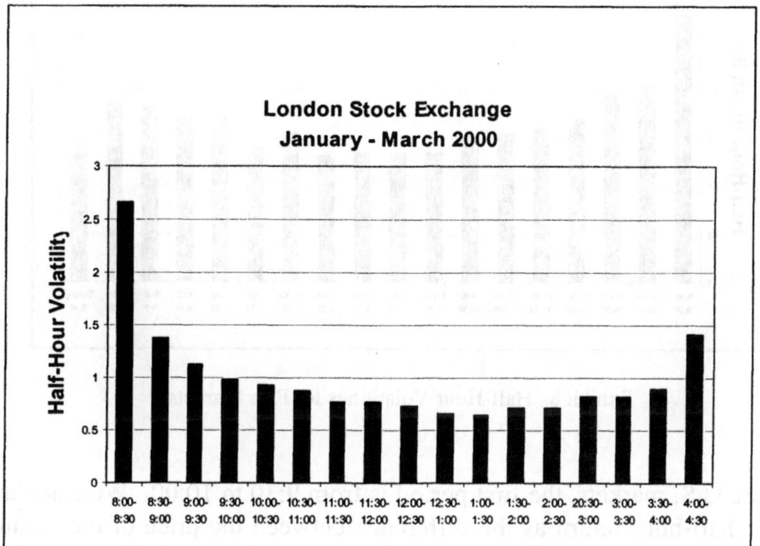

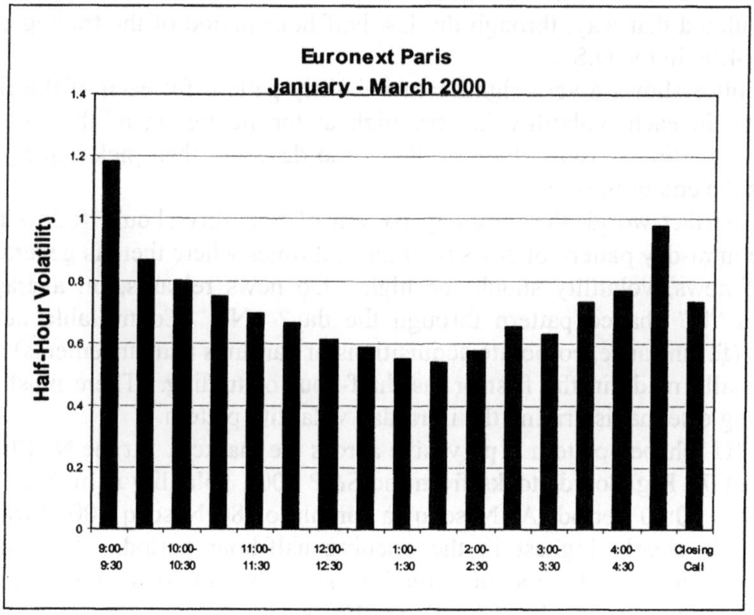

Exhibit 8. Half-Hour Volatilities for Five Markets

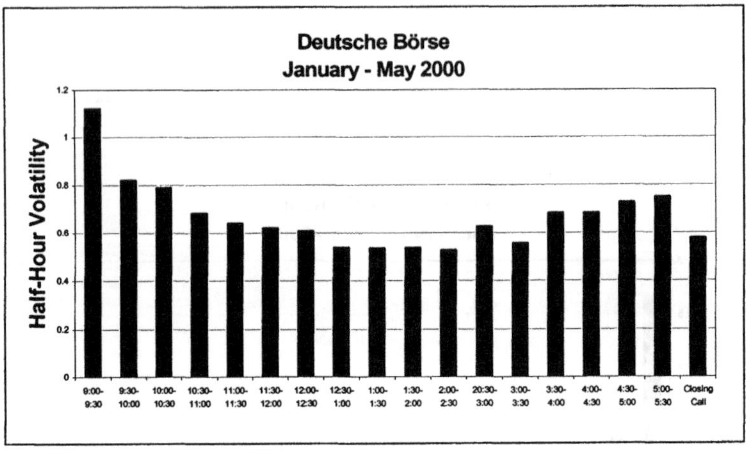

Exhibit 8. Half-Hour Volatilities for Five Markets

In the U.S. markets, the first period is from 9:30 to 10:00. We calculated the first half-hour return as the difference between the price of the opening trade and the price of the last trade in that first period. For the second half-hour, the return is the difference between the price of the first trade after 10:00 and the price of the last trade before 10:30. The half-hourly returns are calculated that way, through the last half-hour period of the trading day (3:30 to 4:00 in the U.S.).

Exhibit 8 shows a very significant volatility pattern for each of the five markets. In each, volatility is very high at the beginning of the day. It gradually declines through the middle of the day, and then picks up again towards the end of the day.

In a perfect world, the intra-day pattern of volatility should follow the average intra-day pattern of news releases. At times where there is generally a lot of news, volatility should be high. Do news releases, on average, follow a "U" shaped pattern through the day? No. Controllable news releases (for instance, corporate acquisitions or earnings announcements) are not typically made in the first or last half-hour of trading. There must be something else that is driving the intra-day volatility pattern.

The "U" shaped pattern is pervasive across the markets. At the NYSE (a sample of 72 Big Board stocks from the S&P 500), volatility is highest for the 9:30 – 10:00 period. At Nasdaq (a sample of 80 Nasdaq 100 stocks), volatility is clearly highest in the opening half-hour period. The same applies in Europe. The opening volatility spike is highest for the London Stock Exchange (a sample of 85 FTSE 100 stocks). It is also sizable for Euronext Paris (a sample of 39 CAC 40 stocks) and Deutsche Börse (a sample of 28 DAX 30 stocks). Further, for each of these five markets, the second highest volatility reading is in the last half-hour before the close of the trading day.

Now let's contrast the short period and the longer period volatility statistics. For each of the five markets we have examined, we broke the 2000-trading year into two periods. The findings for each market and period are shown in Exhibit 26 (see page 167). Once again, because the volatility measurements have been normalized, in a perfectly frictionless, random walk world, all of the numbers shown in Exhibit 26 would be centered on 1.[9]

Exhibit 26 shows the normalized volatility numbers for the five markets for the first and the last half-hour intervals, for the closing call auction[10] (where applicable), for open-to-close price changes, and for the one-day, one-week, and two-week differencing intervals. For the five markets and two assessment periods, all values for the first half-hour volatility are greater than the benchmark value of 1. For the NYSE, Nasdaq, Euronext Paris, and Deutsche Börse, they are almost two times as volatile as what you would expect in the first half hour. For the London Stock Exchange, prices in the first half-hour are almost three times as volatile. We investigated this issue. We looked at the pattern of volume during the day and it turns out that, relatively volume is the least in the London Stock Exchange. There is almost no volume at the beginning of the day. London is a very institutional market, and perhaps the institutions are holding out for a while before they enter the market. Similarly for open to close volatility, it is accentuated most of the time, a bit. We also see from Exhibit 6 that the volatility values are generally greater than unity, particularly for the last half-hour price changes and the open-to-close price changes.

In summary, the answer to Bob Schwartz's question is, "yes, there is accentuated short-term volatility in markets, and the accentuation exists for a broad array of market structures." At this time, I will pass the microphone to my other co-author. As Bob Schwartz did to me, I will pass it on with a question. "I have suggested that the accentuation of intra-day volatility is an

[9] We normalized the volatility measures in presented in Exhibit 6 by dividing each volatility by the differencing interval length and by the average half-hour volatility for the second to second-to-last half-hour trading periods. See Ozenbas, Schwartz and Wood, op. cit., for further discussion.

[10] The returns for the closing call auction were defined as the difference between the price at the close of the continuous market and the price established at the closing calls. For the three European markets that have closing calls, the auctions were held roughly five minutes after the close of the continuous market.

[illegible]

[illegible]

The first question deals with liquidity.

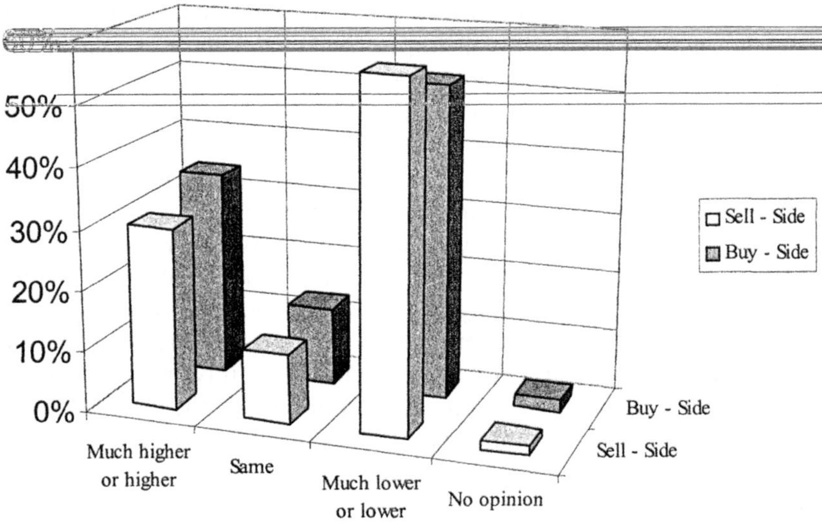

Sell - Side	32%	11%	56%	1%
Buy - Side	34%	13%	52%	2%

Exhibit 9. U.S. Survey: "What is the general level of liquidity of the market in recent months compared with the level of liquidity in the market prior to 1997?"

As shown in Exhibit 9, the predominant sentiment on both the buyside and the sellside is that liquidity has deteriorated.

Survey results reprinted with permission from R. Schwartz and D. Weaver, "What We Think About the Quality of Our Equity Markets," *The Journal of Portfolio Management,* Volume 27, Number 4, Summer 2001, pp. 63-70.

The second question deals with volatility.

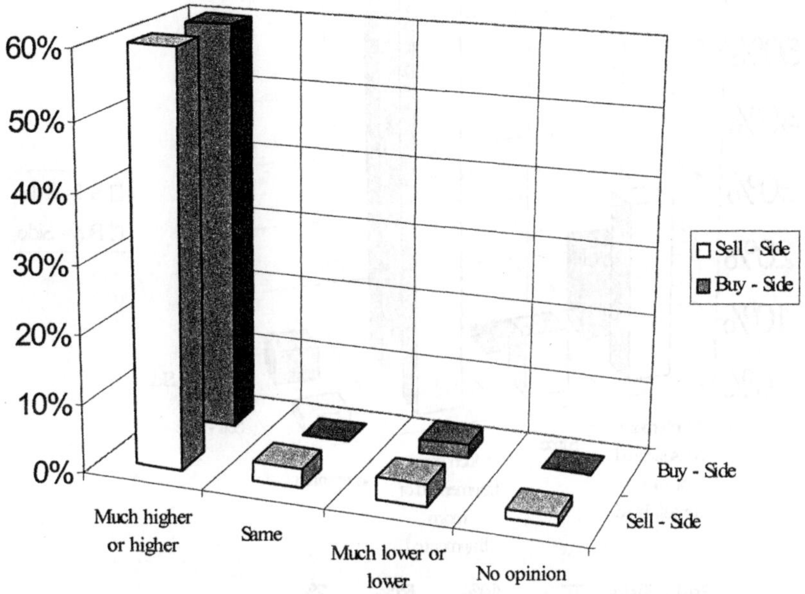

Sell - Side	92%	3%	3%	1%
Buy - Side	98%	0%	2%	0%

Exhibit 10. U.S. Survey: "How do the levels of intra-day volatility experienced in recent months compare with the levels experienced prior to 1997?"

As shown in Exhibit 10, there was virtually unanimous agreement in the U.S. that volatility has increased in the U.S. markets. This is quite interesting to me because in my research, and in other research that I am aware of, we do not see that volatility has increased. This causes me to wonder whether we academics are approaching the study of volatility properly. What do the practitioners see that we do not?

Next are the issues of consolidation and fragmentation.

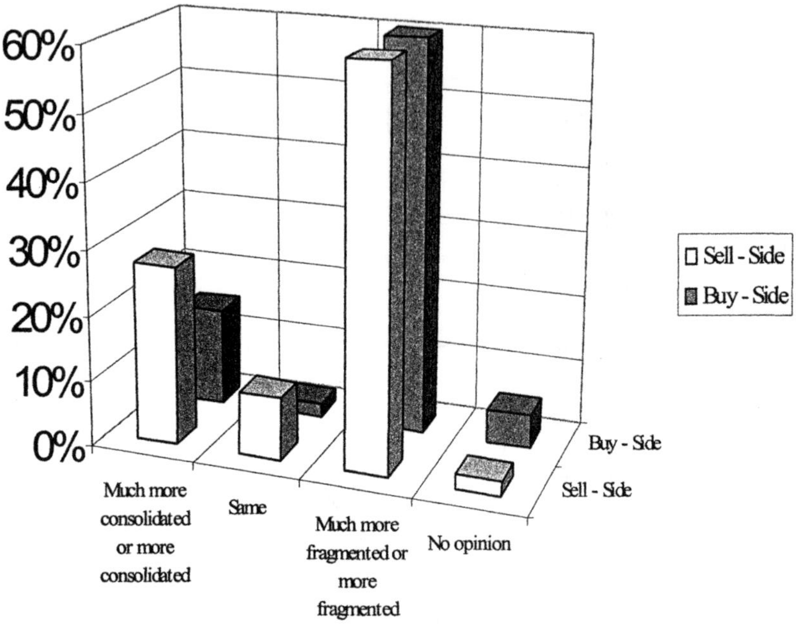

Sell - Side	**27%**	**10%**	**61%**	**2%**
Buy - Side	**15%**	**2%**	**79%**	**5%**

Exhibit 11. U.S. Survey: "Are markets more consolidated or more fragmented than they were prior to 1997?

Exhibit 11 shows that both the buyside and the sellside feel that markets are more fragmented. Another dimension of fragmentation involves the breaking up of orders for sequential execution over a series of trades.

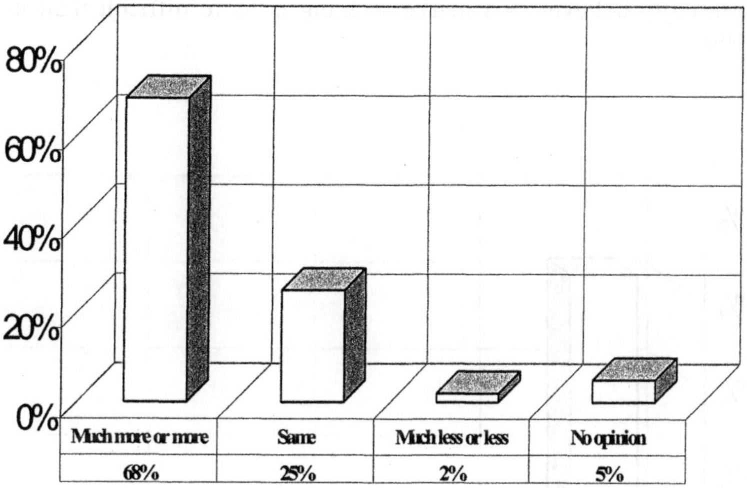

Exhibit 12. U.S. Survey (BUY-SIDE): "Are you more frequently breaking up your large orders for submission to the market into pieces compared to before 1997?"

Exhibit 12 shows that buy-side participants are more frequently breaking their orders up for submission to the market over a succession of trades. Consistently, Exhibit 13 reveals that sellside participants are being shown less of total order size compared to before 1997.

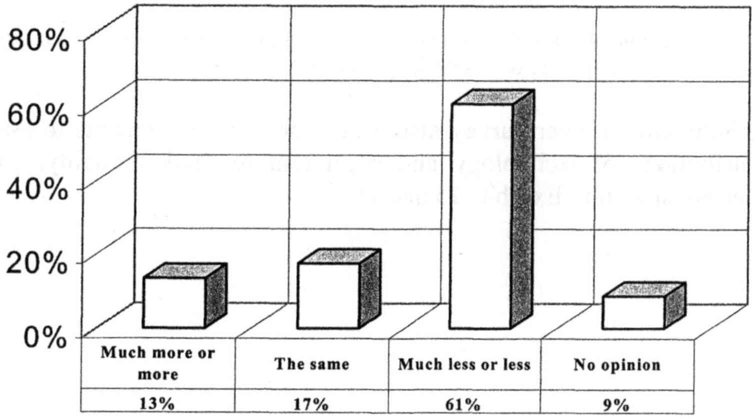

Exhibit 13. U.S. Survey (SELL-SIDE): "How much of total size are investors showing you compared to before 1997?"

What is the impact of this? The markets are less transparent. Further, as a consequence, the answers displayed in Exhibit 14 indicate that the sellside overwhelmingly believes that market making is more difficult than it was before 1997.

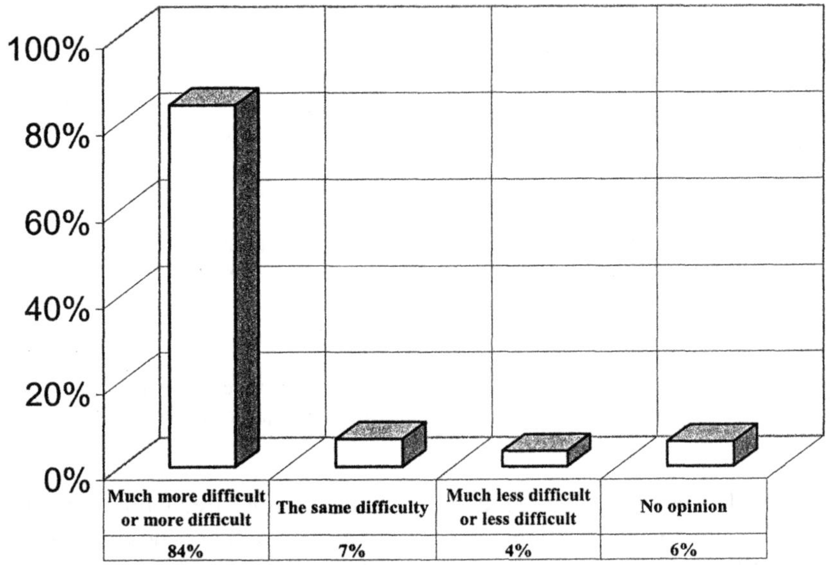

Exhibit 14. U.S. Survey (SELL-SIDE): "From your perspective, is market making more or less difficult than it was before 1997?"

The Schwartz-Weaver survey also asked the U.S. participants to assess the contributions of technology and regulation to market quality. The responses are shown in Exhibits 15 and 16.

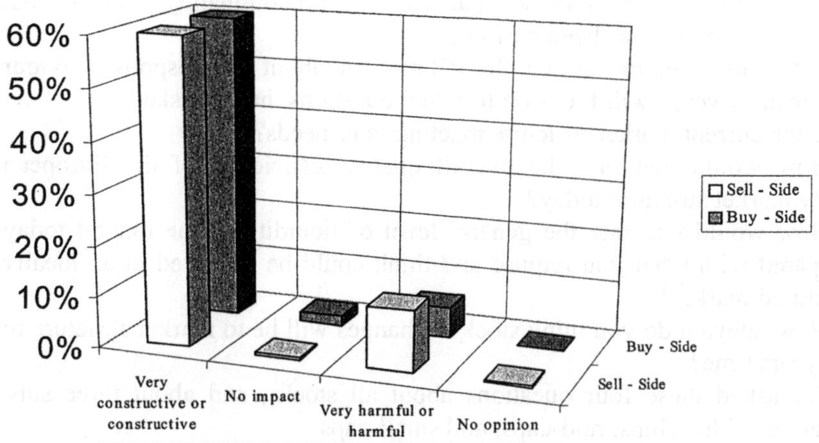

Sell - Side	88%	1%	11%	0%
Buy - Side	92%	2%	6%	0%

Exhibit 15. "What is the broad contribution that technology has made to the quality/efficiency of the U.S. equity markets in recent years?

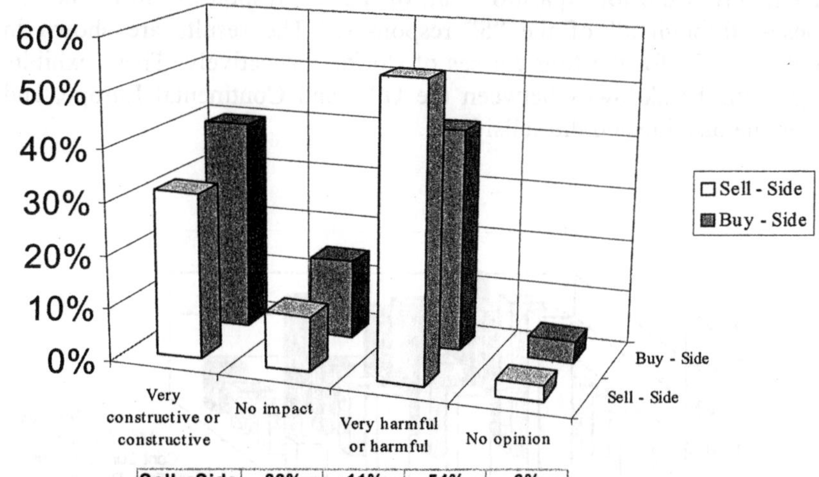

Sell - Side	33%	11%	54%	3%
Buy - Side	40%	15%	42%	4%

Exhibit 16. "What is the broad contribution of regulation by Congress and the SEC to the quality/efficiency of the U.S. equity markets in recent years?"

Participants on both sides of the market are in virtually unanimous agreement that technology's contribution has been positive. Opinions about regulation's contribution, on the other hand, are mixed. The buyside is fairly evenly split, while sellside participants predominantly stated that regulation's impact has been harmful.

Let's move on to Europe. In telling you about the responses to our European survey, I will focus on four key questions that we asked:

Is the current market structure meeting your needs?

How would you rate the overall quality, efficiency of the European equity market structure today?

How would you rate the general level of liquidity of the market today compared with what you require and think could be achieved in an ideally structured market?

How relevant do you think stock exchanges will be to market structure in five years time?

We asked these four questions about all stocks, and about three sub-categories: blue chips, mid-caps, and small-caps.

For each of the four classes – all stocks, blue chips, mid-caps, and small-caps – we aggregated the answers to the four questions. We did so as follows. The most positive response to each question was assigned a value of 1, the second most positive a value of 2, through to the most negative response that was assigned a value of 5. To get a composite, we then summed, across the four questions, all of the "1" responses, all of the "2" responses, through all of the "5" responses. The results are shown in Exhibits 17 – 20 for the four classes of stocks, respectively. These exhibits also give the breakdowns between the U.K. and Continental Europe, and between the buyside and the sellside.

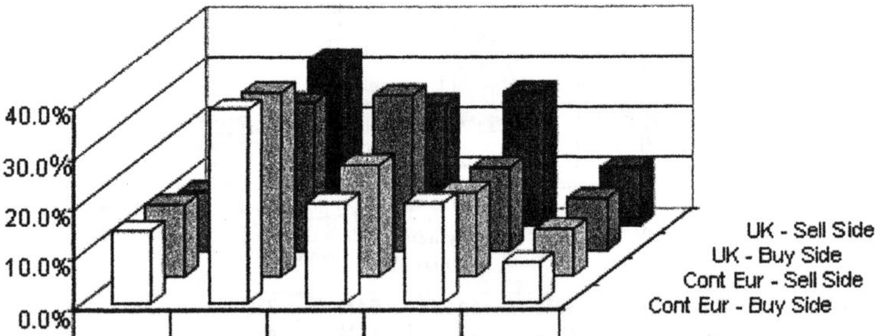

	Very High	Hig	Neutral	Low	Very Low	Average Score
Cont Eur - Buy Side	14.3%	38.5%	19.8%	19.8%	7.7%	2.7
Cont Eur - Sell Side	14.5%	36.7%	22.4%	16.9%	9.5%	2.7
UK - Buy Side	12.0%	29.6%	31.2%	16.7%	10.5%	2.8
UK - Sell Side	4.6%	32.9%	24.3%	26.6%	11.6%	3.1

Exhibit 17. European Survey, All Stocks

Exhibit 17, for all stocks, shows a fairly dispersed distribution that is skewed to the left (towards the more desirable ratings). Digging deeper reveals some interesting things.

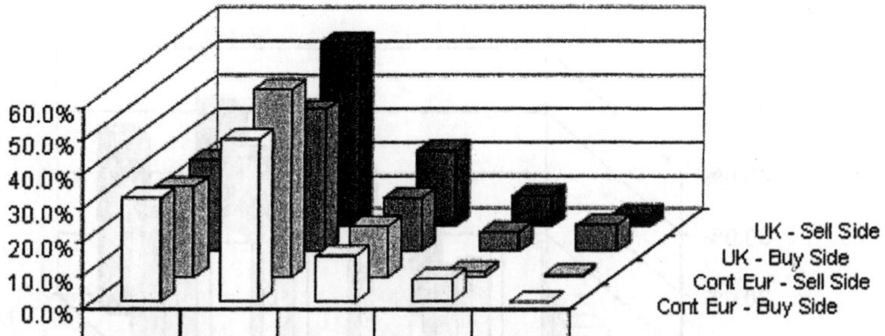

	Very High	High	Neutral	Low	Very Low	Average Score
Cont Eur - Buy Side	31.0%	48.3%	13.8%	6.9%	0.0%	2.0
Cont Eur - Sell Side	26.7%	55.7%	15.3%	1.5%	0.8%	1.9
UK - Buy Side	27.3%	42.4%	16.2%	6.1%	8.1%	2.3
UK - Sell Side	9.4%	54.7%	22.6%	9.4%	3.8%	2.4

Exhibit 18. European Survey, Blue Chips

The responses shown in Exhibit 18 for blue chip stocks are predominantly positive. For the blue chips, the modal response is "high," and the second most frequent response is "very high."

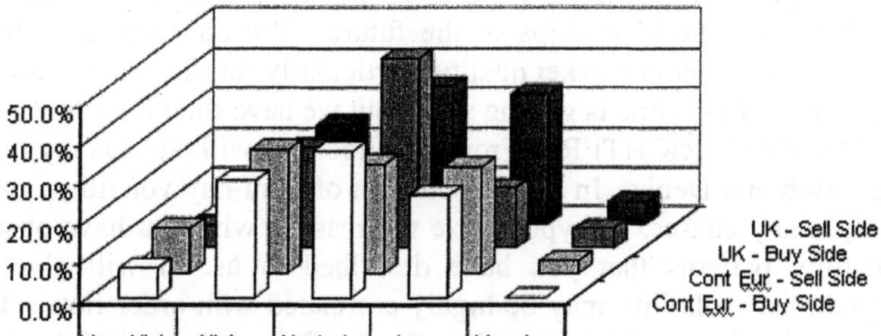

	Very High	High	Neutral	Low	Very Low	Average Score
Cont Eur - Buy Side	7.4%	29.6%	37.0%	25.9%	0.0%	2.8
Cont Eur - Sell Side	11.5%	31.3%	27.5%	26.7%	3.1%	2.8
UK - Buy Side	6.1%	25.5%	48.0%	15.3%	5.1%	2.9
UK - Sell Side	1.9%	25.0%	34.6%	32.7%	5.8%	3.2

Exhibit 19. European Survey, Mid Caps

Moving to the mid-caps, in Exhibit 19 we see that the distribution is shifted to the right (towards the less desirable ratings). Overall, for the mid-caps, the distribution is fairly balanced.

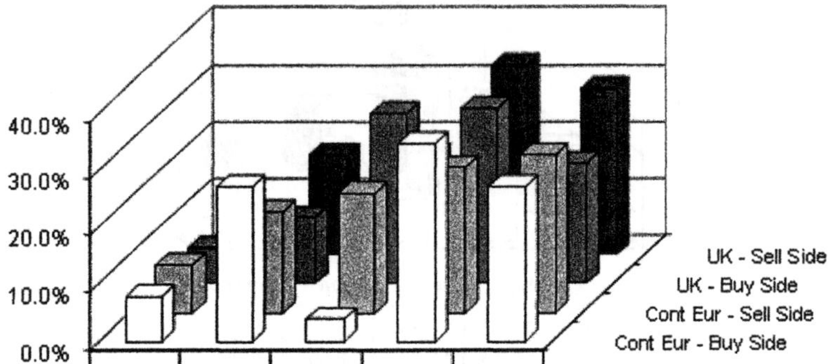

	Very High	High	Neutral	Low	Very Low	Average Score
Cont Eur - Buy Side	7.7%	26.9%	3.8%	34.6%	26.9%	3.5
Cont Eur - Sell Side	8.5%	17.7%	20.8%	25.4%	27.7%	3.5
UK - Buy Side	6.4%	11.7%	29.8%	30.9%	21.3%	3.5
UK - Sell Side	2.0%	17.6%	17.6%	33.3%	29.4%	3.7

Exhibit 20. European Survey, Small Caps

For the small-cap stocks in Exhibit 20, the distribution is shifted further to the right. This is not a good assessment. The small cap market is the incubator for the blue chips of the future. We conclude that, in Europe, concern exists about market quality, particularly for the small-cap stocks.

BENNETT: Time is getting short, but we have time for a few questions.

MICHAEL RICHTER[12] [From the Floor]: I will address my question to Bob, Bob and Deniz. In your discussion of intra-day volatility, you did not analyze any causes, or hypothesize the reasons why you have observed the volatility patterns that you have described to us. I will give you one hypothesis: volatility may be highly correlated with order flow. There is a lot of order flow at the open, a lot of order flow at the end of the day, and it is slower in the middle of the day. If you could study that, that might give you one hypothesis as to the pattern.

OZENBAS: Thank you for your observation. That was our expectation as well, and we did look at intra-day volume patterns. That is why we were surprised to see that, at the London Stock Exchange, the volume was really

[12] Michael Richter is CEO of Lime Brokerage.

small at the beginning of the day – almost non-existent, in fact – and that volatility was the highest at the beginning of the day.

SCHWARTZ: I would add to that. I see the accentuation of volatility at the opening as being related to the complexity of price discovery at the open. Another way to look at it is to ask, if you had good, crisp price discovery at the opening trade, would you continue to see the heavy order flow for the first half-hour, and would you still see the price volatility spike at the open that we have observed?

There is another way to state this. We know that the market opens in a technical sense with the first trade. But, if by opening the market for a stock we mean achieving the price that best reflects the broad market's desire to hold shares, I suggest that, in each of the five markets that we have studied, it takes the better part of half an hour to open the stocks.

BENNETT: Let me add to the answer. I notice that my old colleague from the New York Federal Reserve Bank, Mike Fleming, is here. Mike did a study of what happens at 8:30 when the bond market opens, and there is a big employment announcement.[13] Mike found that price did not immediately go to a new equilibrium value. The bond market, of course, is a dealer market, but the basic reaction to news is no doubt quite similar in the equity markets. It takes a little while for trading to pick up. What is interesting, as I recall, and correct me if I am wrong Mike, is that there is not a lot of trading volume until the price gets at least in the neighborhood of the new "right price" for the day. It takes the market a while to figure out what the right price is.

SCHWARTZ: Mike's paper was very helpful to me. In particular, I would like to underscore its demonstration that protracted surges in price volatility and trading volume attend major news announcements in the U.S. treasury market. This is consistent with our having found a volatility spike in the first half-hour of the trading day. Presumably the spike is part of the protracted process of price adjusting to overnight news events.

SHARON SALAMON[14] [From the Floor]: I have one question for the group. Regarding your European survey, for the small-cap part of the European market, the respondents feel that there are a lot of inefficiencies in the way that the exchanges are structured. Do you feel that a consolidation

[13] Michael J. Fleming and Eli M. Remolina, "Price Formation and Liquidity in the U.S. Treasury Market: The Response to Public Information," *Journal of Finance* 5, 1999, pp. 1901-1915.

[14] Sharon Salamon is currently Director of Institutional Equities for Product Management at Thomson Financial. At the time of the conference, she was the Senior Sales and Marketing Executive at NeoNet Securities.

of the exchanges – with Euronext being a perfect example – is affecting their responses? Do you think that consolidation would hurt or help market efficiency?

SCHWARTZ: I could respond to that, but I have a better idea. Luca Filippa is here from the Borsa Italiana. Luca is a lot closer to what is going on in Europe. Luca, would you care to answer?

LUCA FILIPPA[15] [From the Floor]: Sure, thanks, Bob. Sharon Salamon has posed the one million dollar question in Europe. The efficiency of price discovery in European exchanges is quite good now. As you know, we had a large discussion in the year 2000 on a potential alliance between the eight major exchanges. That discussion, due in part to political and business constraints, ended in no alliance. But we did achieve an agreement on what we call the European market model. We agreed to have the same kind of structure in all of the European markets.

The microstructure of the various European exchanges is basically the same now, although some small differences still exist. The need for consolidation is high, but there is a major difference. We always talk about fragmentation of markets, and in Europe, this is true. But the markets are fragmented in a different way than in the U.S. This is because we may have different liquidity pools, but nevertheless have really liquid pools for the individual stocks. Italian shares are really liquid – in Italy. German shares are really liquid – in Germany. And so on.

There are a few examples of fragmented liquidity for single stocks. A good example is Nokia. 65% of the trading volume on the Helsinki Stock Exchange is accounted for by Nokia. Nokia accounts for some 20% of the volume in Stockholm. Nokia also has large volumes in London and New York.

The consolidation matter is basically a political one. The homogeneity of the structure now allows most users to access a virtual book. And there are a lot of information service providers that connect the single intermediaries to the different exchanges. Basically, the discussion in Europe has moved from trading integration to post trading costs. With regard to post trading issues, the role of domestic settlement institutions has remained large and the cost of cross-border clearing and settlement is still huge.

SCHWARTZ: Luca I have a quick extension of your response. Whether it is Europe or the U.S. does not matter. When the dust settles on market structure, we will see that the small-cap market is not of the same quality as the mid-cap or the blue chip markets. That will, obviously, always be the

[15] Luca Fillipa is Head of Research & Market Analysis at the Borsa Italiana.

case because of the nature of the beast. On the other hand, I personally feel that market structure can be improved across the board.

BENNETT: We have time for one more question.

RICHARD REPETTO[16] [From the Floor]: I want to follow up on the discussion about volatility at market openings and closings. The way that I would interpret it is that price discovery is difficult at the open because of overnight news events, and that it is difficult at the close because risk becomes a big driver as traders seek to close out their position. So if we had a market structure – and I do not know what it would be – where price discovery was more uniform in quality over the trading day, we would not see the volatility patterns that you have shown us.

SCHWARTZ: Yes. I would say yes to that. Holly, how would I answer Rich's market structure question?

HOLLY STARK[17] [From the Floor]: I think that was a set up for Bob to make the case for call auctions at both the open and the close.

SCHWARTZ: Call auctions? That is a wonderful idea (laughter).

BENNETT: I thank our panelists, and I thank the audience for a good discussion.

[16] Richard Repetto is currently Associate Director at Sandler O'Neill & Partners, LP. At the time of the conference, he was a Managing Director at Putnam Lovell.

[17] Holly Stark is Principal and Director of Trading at Kern Capital Management.

CHAPTER 2: INTRA-DAY VOLATILITY: FRIEND OR FOE?

Moderator – David Krell, *President and CEO, International Securities Exchange*
Thomas Cardello, *Managing Director, Morgan Stanley*
Avner Wolf, *Chairman, Department of Economics and Finance, Zicklin School of Business, Baruch College, CUNY*

DAVID KRELL: We are very fortunate to have two panelists in this session who are experts in the field of volatility. This panel is, therefore, balanced, unlike the previous panel, which consisted mostly of academics. Here we have a 50/50 balance between the practitioner community and the academic community. Thomas Cardello, managing director at Morgan Stanley, is in charge of the automated market-making department. He is also involved in market making in the U.S. as well as overseas. Our other panelist is Professor Avner Wolf, Chairman of the Economics and Finance department here at Baruch College. Both of these individuals have had extensive experience in derivatives trading. It is a pleasure for me to be the moderator of this panel.

First, I would like to meander a little bit beyond the discussion that Bob and I had talked about. Our primary objective on this panel is to talk about intra-day volatility. In the options business, we are very much concerned about volatility in general. If I can present an overview of volatility first, and some definitions of volatility, then we can get to the real topic, the essence of what we would like to talk about this morning – the impact of market volatility on market quality.

In the options business, as you well know, all of the theoretical option pricing models include six basic factors. Five of them are pretty well known. They are the underlying stock price, the exercise price, time to maturity, interest rates and dividends. All five of these factors are known at the outset. The sixth factor is volatility. Volatility is the one that we spend most of our time thinking about, dreaming about, and analyzing.

What do we mean by 'volatility?' What do we mean by 'implied volatility?' We can use any one of the various models – Black-Scholes[18], the binomial[19], or any of the derivatives thereof – and solve for what we call 'implied volatility.' I selected AOL as an example. Look at Exhibit 21.

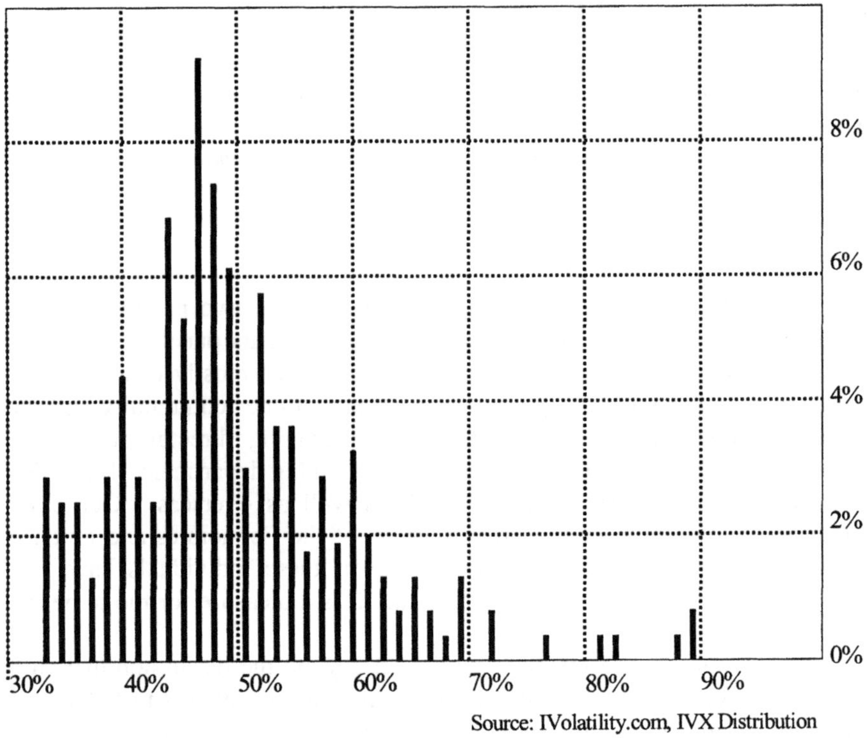

Exhibit 21. AOL 2001 Implied Volatility Index (30 Day)

18 A model used to calculate the value of an option, by considering the stock price, strike price and expiration date, risk-free return, and the standard deviation of the stock's return.

19 An option pricing model in which the Underlying asset can assume one of only two possible, discrete values in the next time period for each value that it can Take on in the preceding time period.

What we see from this histogram is that, in 2001, the 30-day implied volatility from the options price, ranged from about 35% annually to about 90% annually. About 2/3 of the time, volatility was between 40% and 50%, and indeed the highest individual bar is about 45%. This is a pretty tight compression of volatility as we measure it in the options business. We can also look at the implied volatility and compare it to the historical volatility of an underlying stock. Exhibit 22 shows an overlay of both the implied volatility (in this case it is a solid line), and the historical volatility (a dotted line).

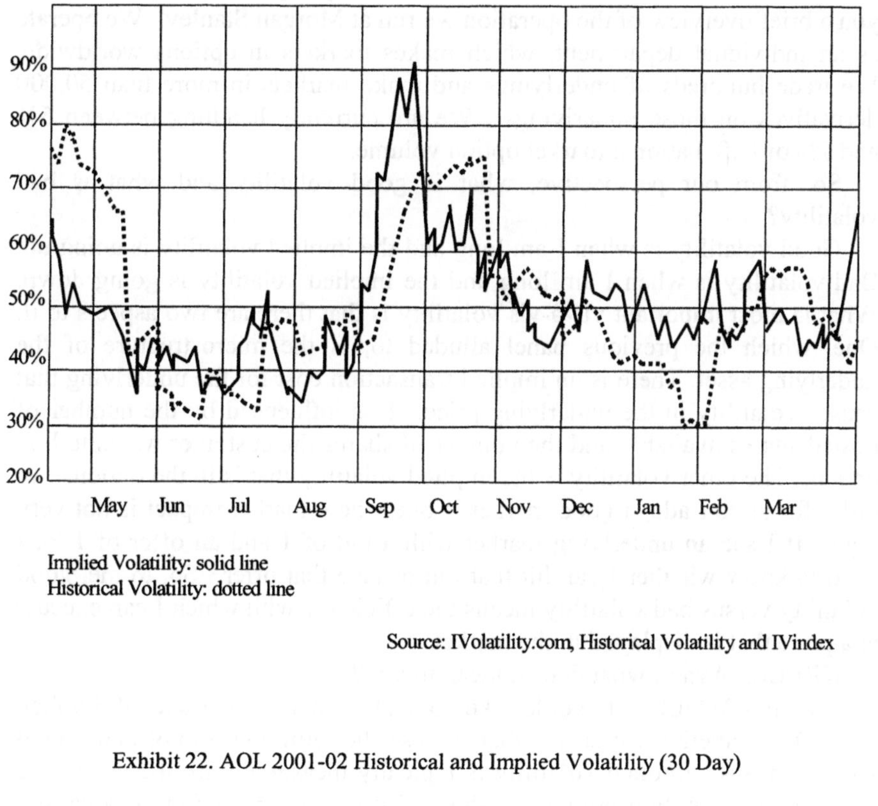

Exhibit 22. AOL 2001-02 Historical and Implied Volatility (30 Day)

In 2001-2002, volatility ranged from a low of about 30% to a high of about 90%. It is not surprising that the highs of around 90% occurred in

September 2001.[20] The historical volatility deals with what happened in the past. It measures the previous 30 days. The implied volatility, on the other hand, is a forecast of what options traders think volatility will be for the remaining life of the option (in this case, about 30 days). Our measure of historical volatility is the variance of stock price returns over a period of time. Bob, Bob and Deniz discussed this in the previous panel. We frequently use a 20- or 30-day time slot, depending on the life span of the option.

That is an option trader's basic perspective. I would now like to ask our panelists their views. Let me turn first to you, Tom. What does volatility mean to you? Specifically, what does it mean to you as an option trader who needs to make markets in 400 different securities and options at any give point in time?

THOMAS CARDELLO: To provide some perspective, I will first give you a brief overview of the operation we run at Morgan Stanley. We operate as an individual department, which makes markets in options worldwide. We trade hundreds of underlyings and make markets in more than 50,000 derivatives on those underlyings. We are currently handling between 5% and 7% of U.S. national market option volume.

So, from our perspective, what is good volatility and what is bad volatility?

Good volatility is when I am long and the implied volatility is going up. Bad volatility is when I am long and the implied volatility is going down. What is most important vis-à-vis volatility is that there are two aspects to it. One, which the previous panel alluded to, is the microstructure of the underlying asset. There is an implied transaction cost for the underlying that causes volatility in the underlying price. It is influenced by the number of posted shares available and the number of shares the customer wants to buy or sell. The other volatility is the implied volatility that is in the options. In order for us to trade, a good market is one where market impact is not very high. If I see an underlying market with a bid of 1 and an offer of 1 ½, I need to know whether I can hit that bid or take that offer. So, to me, good volatility versus bad volatility means the efficiency with which I can execute at a price that is displayed in the market.

KRELL: Avner, what does it mean to you?

AVNER WOLF: I would like to elaborate on the issue of implied volatility. Sometimes it seems that we use the term and do not understand what it means. Implied volatility is typically measured with the use of the Black-Scholes option-pricing model. Instead of plugging a volatility

[20] The tragic events of September 1, 2001 created fear and uncertainty in the market. Krell picks up this theme later in the session.

estimate into Black-Scholes to find the price of an option, the market price of the option is plugged into the formula and a value for volatility is 'backed out.' The value that is backed out is the value that is implied by the Black-Scholes formula, given the market price of the option.

David, I would like to mention something that you alluded to in passing. It is something that I emphasize in my teaching. The volatility that we use in options pricing does not reflect what happened yesterday. Rather, it is the expected standard deviation of a stock's rate of return between now and the expiration date of the option. Volatility is not something that we can take from history. I gave a presentation in Chicago a number of years ago, and a trader came up to me and proposed that I become his partner if I could come up with a model to forecast and quantify volatility, (laughter) which is very hard.

The title of our session is 'Volatility: Friend or Foe.' I would like to mention Bob's presentation, and try to come up with a definition. It seems to me that good volatility has to do with market information. When new information comes to the market and sparks trading, it generates good volatility. Prices should adjust to new information. But if the volatility were the result of market imperfections and transaction costs, I would call it bad volatility. This is an academician's definition. But please understand that this academician clearly sympathizes with what you perceive as good and bad volatility from your perspective as a trader.

KRELL: I want to make sure that, when we talk about volatility in the options or derivatives business, it is understood that we are not talking about Beta. Beta is a relative measure of performance. Beta measures the performance of a given stock against a broad based index, such as the S&P 500 or the NYSE composite index. In the options business, we measure the absolute volatility of that underlying component. We only look at the returns and the variance (or standard deviation) of those returns. I think that is considerably different than what you in the academic community, or in the equities world, might think about variability of returns.

I will mention one thing that pertains to the discussion in the previous panel. Paul Bennett talked about different views of market quality. Last year, the SEC requested comment letters pertaining to the proposed rule that Paul Bennett mentioned, Rule 11Ac 1-5. We sent a comment letter to the SEC. It was a tongue-in-cheek comment letter where we created a phantom airline called Fly by Night Airline. Fly by Night had the cheapest fares. However, it only flew between 1 a.m. and 5 a.m. It had a poor safety record. It had a departure and arrival timeliness of 0. It had very poor terminal service. No food or drink was available, and you had to rent your seat belt from them at an additional cost (laughter). Do you want to fly on that kind of an airline?

If the government forced you to go to the cheapest provider, is that the best for you as a consumer? That is the underlying question we are all facing in our businesses today. Is the cheapest cost the best for you at any given point in time? The previous panel talked about price, liquidity, speed, service, transaction costs, transparency and anonymity. These are all components of what is important to certain people at certain points in time. And yet, while price may be an overwhelming desire at some points in time, for large traders it may not be the only component that is important. Just measuring bid-ask spread differentials is not enough. We have to go beyond that price to see what is driven by the desires, the objectives, of users.

I have another question. Does volatility mean revert intra-day? Does it trend?

CARDELLO: Yes, volatility exhibits strong mean reversion.[21] The question is, how do you exploit that mean reversion? There are two volatilities that exhibit mean reversion – the historical volatility of the underlying object, and the implied volatility. They both seem to mean revert during the day, but the interesting thing is that they by no means move in lock step with each other. If you have noticed, one may revert back to its value earlier in the day. The other might not follow.

KRELL: Avner, any observations?

WOLF: The study described by Bob Wood, Bob Schwartz and Deniz Ozenbas, showed clearly that there is some kind of pattern of short-term volatility, at least intra-day volatility. I am not so sure about long-term volatility. I would agree with you, Tom, that there is some kind of mean reversion structure to volatility. There is also a lot to study with respect to volatility, both historical and implied. How do the two work together in helping us to predict future numbers? I want to emphasize one other issue. The question you asked me earlier, what does volatility tell you, or what does it mean to you? I looked at your numbers in Exhibit 21 for AOL (see page 36). It was what, about 45% for 30 days volatility?

KRELL: Yes.

WOLF: Just think what that means. AOL was trading around 50 for a long time. Fifty percent volatility means that, within one year, the price could go up from 50 to 75, or go down to about 33. That is what volatility tells you on an annual basis. I can use the normal distribution to get an idea about the annual price range of the underlying stock price. So the volatility conveys information that may be used in options as well as in equity trading.

[21] Mean reversion (reversion back to the mean) refers to reversal behavior. Namely, when a variable deviates from its mean (is either higher or lower), it tends to reverse direction and revert back to its mean (average) value.

It suggests what the average investor thinks about the range of stock prices within a given period (one month, three months, six months, one year, etc).

KRELL: Good. I have some more questions. First, how do you measure volatility?

CARDELLO: How we measure volatility is again two fold. The naïve way is to model the returns generation process of the underlying stock. Volatility would be the second moment of the returns distribution that I am modeling. The other way is to look at the option prices, describe the process that defines an option's price, and back out the implied second moment. Generally, you end up with two different measurements.

The interesting thing is that, as the previous panel said, there is an awful lot of noise in these measures. Getting back to your other question about the reversion of volatility during the day, I again note that there is an awful lot of noise in these measurements. Something as simple as changing the time frame for measurement can give you different answers.

WOLF: If there is a stock or an option that is not traded on an exchange, you cannot use implied volatility. I hope everyone understands this. There is no way to use Black-Scholes to estimate the implied volatility since there is no price that is disseminated throughout the day. You need to do your own calculations and estimation of the volatility. If it is an exchange traded option, where prices are available, I would typically use what the options market tells me the volatility is. This is the easiest way to get information from the market.

KRELL: Over what period of time do you measure volatility? Is it a specific period?

WOLF: When it comes to options, I would typically use 30 days to three months. What is the highest volume of options traded? One-year options? Half-hour options? No. It is typically one-month, two-month, or three-month options. This would be my guideline for the length of time I would use to study volatility.

KRELL: Is volatility inherently good or bad, generically?

WOLF: I will answer with a story. Years ago I attended a conference at Columbia University. There was a big discussion between a Nobel Prize Laureate, Kenneth Arrow, and a yet to be Nobel Prize Winner, Myron Scholes. The topic was, 'Is Volatility Good or Bad, or Do We Need Volatility?' Without volatility, there would be no market. If we lived in a world of certainty, there would be no interest on our part in trading anything. Information would mean nothing. Volatility is necessary for markets. The question once more is, what is bad, and what is good. I gave you my answer before.

KRELL: Tom, any comments?

CARDELLO: I think that volatility, per se, is neither good nor bad. What matters is the costs involved in transacting. You can have two markets that each have a measurable volatility of 40%, and bid-ask spreads of equivalent magnitude. What matters is whether you can actually execute in reasonable size on the bid and offer that is displayed in that market. If I can only trade 200 shares at any one time in one of the markets, and in the other I can trade 100,000 shares at any one time, the second market is going to be much more conducive, not only to higher volumes, but to more orderly markets. In the first market, where you can easily transact only 200 shares at a time, your transaction costs for doing 100,000 are going to be much larger.

ROBERT WOOD[22] [From the Floor]: Back to your comment on how you calculate volatility. When you are calculating it as a second moment, you are implicitly assuming that the first moment is stationary.

CARDELLO: No. Why do you say that? I have to ask a question to answer a question (laughter).

WOOD [From the Floor]: Because you are assuming that the first moment is stationary when you are calculating deviations from the mean.

CARDELLO: You have to assume that it is stationary during a certain time period. If I am calculating volatility over a period of, let us say, 30 minutes, yes I have to assume some kind of stationary mean. But I take it during that short time period.

WOOD [From the Floor]: Supposing that, in the 30-minute segment, news arrives that significantly changes the mean expected return for that company over its lifetime. Is that assumption of stationary in the first moment justified?

CARDELLO: No, not in that particular case. But that is just one reason why measuring volatilities is so noisy. In a prior world, I was an experimental physicist. If that was a noisy set of data, I would throw out that particular half-hour period. You have to be very careful about picking periods of data. If you are going to do this analysis, do it when the Federal Reserve does not come out with any news during that half-hour period.

WOOD [From the Floor]: How do you know when you are justified in the assumption that the first moment is stationary?

WOLF: I want to refer to the first study in that area by Fisher Black. It was in 1975. Black had discovered that volatility is not fixed.[23] This is a strong violation of one of the basic assumptions of his model, which, as you may know, got his co-authors Myron Scholes and Robert Merton the Nobel

[22] Robert Wood is Distinguished Professor of Finance at the University of Memphis.

[23] See Black, Fisher: "Fact and Fantasy in the Use of Options," Financial Analysts Journal (July/August 1975) pp. 36-41.

Prize for options pricing theory. This is a challenge. Most of the models that are currently being used by almost everyone –correct me, David, if I am wrong, even by your exchange – to price options makes the assumption that volatility is fixed. Otherwise, you cannot come up with a closed form formula to price options. Everything else is either too slow, or too inaccurate, or gives results that you cannot interpret.

I do not have a clear answer. I do not even think you can use time in Black-Scholes and find a pattern to the volatility. As you just said, when information comes half an hour later on AOL, or any other company, it may change your initial assumption about the stationarity of the first moment. To a degree, your model is flawed. Nevertheless, we keep using Black-Scholes. I would estimate that 90% of the time market users, with some modification, are still using Black-Scholes in one form or another.

I would like to allude to another issue. What if we have one stock that trades, on average, every 10 seconds, and another that trades, on average, once a minute? The question is, can we use implied volatility for both of them? Once again, implied volatility is taken from options prices. So, if you have a set of stocks with this kind of a delay in trading, you need to look at the underlying stock. You must also know what the liquidity is in the options market. Then ask the question, can implied volatility be used?

Sometimes, if there is no liquidity – and, Tom, correct me if I am wrong – the implied volatility means nothing. Perhaps you have bid and ask quotes. You still do not know what it means, what price to put into your Black-Scholes model for backing out implied volatility.

KRELL: That is right. Option traders take that into account. If you have a stock that is trading within a one point range every 10 or 15 minutes, versus one that is trading every 10 seconds, that will be taken into account in the pricing of that option.

CARDELLO: I have a further thought about the stationarity of the mean. I view any given data sample in segments that are piece-wise stationary. That way, I can make an assumption that the mean will be stationary over small subsets of the overall data sample. In that way, I can get a statistical estimate of the second moment of the distribution. It is the shape of the distribution that you assume is going to be changing. It is going to be varying over longer periods than the mean. The mean itself varies. The idea is that implied volatility is varying more slowly than the actual price.

KRELL: I might point to this chart that is up there (see Exhibit 22 on page 37) to show you how a traumatic event like September 11th effected option pricing, not just for AOL, but for the overall market. Volatility went up for everyone because of the event. You see that dramatically illustrated here. The 90% annualized volatility of AOL in September was indicative of that.

WOOD [From the Floor]: Our tools for measuring volatility are pretty primitive. I wish we could do better.

KRELL: We agree with that.

CARDELLO: Yes, we agree. Absolutely.

PAUL DAVIS[24] [From the Floor]: To change the subject just a bit.

KRELL: It is not in the script.

ROBERT SCHWARTZ[25] [From the Floor]: That's volatility (laughter).

DAVIS [From the Floor]: We are talking about market quality. I am interested in knowing how the International Securities Exchange is growing, and how Tom's desk plays into that. How has having the ISE available changed what you do?

KRELL: This is a commercial for the ISE (laughter). The ISE is going to be two years old on May 26, 2002. We trade stock options on about 500 individual stocks. Our market share this month is about the highest in our history. Our market share, for the entire market, is about 21%.[26]

Yesterday was an event for us. It was the first day that we traded more volume than two of our competitors combined. We have been very happy about the acceptance of our market structure, which is a hybrid. The ISE is a screen based, agency-auction market. We do not have a floor. We are fully electronic. We also have dealers like Tom and Morgan Stanley, and others as well, who are required to provide liquidity to our marketplace. With that, I will turn it over to Tom and let him share his experience with us.

CARDELLO: The market share numbers I quoted were volumes exclusively on the ISE. We have significant national market volume by participating primarily on the ISE. We expected, two or three years ago, that the markets in this country are likely to go electronic. Because of that, we put tremendous effort into developing a market making capability for the electronic markets in the U.S. Two years ago, it was a risky decision. More and more, it is turning out to be the right decision.

One of the most valuable things about being able to transact electronically worldwide is the immediacy that electronic trading gives. We

24 Paul Davis is Senior Managing Director at TIAA-CREF Investment Management.

25 Robert Schwartz is Distinguished Professor of Finance at the Zicklin School of Business, Baruch College, CUNY.

26 The ISE, which is the second largest U.S. options exchange, reported strong gains in February 2003, and according to a published release it was the largest U.S. equity options exchange in that month. An analysis of trading volume showed the ISE traded more equity options than any other U.S. options exchange, and its equity options market share was 27%, up 42% from 19% for the same period 12 months earlier. ISE lists 533 options classes.

find that market impact is significantly lower, largely because we do not extend a free option to specialists or to other market participants during the time that elapses between when we first put in an order and when we get that order filled. And now there are enough participants on the ISE and the electronic markets for us to start ramping up our sizes.

Among the many factors which drive the success of a market, especially an electronic market, are the number of participants. Also important is the quality of the participants and the quality of the market makers. We can provide a significant amount of capital. Consequently, the market impact suffered by customers and clients is far less when they come to the electronic market than to an open outcry market. Because of that, we are noticing that our profitability, our market share, and our market volumes are continuing to go up. They are going up by virtue of us providing better markets. I hope that answers your question.

KRELL: Just one more slight commercial. We measure some of our own quality by looking at the spread differential in all of the options we trade. We trade more than 40,000 different series in these 500 different names. Almost 70% of the time we offer the tightest spread. Almost 90% of the time, ISE spreads are equal to or better than the spreads offered in the other four markets. That is another measure of how we think this market will evolve, and why we think that we offer a successful model.

We provide one other thing that I should note. We have intra-market competition among our dealers. Tom is constantly competing with other market makers in our market. This is part of what creates tighter markets and tighter spreads.

CARDELLO: One other comment. There are electronic market structures other than the ISE. U.S. market structure in the future is not necessarily going to be identical to the current ISE market structure. However, I suspect that David will be guiding how the broader U.S. market structure evolves.

WOOD [From the Floor]: What has decimalization done to the noise in volatility that you have talked about?

CARDELLO: Interesting question.

KRELL: Generally, in the options business, we migrated to decimal trading together with the underlying securities moving to decimal trading. However, we did not move into a penny increment environment. Not yet, anyway. In the options business, we still have a minimum tick of 5 cents. This is our minimum increment in trading.

CARDELLO: We trade in both the option and the underlying market. We have observed that decimalization has made the apparent book – the displayed market – more real in the stock market. What is the apparent book? By the apparent book I mean I can trade 100 shares at a 0 spread. I can trade 500 at a 1-penny spread. I can trade 1,000 at a 2 pennies spread. I can trade 10,000 at a 4 pennies spread and 100,000 at 6 pennies away. Decimalization has just made that a reality. To trade 100 shares you can now trade at a spread of 1 cent or less, and you do not have to get to the level where there is a 10,000-share market which may be 6 cents wide.[27] I no longer have to trade 100 shares at the 6-cent spread. I now can trade the 100 shares at the narrowest piece. Consequently, decimalization has apparently narrowed spreads. But it probably has not done that much to the real market in terms of being able to get volume at a given price.

KRELL: We will open the discussion up to other questions. Anthony?

ANTHONY NEUBERGER[28] [From the Floor]: I want to return to the relationship between the quality of the underlying market and the quality of the options market. There seems to be some belief that a poor underlying market is characterized by excessive volatility, and that, somehow, this is good for options traders because options traders like volatility. In reality, poor quality in the underlying market makes it much more difficult to arbitrage between the options market and the underlying market. Therefore, the extra volatility which is induced by poor market quality in the underlying presumably translates into poor underlying quality in the options market. I was wondering to what extent this is what you actually observe.

CARDELLO: Two factors come to mind. First, if you have an underlying security that is uncorrelated (or is only weakly correlated) with any other underlying security, then the illiquidity affects the spreads in the options themselves. This is because of the transaction cost inherent in hedging the option. And there is a continued excess transaction cost associated with the dynamic synthesis of the option. If you are going to synthesize an option – if you are long or short an option – you can hedge that option by trading stock against it, according to a prearranged trading strategy in the Black-Scholes model. On the other hand, let there be a high correlation between an underlying security that has very low liquidity and another security that has very high liquidity. For instance, assume that some low liquidity stock has a high correlation to some high liquidity stock such

[27] Decimal pricing on the NYSE, for instance, has narrowed spreads. On the negative side, academic studies show that the depth of the market – the number of shares offered at a specific price – has decreased sharply from the levels in the pre-decimal market. The reason cited is that investors have more pricing options than under fractional pricing. Decimals have made it cheaper to trade in small quantities of stock but harder to execute much larger orders.

[28] Anthony Neuberger is Associate Dean of the Full-time Masters in Finance Programme at London Business School.

as General Electric. Then I can effectively hedge the option using the high liquidity stock. Because it is liquid, it enables me to put on the position with lower transaction costs. So the answer to your question is, yes-no (laughter).

WOLF: The answer, in my view, is very clear. If there is no liquidity in the underlying stock, there is an accentuated volatility for the underlying stock. This is an increased volatility for the options trader, and volatility is very important for options trading. However, as Tom just said, people do not trade options just for the sake of trading and speculating. Some participants trade to hedge. You cannot establish the hedge very easily in an illiquid market. In that respect, what you alluded to as bad volatility won't help the options market at all.

WOOD [From the Floor]: Tom, are you saying that your hedging costs have not been reduced by decimalization?

CARDELLO: No, I am saying that the apparent liquidity has not changed. But if I trade 1000 contracts and my hedge ratio is 20%, I really only need to hedge a certain amount of stock. I will be able to hedge that stock at a better price if it is within the apparent market.

I have to translate that into English. If I trade one option contract on 100 shares, the underlying amount that I have to hedge is 20 shares. If, in the old regime prior to decimalization, that market was 1000 up 6 cents wide, I will be better off now because I can probably get the 20 shares off at 1 penny. But if I trade 50 times that amount, I am no better off because my liquidity is not at a penny wide. It is still at 6 cents.

WOOD [From the Floor]: Given the size range that you are in, can you provide us with a feel for any change that decimalization has had in your aggregate trading cost?

CARDELLO: Our operation started about two years ago. When we started, we were trading 10 lots. In those days, when decimalization was coming in, it made a difference. But nowadays, with the sizes that we trade, we are typically several thousand up on liquid names, on individual posting, and maybe even five times that on facilitation type orders.[29] So decimalization helps to the extent that it brings in more liquidity, but I would not say that it makes much of an impact given the sizes we are trading now.

KRELL: We have time for one more question.

NARI JOTE[30] [From the Floor]: Someone had said that, if there was no volatility, there would be no stock market. Is there any relationship between volatility, transaction costs, and the cultural behavior of the individuals? I

[29] A facilitation type order occurs when a broker dealer takes some fraction of the "other side" on an order to trade a number of contracts at a certain price.

[30] Nari Jote is Management Consultant and Global Business Coordinator at Jote & Associates.

have worked in India, in the U.K., and in this country. I see that people have a different behavioral sense when it comes to volatility. What do you correlate that with?

I also have a second question. What part does an Enron type disaster play in volatility?

KRELL: I didn't really understand the first question. Let's move to the second one.

JOTE [From the Floor]: OK.

KRELL: Does anyone wish to comment on the changing volatility in an Enron-type situation? How is that taken into account in options pricing?

CARDELLO: Obviously, volatility goes up immediately. The interesting thing about something like an Enron is that, since the news did not all come in one sudden instant, and since the price did not instantaneously go to its lowest level within 20 minutes (it took a couple of days), and because there was a liquid underlying market, we were able to continue making markets in Enron even though the option volatilities went way up. The implied skew of the option – the expectation that the stock price would decline instead of rise – was also immediately changed. We saw that we were able to conduct orderly market making activity in Enron while the stock was open on the stock exchange. The options prices went way up. This was largely because there was liquidity in the underlying stock during that time, and the price movement did not occur all at once. Contrast this with a case where a merger or an acquisition is announced and, all of a sudden, the stock immediately goes up 10 points and stays there forever. That is an un-hedgable event.

KRELL: I believe your first question was…

JOTE [From the Floor]: My first question was cultural. Isn't it a cultural factor that different countries have different volatility factors?

CARDELLO: A quick answer to that is to contrast the U.S. with Hong Kong. There is a very large speculative interest in Hong Kong. You see high volatility markets. You do not see very high liquidity except in some of the indices. And, in the U.S., because you do not have that level of speculative mentality, you have other institutional players in there. Consequently, the U.S. markets are not as 'choppy.'

KRELL: The other issue pertains to market structure. In India, for example, until recently, you had a product called 'badla.' Basically, badla was a way of buying and selling stock without paying for it. It is called 'kiting' in the U.S., and it was outlawed after the Crash of 1929 because it was cited as a contributing factor. But in India, it was legal and prevalent, extremely prevalent, until it was outlawed within the last year or eighteen months. Now I think it is much more likely that you will get a situation where you have true derivatives trading in India. But that was a way of trading a derivative without trading on an organized exchange. Badla was basically a bet between two individuals on the price of the underlying stock. It was like a swap. And then the payments would be equalized. Am I correct on that?[31]

JOTE [From the Floor]: That is true. And it is changing fast with the global economy integrating together.

WOLF: In academia, and I believe also in practice, we find that when the market is down, volatility is up, and visa versa. Right now, we are going through a different phase. The market is down and volatility is down. Putting this together, how would this effect the trading of options based on what we see right now?

KRELL: We are recently undergoing a consolidation in the options industry. You can read almost every week about the prices of memberships at various exchanges, and about various trading groups consolidating. We are in a unique situation. The competition between and among the markets is so intense, that spreads have narrowed to their tightest levels in options trading in a decade. And volatility is at an all time low. That is not a good combination to have from an options trading perspective. It is all three plagues happening at the same time: industry consolidation, narrower

[31] Kiting was prevalent in the U.S. prior to 1929, according to financial historians. It had an unsavory connotation because kiting was used to prop up "bucket shops." It allowed speculators to buy and sell stocks without putting up any cash. For example, an investor could buy a stock through a broker dealer for $10 without putting up the money and then, an hour later in a rising market, sell the stock for $11 dollars and pocket the difference of $1.

spreads and volatilities at new lows.[32] As a result, we are undergoing tough trading times from a trader's perspective. From the customer's perspective, it is terrific, but from the trading perspective it is very, very difficult.

I would like to thank our panelists, Tom and Avner, for a terrific job. Thank you all very much.

[32] The larger, more capital-intensive firms in the U.S drive industry consolidation of small options specialist firms. The multiple listing of stock options on various exchanges has hurt these small firms. Consequently, there are fewer traders on the floors and demand for seats has softened in part because of this trend. Decimal pricing has also hurt floor traders. In early 2003, there were five U.S. options exchanges and a sixth pending a launch in mid-year. These six are the Chicago Board Options Exchange, the International Securities Exchange, the American Stock Exchange, the Philadelphia Stock Exchange, the Pacific Exchange and finally the Boston Options Exchange, which was expected to become the latest.

CHAPTER 3: VIEW FROM THE TRADING DESKS

Moderator – Robert Schwartz, *Speiser Professor of Finance, Zicklin School of Business, Baruch College, CUNY*
Andrew Brooks, *Vice President and Head of Equity Trading, T. Rowe Price Associates*
Christopher Killeen, *Senior Trader, TIAA-CREF Investment Management*
Mark Madoff, *Director of Listed Trading, Bernard L. Madoff Investment Securities*
Barry Small, *CEO, Weeden & Company*
George Sofianos, *Vice President, Goldman Sachs*
Bruce Turner, *Managing Director and Head of U.S. Equity Trading, CIBC*

ROBERT SCHWARTZ: The seating, like the program, is in alphabetical order. Fortuitously for us, it meshes with another purpose I have in mind; clustering. My panelists are arranged in three clusters. First we have Andy Brooks and Chris Killeen, who are on the buy-side. Next we have Mark Madoff and Barry Small, who are on the sell-side. Finally, we have George Sofianos and Bruce Turner, who are on both sides (laughter). But not at the same time – they both have had the pleasure of working for a major market center, and also for a broker dealer firm. The only thing that is missing from the panel is some people from the listing companies themselves. They never appear on these panels because they don't know what a limit order is (laughter).

Let me start with the buy-side cluster. You guys are the ultimate customers, aren't you? Chris, by the way, was a little late getting here this morning because he was actually present at the volatility spike in the first half hour of trading today. And, since he was trading my funds, I hope he got a good execution

CHRISTOPHER KILLEEN: I tried.

SCHWARTZ: Andy and Chris, can I ask both of you first to give us a quick description of your orders? I know that you occasionally trade 1,000 shares or even 100 shares. I do not care about those small orders. Tell us about the tough ones.

ANDREW BROOKS: I would like to start by emphasizing that *market quality,* which is the title of today's conference, has become a big issue. For many of us, a very big issue.

In response to your question Bob, we certainly do have 100 share orders. We try to process and route them as efficiently and as economically as we possible can. We try to allow traders the opportunity to focus on the larger, tougher orders; the orders that are 20 times average daily volume. An order of this size can represent 2% of a company's outstanding shares. These orders are really difficult to handle, especially when there is news out or an event. They are also difficult when there are lots of buyers and we are the only seller, or when there are lots of sellers and we are the only buyer.

Implementing an effective trading strategy in this situation is very difficult. It may sound easy if there are lots of buyers and you are the only seller. You should not have a problem in selling but the issue becomes, at what price do you sell? You'd think you could sell higher but how high is high? You need to know if you have the luxury of patience. When we are a buyer, the answer would involve a conversation with the portfolio manager about how to initiate a certain strategy to buy the shares for this large order. When we are a seller, if there is no luxury of time, for instance, you have to sell right away.

SCHWARTZ: Could I quickly break in and ask Wayne Wagner something? What Andy is saying is common, isn't it, Wayne? I have seen your statistics on the number of orders that are bigger than average daily volume. I do not know about 20 times daily volume, but bigger than 100 percent of daily volume is very common.

WAYNE WAGNER[33] [From the Floor]: We find that 80% of institutional orders are for more than half a day's volume.

SCHWARTZ: Let us talk about market quality in this context. This is a fun one. Andy, back to you.

BROOKS: For the big orders, what you think you will be able to do is often impossible to achieve. I am sure that we have representatives of people who gauge or assess the transaction costs on a particular stock. For example, this morning it might cost you 9 cents to buy 300,000 shares of 'telephone.' But the market is up 100 points, and I bet it will cost you 29 cents. (I do not know where 'telephone' is trading right now, I am just guessing.) Invariably that is the world we live in. You think you can be

[33] Wayne Wagner is Chairman of Plexus Group.

patient, you think you can trade tight. But it is not always possible to trade at a level that you think is initially possible.

I am delighted that we are, perhaps, starting to focus less on the narrowing of spreads, and more on this intra-day volatility. Intra-day volatility is really making our jobs very difficult. It is making it very hard to trade, and our orders are indeed large.

SCHWARTZ: Chris, how do you feel about this, and about what happened this morning?

KILLEEN: Our problem is that we have these institutional sized orders in a market that has been designed for retail investors.

SCHWARTZ: Could you repeat that? I didn't hear you (laughter).

KILLEEN: It seems as if the cards are stacked against the institutions. This is because the market has been designed for retail order flow.

SCHWARTZ: Do people in the audience agree? Raise your hands. Thanks. I see a lot of agreement.

KILLEEN: I would like to say something about what happened this morning. We participated, with volatility, on the open. We had a buy and a sell swap trade, in the same industry, and both stocks opened up higher. As far as participating on the open, which I know we want to talk about later, you have to take every trade, one by one. With the easier trades, we try to handle and route them electronically for execution to save time for the more difficult trades.

When a trader considers participating on the opening price on the floor of the NYSE, every order must be evaluated individually to satisfy the best execution of the trade, using normal trading volume and price volatility as a guideline. The decision of whether or not to participate should be based on how that opening price and volume would impact trading in the stock. If the stock isn't very liquid and it looks as if a relatively large volume of stock will trade on the open, then it would be wise to participate. It may be wise to participate even without a great deal of volume. On a final note, this decision can be made with the help of a 'look' from a floor broker at the booth where the stock is about to open. Included in this look is an indicated price spread along with the size of the orders, to buy and to sell. Of course, since the NYSE operates under the auction method, this look is subject to change before the stock actually opens, but it is nonetheless the best and only information about where the stock will be trading when it officially opens.

Getting back to this morning, I had two stocks that opened up. One opened up \$3 higher (about 2 ½ % higher) and the other one opened up \$1 higher. Common sense told me to stay away from the open on the stock that I wanted to buy, and to sell into the strength of the one that I wanted to sell.

SCHWARTZ: Did they then come back?

KILLEEN: They did come back for a short time.

SCHWARTZ: They both mean reverted?

KILLEEN: Right, they did revert. Then, at 10: 00, some consumer confidence numbers came out that buoyed the market a little bit, and the market for all stocks strengthened. I tried to take advantage of that. It was a volatile period, the first half hour today. It was a big open. I came in and tried to snatch up some stock before they ran away. Meanwhile, I was keeping up with the sell-side and trying to take advantage of the market while it was hot. There was news related to the stock I was interested in, so it might hang out there all day in a strong upward move. By 'hang out there' I am referring to the strength of the move in the stock's price. The news out that particular day had created an upward bias in the price of the stock. I didn't want to compete my order too early and miss higher prices to sell at, so I began pacing myself with the strength in the overall market.

That is the challenge. We spend most of our time on the difficult trades. I search for liquidity because the market is not built for trades of hundreds of thousands of shares. You can get a typical order that can be half a million shares, and the stock might trade 50,000 shares a day. That huge order is going to take time. You have to find the contra side of the trade, and that is a battle. But we do have a number of tools and protocols that we use in the search.

SCHWARTZ: Thanks, Chris. Mark, let me move quickly over to you. We are talking about market structure with regard to institutional needs versus retail needs. What are your thoughts?

MARK MADOFF: Our focus is solely on the retail order. As Andy mentioned, while he is trying to devote more time towards larger size trades, we try to become a destination for the smaller trades. That is what we focus on. The average retail investor either comes in through a mutual fund, or comes in through an individual equity trade. We all need to do our job well. Everybody needs to focus on best execution from his or her own perspective, and we need to focus on it from the individual side. That is how we try to approach things.

SCHWARTZ: As you made that comment, which I do resonate with, I noticed you flinch a little. I was not surprised, because I know that you are at a different end of the order size spectrum. But there is a thought that I have had. I was thinking about it late yesterday, and an image came to my mind.

How many of you remember that old, very famous folk blues singer, Lead Belly? Are we dating ourselves on this one (laughter)? There is a song that Lead Belly sang which is pretty meaningful. It is meaningful for Mark Madoff's operation, and for you guys on the institutional side who are having trouble working your orders. The big players can be incurring market impact, and they see it as a cost. But how does it affect the market for the retail order flow? Here is Lead Belly's answer. The song is, 'We are in the Same Boat Brother.' The key line of the song is, 'if you shake one end you will rock the other, we are in the same boat brother.' If you big guys are knocking price around, how does it affect what others, including retail, are seeing and feeling?

MADOFF: It is hard for us to assess that. Decimalization has brought the average spread in the stocks in the S&P 500 from somewhere in the vicinity of 10 cents down to 2 cents. The decline is dramatic. But the shrinking of the spread, and the shrinking of the size at the spread, has had a much smaller impact on the small order than it has on the large trade. The average retail trade, globally in the industry, enjoys about a five-second-turnaround time. This means that they are achieving a level of automatic execution. Those orders are coming in, and are being returned quickly to the investors as completed trades.

But it is difficult for us to assess exactly what the impact would be if a retail order came in along with a 200,000 share institutional order. What would happen to the small order? All we can do is focus on the small order. We can make sure that, at the point of entry, we take a snapshot of the market, execute that order, and return it to the customer. And we can look at market impact versus the time lapse between order entry to the time of order execution.

SCHWARTZ: Mark, you are talking about a five second turnaround. Andy, what are you guys thinking about when your order is equal to average daily trading volume, or, perhaps, 20 times daily volume? What is your turnaround time?

BROOKS: It varies. It all depends on how quickly you can locate the liquidity at the price point that you …

SCHWARTZ: Five seconds?

BROOKS: Certainly not five seconds (laughter).

SCHWARTZ: Five minutes, five hours, a day, more?

BROOKS: It depends. Sometimes you could be initiating a position or disposing of a position over several months. If a decision is made to dispose of a stock, it could take several weeks or several days to complete. It could take five seconds or 10 minutes if you get a hit in a crossing network, or if you call, for example, Weeden & Co. There is a random element and sometimes you don't know what you could trade in the market until you try. But the question would then become, are you comfortable with the price at that time? The answer is, you'd better be before you trade it all. You'd better be comfortable in your investment decision and be comfortable that the price you are trading at is a fair price.

There is a myriad of choices to search for liquidity in this process. You should look to see where the stock has been trading and how much volume has been done. There are market data facilities such as AutEx and Bridge, as well as Nasdaq market maker data to show who is the largest dealer in particular stocks. On the NYSE, you might check with a floor broker to see who was the dominant player in a stock.

SCHWARTZ: There are two dimensions to think about. One is the size of an order, and the other is the price of a trade. What happens to size and price when things get turbulent? Isn't one of the causes of turbulence your elephant size orders? And how do you handle your elephant size orders in turbulent times?

Let's consider market quality in the context of a relatively stressful time. In particular, let's focus on the first half hour of the trading day. That is typically a stressful time. How many of you knew already that volatility is higher in the first half hour? Thanks. Great, a good show of hands. Isn't that a wonderful thing about rigorous statistical analysis? It tells you that what you always knew to be true is indeed true at the .05 level.

With that as background, I want to ask Chris and Andy another question. When you get an order to work that exceeds average daily volume or a multiple thereof, what do you start thinking about? What goes through your mind?

CHRIS: What I think about is accessing institutional size liquidity. I might first try the stealth approach and enter my order in a crossing network such as POSIT and/or Liquidnet. I would then take a look at the previous day's trading history to find out what broker was involved in the name. I might then call that broker and have a discussion about the availability of stock without tipping my hand to the exact size of my order. In extreme cases, we might even contact the company directly to obtain stock. In the absence of luck on these fronts, we usually expose small amounts to the floor and work them patiently until the order is compete.

BROOKS: In the context of the opening, you think about how big your order is relative to what is traded. Do you think you will be able to get it done in a reasonable time frame? Is there a sense of urgency? Have you been instructed and communicated with your portfolio manager? Do you have a strategy that he or she has bought into?

Like you, Bob, I was giving some thought to this yesterday, and I came up with an analogy. The first half hour is similar to the breaking of the gate at the Preakness. All the horses charge out and they are looking for position. Somebody wants to be on the inside rail. Somebody is holding back because they know that they will finish strong and they think that the start was too quick. Chris talked about that today, about a stock opening up \$3. If you are a buyer, do you want to be in on that part of the race, or do you want to lay back? That is part of the reason why there is so much volatility at the opening. There is so much confusion. You have all of these horses scrambling and trying to figure out what strategy they want to employ. And that strategy changes every day, based on God knows what – news, the environment, feelings, the weather, and lots of other things.

SCHWARTZ: I know, Andy, that the opening is a period of particular interest to you. I have empirical validation of that. Last week I was involved with putting my material together, forgot to look at the clock, and called Andy at 9: 32. He could only pronounce the first two letters of my name (laughter). We continued the call later.

One thing that you definitely think about is the time frame, right? How quickly do you want the job done? In light of this, there is one question I have always wanted to get my arms around. I have talked to various people about it, and rarely get a straight answer. The open, the first 15 minutes, or the first half hour- is it a particularly difficult time, or is it not a particularly difficult time to trade in?

KILLEEN: It is a very difficult time.

BROOKS: It is difficult because there is a lack of information. Stocks can get three different looks in that time span. In a rapidly changing marketplace, a stock could get many different looks. By a look I mean, at least on the floor of the exchange, that buyers and sellers will put their orders in and then cancel out in that time frame. There is an information lag there. If you have a market order, you have to be very careful with it. You have to make sure that the person you give your market order to understands what you are trying to accomplish and that he knows the price you are comfortable with.

SCHWARTZ: You want to look and go carefully. Is it because you are uncertain about the prices that you are seeing?

BROOKS: That could be one part of it. It could also be that I do not want to dominate the volume. That is, not unless I am very confident in my approach. If I have a new order, I am going to look at it from a top down approach. I am going to say to myself, where is the order coming from? What industry is it? What is the characteristic of the portfolio manager, or of the portfolio itself? Is it to add to an existing position, or is it a new position? I will quickly think through all of that. Based on that, I will get the look from the floor. If I think it is beneficial for us to participate, I will be a good part of the volume.

SCHWARTZ: Especially if the market is coming to you. If you want to buy, and you just know it, and if prices happen to be lower, then you will take advantage of the situation. Correct?

BROOKS: But we also know from the work that you all have done, that the first hour of trading is a big part of the volume for the day. That is important to us. I also think that the specialists, or the people making the markets, can profit the most in that opening 10 or 15 minutes, and maybe at the close as well. So your question, Bob, how do you feel about the prices, is a very good one. It really comes down to how confident I am of the order and what I have to do. And also how confident I am of what I really think is going on in terms of supply and demand that has not come to the market. I am referring to the latent trading interest of those who are just looking. You know, those people who are staying out of the opening and who might show up at 10: 30.

SCHWARTZ: Yes, the unrevealed orders. This relationship between volatility and volume is a tricky one. It came up in the previous panel. You see a lot of volume in the first half hour, and that volume drives volatility. However, on the other hand, volatility can discourage volume. That is like the identification problem that Paul Bennett was mentioning. Which way does it really go? Do you guys like to go in at the open, yes or no?

BROOKS: In general?

SCHWARTZ: In general and relative to other times. Is there something in you that holds you away from the opening?

BROOKS: I would say my opinion on that has changed in the last few years. I have a positive bias and would probably want to be there on a stock that has decent trading characteristics. By decent trading characteristics, I mean, if it has a decent trading volume on an ordinary day. That is predicated on my confidence, and on whether or not I wanted to get the big piece of volume done relative to the order that I have on the desk.

BROOKS: One of the challenges is, if you are interested in buying or selling a stock, and if there is going to be price dislocation and you are not there, you are not represented. I had a situation ten days ago that should never have happened, but it did. I missed the opening. The stock opened up a dollar, and I was not there to sell my 17,000 shares. I am still irritated about it. It was a lack of communication (laughter).[34]

But that was a terrific opportunity. If we had been there, maybe it would not have opened up a dollar. Maybe it would have opened up 40 cents. That is part of the gamesmanship going on. What cards are you showing, what are you holding back? But invariably, you do not get to benefit from a price dislocation unless you are there in the first place.

KILLEEN: You have to be careful of price dislocation, which is a big move in the price of a stock since the previous day's closing price. If you

[34] Chris Killeen notes that whenever a human broker working an order for a buyside trader neglects to give this trader a 'heads up' on a price dislocation, the broker is usually sent to the 'penalty box' by the trader. He used the sports metaphor to mean that the trader would temporarily stop using the services of the broker as a sort of professional reprimand.

have an illiquid 'open' order on your desk, you would most likely want to participate when this happens, if only because it is usually associated with large volume causing the price movement. You don't want your portfolio manager asking, 'How come you weren't there?'

SCHWARTZ: Do you have any particular opinion about the open?

KILLEEN: I see more retail activity at the opening, and I see more overseas activity at the opening. The institutions are much more cautious. As Andy said, if they see a dislocation, they will take advantage of it. But I know the institutions do not want to go in, be in the opening, and have these specialists provide the liquidity. They do not want that to happen. But if there is natural liquidity there, that is to their advantage. Then they will play.

BARRY SMALL: We see that a tremendous percentage of the market's daily trading, probably around 20% to 25%, takes place on the opening, pre-opening market orders. A lot of the action comes from retail customers who have spent the evening digesting the news that has taken place. It is probably their best opportunity to be on an equal footing based on news. This is very important. We also see a lot of institutional buyers come in. It is the small institutional players who prefer to put their orders in on the open. They do not want to leave any subjectivity to a trader. Their attitude is, get me the open and let me go home. The time difference also plays a factor on orders from overseas. These investors want to go home, and get their stuff done.

SCHWARTZ: That is interesting. We see similar statistics from Europe, where electronic trading platforms characterize the markets, and electronic call auctions are the formal opening procedures. Order flow at the European call market openings is predominantly retail.

I keep thinking about the heavy volume that we see in the first half hour. There are a lot of orders there that could have come in earlier. They could have come in at the open. But they don't, because they are part of the horse race. Is that fair Andy?

BROOKS: It is absolutely fair. We are fond of describing some of what we do as that big poker game in the sky. When you play that game, you take your time putting your cards down. You are careful how you do it.

SCHWARTZ: I want to interrupt this discussion. There is a question from the audience. Natan, what is it?

NATAN TIEFENBRUN[35] [From the Floor]: My question relates to the lack of confidence around the open. It is a U.S. problem. From my experience trading in European markets, it is not a European problem. It has

[35] Natan Tiefenbrun is Senior Vice President at Instinet Corporation.

to do with a lack of confidence in the price formation process. On the floor of the New York Stock Exchange, you have no idea where that price is coming from. You do not know if it is a specialist applying liquidity, or if it is natural liquidity. Consequently, you have no confidence and you back off to see what happens.

In Nasdaq, the problem is that you have so many small retail orders, so many little spikes, and so much noise. It is really hard in Nasdaq to see the true price formation that is going on.

Across most of Europe, the open is liquid and transparent. Participants have great confidence. Institutions do go in at the open in Continental Europe, although perhaps not in the U.K. where there is still a dealer culture rather than an electronic order book culture. I would say that this is a market structure problem in New York. Price formation has just too little transparency. I would love to hear the buy-side firms respond to that.

SCHWARTZ: Or the sell-side.

TIEFENBRUN [From the Floor]: Either or.

BROOKS: We are dodging something in this part of this discussion – price. Every day we have, say, GE, and its fundamentals might change – at glacial speed, I grant you. Yet intra-day GE's volatility is 5%. Knowing this, do I want to have completed my 100,000-share order at 9:37? I had better have a pretty strong feeling to do so. I am sure Chris would say the same thing. Actually, so would everyone on the panel.

We are keeping our cards close because we are wondering about the legitimacy of the prices that we see. It is not because of the specialist or anybody else. It is just the way the markets are. Everybody at the table, as the options guys were describing, seem to make a lot of money from intra-day volatility. I think that runs counter to long-term investing. I am not saying that one is better than the other, but intra-day volatility is a very scary thing for long-term oriented investors.

SCHWARTZ: I am not sure that the options people on the previous panel were saying that the accentuated intra-day volatility is good.

BROOKS: I think that is how they make their money.

SCHWARTZ: I don't know. I was going to ask David Krell one more question, but we were running late. I will ask it now. David, if you accept that the first half-hour and the open-to-close volatilities are accentuated, that the accentuation is related to trading costs, and that we could mute the accentuation with better market structure, what effect would this have on option prices? What would your answer be?

DAVID KRELL[36] [From the Floor]: From an option trader's viewpoint, the accentuated volatility hurts the options markets because the layoff on the stock, which is what the hedge is, costs you more money. As a result, you have to build that into the price of the option. I think that higher gradual volatility is probably helpful. But accentuated, short-term volatility (intra-day volatility) is probably negative.

SCHWARTZ: As we talk about accentuated volatility in the first half-hour (or from open-to-close, if you wish), is it reasonable that the accentuation is a reflection of market quality? Is it reasonable to expect, if we had improved market structures, that we would see less of this volatility accentuation? George, I would like to hear what you have to say.

GEORGE SOFIANOS: I would first like to introduce a new concept that I think is very useful when we talk about large orders. When we talk about very large orders, it is important to distinguish between volatility and what I like to call 'stock momentum.' Volatility is essentially price fluctuations around the trend. What I call 'stock momentum' is the change in the stock's price over the horizon of a trade. We are talking about a large trade that may actually take several hours or several days to complete. Looked at in this context, intra-day volatility around the trend is a very small component of the trading cost.

The biggest component of the trading cost (I think Andy alluded to it) is momentum, the direction of the market. If you are buying, and the market is rising, and you are slow, you get killed. If you look at the numbers and try to decompose them for the volatility and the momentum, you will find that, for the very large orders that take time, momentum is everything. This is very important.

I have a controversial statement that I will make to generate discussion. For very large orders, for orders that are multiples of average daily trading volume, market structure does not matter. Momentum, as opposed to intra-day volatility, is not so sensitive to market structure. For these very large orders, what you want to tap is the non-displayed liquidity on the buy-side. There is no system out there, no market structure that would make the buy-side reveal its non-displayed liquidity. Those very large orders are beyond the realm of market structure.

SCHWARTZ: I agree with a lot of what you said. Momentum is a big cost. But I also wonder where the momentum comes from? Is it because of a butterfly that flapped its wings in Mexico? Is its genesis in the operations of the retail market? Is it the result of larger orders that are broken up? When a large order is broken up, the trader is bringing similarly signed pieces – buy, buy, buy, or sell, sell, sell – to the market, over a period of time. Does that become a foundation for momentum? Yes, or no? Bruce?

---

[36] David Krell is President and CEO of the International Securities Exchange.

BRUCE TURNER: Absolutely. You cannot keep feeding orders in and not expect them to impact what is going on. I mean, you have an order that is 100% of average daily volume, and you keep dropping in 50 thousand shares at a time, you are telegraphing what you are doing.

SCHWARTZ: We are, of course, in an academic environment. We are on the 14th floor of a business school that teaches finance courses, and that gets into issues such as capital markets efficiency. What is the standard thing we keep hearing from academia? The classic concept of an efficient market is one where prices follow a random walk. Now here we are, talking about momentum. Momentum is not random walk.

I ask my class, how many of you believe in random walk? Boy, are they quiet. Nobody raises his or her hands. I would not raise mine either. How many of you here believe in random walk? No hands being raised? I am not surprised. People who believe in random walk usually do not walk into conferences of this nature.

I am dwelling on this a bit because momentum trading is in conflict with random walk and hence market efficiency. I would like to know more about how momentum might relate to psychology, especially the psychology of the retail customer. But there is something more tangible involved. There is the slicing and dicing of the institutional sized orders.

If what I just said is correct, doesn't it imply that market structure does matter? Doesn't market structure matter if momentum starts with institutions having to slice and dice their orders and work them over a period of time in order to get to the liquidity pools?

MADOFF: Are you assuming that a liquidity pool is there on the other side?

SCHWARTZ: Perhaps. But, where is the liquidity pool on the other side? We talk a lot about connecting with liquidity pools on the other side. Are they there?

MADOFF: It depends on the genesis of an institutional order. The way in which information is disseminated now, it goes to everybody, and it does so quickly. What has triggered the institutional order? Why is the investor a buyer of stock? Today, the individual who is buying 200 shares of a stock is reading a research report, in all probability on the Internet, and he or she may have the same reason to buy that Andy has. And now Andy's horse race has a lot more players in it than it used to. Before it meant about ten institutions doing the same thing. Now you may have 10 large institutions and 50 small institutions all of which may, for some reason, have an order similar to Andy's. Plus, you may also have a host of individual investors, all with similar market access. Now, suddenly, everybody has direct access, or some direct access like product.

SCHWARTZ: There is a term I first heard in London a decade or so ago when I was over there doing some work with Anthony Neuberger. Anthony referred quite a bit to 'one-sided markets.' I remember our discussions of institutions getting similar research reports. This leads to a situation where, when one wants to buy, chances are they all want to buy. When one wants to sell, they all want to sell. Today in theU.S., with more players and more diversity, are one-sided markets more prevalent or less?

BROOKS: The answer is, everything is for sale at a price. Everything can be bought at a price. We are back to the basic challenges that we face – price versus volume, immediacy versus patience, and perfect knowledge versus the random walk. That is the finesse part, the art form that is now more of a challenge because of the number of players that people reference. There are so many more players today in the horse race. Outcomes are not so clear. Yes, we think the stock is cheap and we want to buy it. There might be a natural on the other side size. On the other hand, a decision to buy or to sell could be driven by a stock valuation and not by the natural supply and demand of stock. We may want to initiate a sell order, for example, because the stock is fully valued, or we may initiate a purchase because we found out from doing our fundamental analysis that a new product offering is being well received. Most of the time, we are acting on our fundamental analysis and portfolio decisions. We may want more exposure to healthcare, for example if it looks cheap.

SCHWARTZ: What is your view of it Barry?

SMALL: Andy makes a good point about price. But there is a lot of activity between what you *want* the price to be and what you *expect* the price to be. The role of the intermediary is still important. A big investor like Andy needs a buffer. He needs to find capital to bridge himself from that expectation of price to what is reality. It could be something as simple as, every value trader wants to get out. If so, the value guy could be the natural other side of Andy's trade, but he doesn't want to be the first one in. So there is going to be a lot of intermediary plays in there. Maybe hedge funds come in and bottom fish. There may be market makers. It might be me putting up significant capital for Andy. I could wind up taking on a position and holding it for a period of time. Eventually, price will get to a level where a value trader will stand up and put his bid in, and he will be the natural other side of the trade. Still, the natural other side is elusive. Even if we get a wonderful new system like Seth Merrin's Liquidnet, and Seth gets nice volume on it, there are still not a lot of transactions.

SCHWARTZ: Seth is the person to ask. You are looking for the natural other side, aren't you, Seth? When Andy wants to sell, is it more likely that Chris wants to sell also? How common are one-sided markets? Or, Seth, do you find that there are natural counterparts.

SETH MERRIN[37] [From the Floor]: There are always natural counterparts. Obviously, lots of institutions are always on the same side in our market. But, as more and more institutions come on board, we achieve a higher match rate. When Liquidnet started out, we had a very small match percentage. Now we are showing liquidity in about 20% of all of the orders that people have on their desks throughout our entire community. There are matches, but only about 20%. You could also say, wow, it is amazing! I can get 20% of my orders done through Liquidnet right now!

SCHWARTZ: If you would allow me, I would say 'wow.' Whatever it is that allows somebody who wants to do a job, to find the liquidity on the other side, is pretty good. If something could be improved by superior market structure, if a structural change could enable buyers and sellers to find each other at a price without having to take seven days, or five days, or one to fill an order, I would say that that would be a better quality market.

TURNER: We are talking about how to get as much information out there as we can. Let's face it, we are all playing poker. We have already got about eighteen analogies out there, so I will try not to add to them (laughter). But we are all playing poker, and we all keep our cards close to our chests. So the question is, how do we make people feel more comfortable about what is out there?

The liquidity pools do matter. They are diverse, and there are multiple liquidity pools out there. How can we aggregate them in one spot? Aggregating them would impact on the whole process. As you start to feel more comfortable about putting 3,000 out there, it will be more comfortable for some other person to put 5,000 out there on the other side. Once there is more liquidity in a stock you will feel more comfortable about putting up size because the price is less likely to run away from you. It becomes the game that I think Seth was talking about.

SCHWARTZ: That certainly is the point that I was trying to make. There are people at opposite sides. I do not mean to imply that it will ever be perfect. If you are going to trade that large number of shares, you have to accept that you cannot do it instantaneously. The critical question is, could 'finding the other side' be done better and faster than we are currently doing it? That is where the issues of market structure and market quality intersect.

HOLLY STARK[38] [From the Floor]: The problem is exacerbated when you move down the capitalization levels. Those pools of liquidity are not ponds. They are little droplets. Let's stay with the water analogy now, as

[37] Seth Merrin is CEO of Liquidnet.

[38] Holly Stark is Principal and Director of Trading at Kern Capital Management.

opposed to horses. Your market impact will be much greater as you try to trade an outsized piece of stock. If, as was mentioned, you take a stock to the level where it is going to trade, you will certainly have market impact. It would be much more efficient, especially with those stocks that are highly illiquid, and where there might not be an institution on the other side of the trade, to have another approach. There may be ten institutional holders and the liquidity droplets may be in the retail marketplace. You would have better price discovery and a more efficient market, if you had a call market – especially for those less liquid shares. You didn't pay me to say this, Bob (laughter).

SCHWARTZ: No, but I will (laughter).

STARK [From the Floor]: Truly, there are many more inefficiencies in the small cap market, and your price impact can be so much greater. Especially if you have an outsized order.

TURNER: But Holly, suppose that you want to buy 5% of the daily volume of a stock in a call auction. And you get this call auction at, say, 10: 00 a.m., and everybody submits his or her orders. The liquidity to get your order done may climb to 20% of the then current total volume. So you get it done in one block in the call, but with volume in the stock having increased by quite some percentage points. George is calling it momentum, and you are calling it a call. Whichever, the net result is that you still pay a price if you agreed to buy at the price set in the call. But, as Andy said, there is always a buyer and a seller.

STARK [From the Floor]: Yes, you are pricing the order.

BROOKS: And it is a static moment in time.

TURNER: Right, and your theory being, we know it is a static point in time, and it may not trade again, and so we all have to be there.

STARK [From the Floor]: Yes.

TURNER: I do not know how that would work. We need a continuous market. And you will never get people to reveal 100% of what they are looking to do.

STARK [From the Floor]: Bruce, I agree with you. That is the buy-side conundrum. Everyone wants to see the liquidity, but no one is actually going to put his or her order out there. Everyone wants markets to be transparent, but nobody wants anyone else to know what they themselves want to do. I think someone else mentioned that.

But, regardless, call markets and continuous markets are not mutually exclusive. Certainly, there will always be people who want to trade on a continuous basis. Retail people, for instance, who come in whenever they fire-up their computer. These people want immediacy of execution. Nevertheless, knowing that you might have a better chance of getting a certain amount of liquidity done at certain points in time during the day could be very interesting.

TURNER: But it does not solve the slice and dice problem. What happens now is that people say, OK, it is time for the POSIT cross. Let's put apiece in there. Let's see if we get a hit. If we do, great. If not, we keep going.

STARK [From the Floor]: Bruce, I do not trade on a VWAP basis. I do not want to get into that.

TURNER: No, this is not a VWAP thing. But if you get an oversized order on one of these stocks, you want the benefit of having both a call and a continuous market. The result is that you do not put the whole thing into the call, because people are still slicing and dicing.

SCHWARTZ: There are alternatives other than the call. Liquidnet is an alternative in the continuous market. Liquidity Tracker, to an extent, could be viewed in this context. Fred, would you say a word about Liquidity Tracker?

FRED FEDERSPIEL[39] [From the Floor]: Liquidity Tracker is a new system that will be deployed by Nasdaq this summer.[40] As Bruce says, there is no way you can force any player, buy-side or sell-side, to show his whole hand. But Liquidity Tracker tries to create a system that encourages players to show a little bit more. For instance, you can select the players to whom you will show that information based on what they are actually trading in real time. Liquidity Tracker will be employed by Nasdaq, which hopes it will encourage the process of showing more size. As I said, you can direct the disclosure to specific parties based on their real-time trading activity. And Liquidity Tracker maintains total anonymity on both sides.

SCHWARTZ: Mark Gresack. You have a question?

MARK GRESACK[41] [From the Floor]: First of all, I want to go on record as saying that I like Lead Belly.

SCHWARTZ: Oh, good. Can you sing a few bars?

GRESACK [From the Floor]: Not really (laughter). My question goes to Andy's point about price versus volume, and to your issues, Bob, about

[39] Fred Federspiel is currently CEO of Pipeline Trading Systems. At the time of the conference, he was CEO of e-Xchange Advantage Corporation.

[40] In mid-2003, Nasdaq announced that it was discontinuing Liquidity Tracker, an automated order routing system that allowed traders to direct orders to specific market makers. Volume was negligible soon after it was launched.

[41] Marc Gresack is currently CEO of Glen Eagle Securities. At the time of the conference, he was a strategic consultant at Brut LLC.

market structure. Take Cisco. On a daily basis, Cisco trades 45 or 50 million shares a day, sometimes more. Where are all the orders? They are on a reserve book.[42] My question is, how has the reserve book changed the way in which the buy-side trades? Does it get to the transparency piece, and to how much you are willing to show? Is it because you do not want to show your hand all at once and you slice it? The reserve book is a good tool for doing that. I see on the electronic side that the reserve book has really changed the way the buy-side has traded over the last few years.

SCHWARTZ: If these new systems – Liquidity Tracker, reserve books, Liquidnet, call auctions, or whatever – change the way that people trade, the question is, do they help with the two things that we have discussed: price discovery and quantity discovery? If the answer is yes, then that is a bridge between market structure and market quality. It is a bridge that I like to talk about in the context of volatility more than in the context of the bid-ask spread.

BROOKS: The problem (or the rub) is that the volume discovery does not happen because prices are not trusted.

SCHWARTZ: Can you speak further about the extent to which you do not trust the prices that you see, and about how that effects your revelation of quantity?

BROOKS: It is not just a matter of trusting the price that I see. It is also my thoughts about what price might do going forward. If I declare and trade in size – say I trade 750,000 shares of a stock that trades 50,000 share a day on average – I have gotten the job done, but I have gone way past the average daily volume. The question becomes, for me, as an individual with human traits and an ego, whether I want to immediately look stupid. Can I risk that? Am I confident enough in our investment process, in the certainty of immediately declaring my entire trading interest? Am I confident enough to immediately risk looking stupid? Hopefully, most of the time I am.

SOFIANOS: I guess part of this is due to the continuing trading process. As markets evolve over the trading day, there is more information revealed and the price follows a trend. So you really do not want to put all of your eggs in one basket by having your entire execution done at one point of time.

SCHWARTZ: So, Andy, you do have uncertainty about price. I like how you put it in the context of looking forward.

SOFIANOS: But are the fundamentals of the price more a function of the market structure? It is this distinction that must be made when volatility is very sensitive to the momentum over time. This phenomenon only occurs with very large orders. It is not related to market structure. In short time

[42] A reserve book allows an institution to work portions of a large order without revealing what is behind it.

spans over the course of the trading day the structure of the market will play a much more significant role in the price of a very large order. That's because of the way the order is handled by specialists and others during these short periods. Over the long term, these factors play a much less significant role in the price formation.

TURNER: Andy's issue is about putting up an order of 750,000 to buy and then, seeing nothing around it, having the market go against the order. If you have a market structure that allowed you to put that amount of shares up, a market structure that knows there is some normal line of resistance – that takes into account, for example, a stock that typically trades 50,000 shares a day, so it attracts bids and offers in 5,000 and 10,000-share size at particular prices – then we would have a better solution. This kind of system, for example, would be driven by algorithms that respond to block trading in an anonymous environment, a system that would enable buyers and sellers of large blocks to find each other easily. That would respond in some way to Andy's issue.

What happens now is that the print goes up, it is between two players, a buyer and a seller, but someone misses it – a third party who didn't declare – and all of a sudden they are saying, oh no, I missed it! I got to do something! So they run around trying to see who advertised the trade. They call Andy and Andy does not care. He's concerned about the market impact the new seller will have, resulting in the slicing behavior traders have adopted. It's better to chase a stock than to be embarrassed on the downside. If we had a market structure that got all the players together in the first place, that would not happen. The price discovery process, for example, would factor in the seller of 250,000 shares.

SCHWARTZ: Barry, you are part of the market structure that helps that to happen, right?

SMALL: Absolutely. My reaction is, with Andy and Bruce's discomfort comments, that it is all about limit orders. It is all about the market centers attracting limit orders. Whether it is Nasdaq or the NYSE, we have huge issues here as to whether that market structure will develop. Will they be able to attract and retain limit orders? If SuperMontage is the answer, and it can attract limit orders, we are going to have a very good experience. We will aggregate the market, and fragmentation will be a much less painful experience.

We have a big problem at The New York Stock Exchange, however. The limit orders are disappearing. There are no limit orders. They have instituted a wonderful initiative called the OpenBook[43] but there is nothing

[43] OpenBook is an NYSE product that shows the aggregate limit order volume data for bids and offers in all Big Board issues.

there. We have an open book with no book. I am very, very concerned about the integrity of limit orders coming to the market and being treated fairly. The NYSE has a major problem there.

SuperMontage is on its way to creating a limit order book that will be very viable. If we all had access to that information, if we all saw that the limit orders were being treated fairly, our markets would be less volatile. We would make bolder decisions, and everyone would end up with cheaper trading costs.

SCHWARTZ: Mark, can you respond from your vantage point to what Barry just said about limit orders?

MADOFF: What Barry just said about limit orders is exactly the case. But the next step in limit order exposure is connecting one market to another. The key for us is market connectivity. The major flaw that you have with the New York Stock Exchange is not, in my mind, OpenBook. I think OpenBook is a wonderful step in the right direction. The flaw is the lack of automatic execution that enables access to that book. If you added that step, then, when you see a quote, you would have access to that quote. Then it becomes a real quote. A quote that you do not have access to is not a real quote. If you have to call a broker, or put an order into a system, and then someone has to physically run across a room to get to the liquidity, that is a problem. Even the average turnaround time on a DOT trade is somewhere in excess of 17 seconds. That is a huge issue.

You can see an example of this, and realize why automatic execution is important, if you look at the growth of the triple Qs. The triple Qs trade actively in a number of other venues that provide automatic execution. They have taken a huge amount of volume away from the more traditional auction market environments that are not offering automatic execution. The key now is to go one step further. We must actually connect all of the ECNs and all of the ATSs to a centralized marketplace, similar to the way the ITS system operates. An institution wants to look and ask, where is my liquidity? But it is not only *where* is my liquidity. It is also, how can I actually access it?

An institution should be able to look at a single screen and see an Island quote, a Redibook quote, an Archipelago quote, and all of the exchange quotes. If it wants to get at one of those pools of liquidity, it should be able to do so by pushing one button. Something like the concept of SuperMontage or the ITS, both of which link markets together, could work in practice to solve this problem.[44]

[44] Mark Madoff is referring in his remarks on Island ECN (now merged with Instinet), which is said to 'trade through' the markets in executing customer orders. Island, which is not a member of the Intermarket Trading System (ITS), has lobbied for reform of the ITS.

Today, you must go through any one of a number of private networks to get at that liquidity. And the moment you go into a private network, you run afoul of all sorts of problems. One problem has to do with limit order display and trade-throughs. Are you really getting the best price? By the time I send my order into this system, do I actually get the execution? It is not good for the market, for instance, that one ECN out there will trade outside the quotation posted. This same ECN claims its customers know what is happening. Unfortunately, the investors who are hurt are those whose orders are traded through by this ECN when it is facilitating its own group of customers.

You also need a tremendous IT infrastructure to build these networks. If you want liquidity, you have to build the infrastructure. It is very, very difficult. Getting back to what Barry said, if the limit order display is critical, you must couple the limit order display with connectivity between market centers. Then you have solved a huge problem.

TURNER: I am a big believer in automatic execution. It makes people real. There is an issue with that though. By itself, automatic execution won't get orders in the book. We must incent people to put orders in the book, and automatic execution is part of that incentive. However, the only incentive that will really get people to put orders in the book is the fear that, if they don't, they will miss something. That is really what it comes down to. If you have that fear, people will start putting orders in the book. Then automatic execution will make them all real. Automatic execution is a key component, but we have to go one step beyond automatic execution. Participants must have the fear that they are going to miss something.

SCHWARTZ: In other words, you have to be pre-positioned to benefit from the incoming event. Is that what you are saying?

TURNER: Yes. What we have seen in Nasdaq is, because there is the connectivity and things are really fast, that there is no incentive to put orders in the book. If the market moves, I can go in, zap, in nanoseconds. The turnaround time in SuperSoes is now a sub second, about 2/10 of a second. What is your incentive to put the order in the book when the people who are paying attention are 2/10 of a second away from that execution?

SCHWARTZ: This conversation about limit orders really points something up. The key to improving market structure is to have an environment where people are willing to step forward and preposition themselves. As they do so, liquidity is brought out. It is not just a question of connecting the liquidity pools that are already there. It is a question of having an environment that will allow a liquidity pool to build naturally.

Under the ITS trade through rules, a participant is not allowed to trade a stock at an inferior price to the displayed price in a different market.

SMALL: Absolutely. Look at the fight that has gone on with ECNs and Nasdaq in liquidity rebates. I mean, it is an incredible fight to get that liquidity in the book.

SCHWARTZ: Mark, would you say a word about SuperMontage, and about how it may or may not help?

MADOFF: How does SuperMontage help? SuperMontage makes you fear, 'Oh, I am going to miss something,' because of the way the book processes the orders. SuperMontage can burn through multiple levels, and it freezes people from getting in at the times that hurt investors. In today's world, in other words, you can keep pumping in at the next level down. On SuperMontage, however, you cannot do that. You process what is there, and then you publish a quote. If you want to be represented at the second level but you don't have an order in, you would miss it. The trade would go right through you.

SCHWARTZ: There is another question from the audience. Seth?

MERRIN [From the Floor]: I understand a lot of the things that we have been talking about in terms of aggregating the ECNs up. But, getting back to something that Andy said earlier, we are still talking about small execution sizes. The disconnect that I have always had, that I really do not understand, is between a portfolio manager's desire and his orders, and the trading desk's ability to get those orders filled. I understand from a personal perspective that if you go out on a limb doing 750,000 shares while the average daily volume is 50,000, you can look stupid. So, how do you reconcile the disconnect between what the portfolio manager really wants to do – whether he wants to buy a million shares or sell a million shares – versus the trader's personality conflict in actually being there for the game?

BROOKS: That is a million dollar question, Seth. I would answer it this way. Every portfolio manager, just like every trader including everybody in this room, regardless of what they do, wants to win every single time that he or she comes up to the plate. These guys and gals expect us to properly analyze supply and demand and to stretch it a little bit. Yes, they have made the decision to buy shares, but, gee, if there were sellers shouldn't you have known that? And if it is going lower, shouldn't we be getting a better price? Why did you buy it at all? Because you told me to (laughter)! But I expected you also to know that there were sellers out there.

Our value added as traders is on the margin. For a trader today to stay employed, it is critically important for him to appreciate where his value added is coming from, and to not be an obstructionist. If the portfolio manager wants to sell it, it is generally not the trader's imperative to contradict him.

KILLEEN: There is also a level of trust there. You do not get a blank check from a portfolio manager with an order. If he gives you an order, he is expecting you to work it diligently. It is part of our job and we do not like to lose. We fight for our clients and try to get the best price (if there is a best price). There is a lot of second-guessing, and some portfolio managers are hands on. They call every hour and want to know. Hey, I saw something go by. Was that me? Why? Why not?

SCHWARTZ: What is your perspective George?

SOFIANOS: Andy and Chris' points both also apply to the sell-side traders. What is extremely important is the communication between the portfolio manager, the sell-side trader, and the buy-side trader. There must be a good understanding of what the buy-side wants. There is a desire to act in the context of those instructions. One of the greatest lessons I learned when I moved from the New York Stock Exchange to Goldman, was how important the relationships are between the buy-side and the sell-side. I am thinking of the personal relationships, where they can talk and exchange ideas and provide information and context for each execution.

SMALL: I have another observation. Looking forward, we have got investment returns in the neighborhood of – Buffet expects 6 ½ % for the next five or six years. If so, trading is going to be a very critical part of the investment process. What Andy said about the buy-side trader's value added being on the margin is correct. But the margin can be critically important. If he can add 40, 50, or 60 basis points, that is the difference between a top decile manager and a third or fourth decile manager. You are right, Seth. If liquidity is there, why not just grab it? But (and this is Andy's point), if you can buy part of it and then buy the rest smarter, you can really drive the performance of your organization.

RICHARD REPETTO[45] [From the Floor]: Two questions. First, there are right now front-end aggregators in the Nasdaq market. I would like to hear your opinions about them, specifically the market makers. Second, we talked about limit orders. That is maybe the first phase in driving changes to market structure. My second question is for Bruce. There is an incentive with SuperMontage to add liquidity, you know, the dime per hundred rebates. Do you think that that will incent liquidity? You also get an ECN (say Island), that will pay people a penny more. Do you think you can get to the point where you can really incent material liquidity on the book?

TURNER: That is an interesting story. First, a quick history on the liquidity rebates. Nasdaq pays 10 cents per hundred, and they charge 20 cents per hundred, so we call it one mil two mils. I think the Instinet ratio is 2-3. What has happened is, everyone figures that they can survive with the

[45] Richard Repetto is currently Associate Director at Sandler O'Neill & Partners, LP. At the time of the conference, he was a Managing Director at Putnam Lovell.

one mil net to them. What they are saying is, ok, I will pay 2 and charge 3. Now there is an ECN out there giving 5 and charging 7. That's a two mils spread. At some point this will end if traders and subscribers stop paying the access fee of 7. At some point, the ECN will stop rebating the 5 when subscribers stop paying the 7 mils when they get executed against. You can't pay 5 if you are not getting 7. But the liquidity rebate has been effective.[46]

Look at the statistics behind LightSpeed. They have garnered a lot of flow from the day trading community because of their liquidity rebate. Yes, it is effective. The real issue, though, is the following. You mentioned the aggregators – you have got Lava Trading and you have got a lot of other aggregators out there. They are aggregating what people are willing to put in. All of us on the sell-side have these order books. We only put the top of the file in there. There is a lot of liquidity out there that is not in anything. The trick is to find an incentive mechanism to get those orders into them. So you have got Lava Trading. But if you miss it with Lava, you can still be at the next level. You can still get it in there. SuperMontage has got that extra kick. If you are not in there and the market burns through a couple of levels, you will miss the execution. It may be a slight distinction, but I think that it is an important one.

REPETTO [From the Floor]: Bruce answered most of my question. One additional piece is that the aggregators are only as good as the firms and desks that are willing to provide the information to them. That is complicated and changing. Also, a number of the aggregators will not talk to one another. You have individuals that are trading within one system and, for a host of reasons, that system will not talk to another. That becomes a problem. It is complicated because you could have an individual who has opted to put an order into ECN A, but ECN A does not want to talk to ECN B, and the only way that those orders will ever interact with one another – certainly on the listed side – is if somebody does an arbitrage between the two systems.

[46] As of mid-2003, the liquidity rebates and access fees discussed by Turner were a subject of major debate in the trading industry. These rebates and fees are part of the pricing model used by ECNs and SuperMontage in the U.S. Liquidity rebates are paid to a trading firm each time it submits a standing order – a limit order or quote – that is executed. However, if the firm, seeing a posted bid or offer in an ECN responds by lifting or hitting that resting order, it is charged an access fee. The most common charge is referred to as '3-2', meaning 30 cents is charged for taking liquidity while 20 cents is paid for providing liquidity. Market makers have been lobbying against the access fees, on the grounds that they are inequitable. Market makers are not permitted to charge access fees. Access fees raise another issue. Best execution obligations can force a market maker to use an ECN offering the best price even though the market maker may incur an access fee. This is a motivation for market maker ECN subscribers not to pay access fees.

SOFIANOS: There are some concerns about aggregators. They do a great job for relatively small orders. For an active Nasdaq stock, for example, the displayed inside quote is, perhaps, 100 shares or 200 shares. You can aggregate it all over the place, and the aggregate will still be relatively small. Should the electronic aggregators start walking up the limit order books? The problem is, when you are walking up the books, you ignore the non-displayed liquidity in the market, and the aggregators are not doing a good job with liquidity that is not displayed.

SCHWARTZ: That is Bruce's point.

SOFIANOS: So, there is this tight limit, up to which you can use these aggregators. Actually, it is tight because, for an active stock, to aggregate the inside quote, you do not get very much liquidity. There simply is so little on the inside quote. However, any attempt to go beyond the inside quote with an electronic mechanism causes you to miss all of the non-displayed liquidity. That is where a traditional broker dealer's value-added comes in.

SCHWARTZ: Yes, the non-displayed liquidity is a very interesting component of market quality. And it is very much a function of the systems that we have.

WAGNER [From the Floor]: I want to expand a bit on what Seth was saying. You have to go back to the portfolio manager. When you are talking about market structure, what you are trying to equate is the desire to buy with the desire to sell. The only thing that you have to do that with is price. Price has to move to a point where you equate the number of shares to be bought with the number of shares to be sold.

SCHWARTZ: Yes, but Wayne, you still have to get people to take the orders out of their pockets so that…

WAGNER [From the Floor]: They may not be in their pockets. They may not want to trade until they see the action that is going on in the stock.

SCHWARTZ: Sure. But that is the non-displayed liquidity.

WAGNER [From the Floor]: It is more than non-displayed – it is non-displayable. If you were, say, a hedge fund looking to ride in on some action that is going on in the market at the time, the market action itself is the motivating factor that brings liquidity to the other side.

BROOKS: That gets back to trusting the price, to trusting the pricing mechanism, to trusting that the prospective price is going to be something that you are going to be comfortable with. And as to a point that the fellows down the line here have made, if we can incent people and reward them for displaying orders and for aggregating those orders on a book or on a facility that is accessible, then, just maybe, what moves the price is actually something legitimate.

One of the reasons why you can feel stupid is that, after the 750,000-share print is done, a 3,000-share print moves the stock 25 cents. If it took 75,000 shares to move that price because there were all of these displayed orders at different levels that you have to get through, I would not feel so bad. I would probably be more inclined to put some orders on the book myself. It is when price moves, for no reason, for nothing that makes sense. When simply, because somebody can do it and profit from it, that price moves – that is what causes a lot of us to hesitate to display.

TIEFENBRUN [From the Floor]: The fragmentation issue among ECNs that we talk about today is a red herring. To the best of my knowledge, all of the ECNs are very tightly connected. I do not know of any examples where one ECN will not talk to another when it comes to filling orders. The fragmentation problem, which SuperMontage addresses in part, is that the broker dealers are maintaining order books that they are not publicly disclosing, that they are not providing access to, and that they are not providing visibility to – to anybody.

The ECNs are the good guys here. They publish their entire book, and there are many aggregators. All of the ECNs offer the market smart routing and aggregated views, etc. The problem lies with the traditional broker dealer who has an order book that is not yet published.

VIKTORIA DALKO[47] [From the Floor]: I have two questions. First, according to your experience, what is the minimum sized order that will have a meaningful price impact? We saw statistics of 30 basis points and so on, but do you have a minimum order size that will cause this kind of a price movement?

Second, regarding the market makers, do you find that they can affect the price, or are they completely neutral in the process?

TURNER: Andy, do you want to answer the second one (laughter)?

BROOKS: No, Bruce. I am going to let you handle that one (laughter)?

TURNER: Taking the second first, market makers, of course, can influence the price. Price responds to what is out there. A lack of depth in the book enables people to move prices more than they think should happen in our markets. We need to get more orders in there. More orders would control that movement of, in Andy's scenario, down 25 cents on 3000 shares.

As for the first question, I do not think that there is any minimum size that can move a market. There are too many variables involved. Scenarios

[47] Viktoria Dalko is President of the RICE Institute.

could be created where minimal size could move stocks dramatic percentage amounts, and vice versa.

PAUL DAVIS[48] [From the Floor]: I have an observation. I like the distinction between displayed liquidity and un-disclosed liquidity. My intuition is that the combination of SuperMontage and Liquidity Tracker will be dynamite. You can distinguish between the displayed liquidity on SuperMontage and the un-displayed liquidity that you can get to with Liquidity Tracker. I am very excited about this combination. I am anxious to see it in play.

SCHWARTZ: Thank you.

Time is moving. I would next like to get a closing comment from each of the panelists. Let me give you a little platform to start with. We have had some sizable market structure changes of late. The order handling rules, for instance. Then there has been decimalization and all sorts of technology change. What overall impact has all of this had? Could each of you give us a bottom line on your view of market quality today? Has it improved, or has it deteriorated? Bruce, how about you leading off?

TURNER: I am not sure I can do this in two minutes. We have seen a confluence of events. Best execution is key, and the SEC's 11Ac1-5 and 6 is on everyone's mind right now. You have decimals and order handling rules, and you can combine all of that with what has been a pretty lousy tape. At the end of the day, we must create a better marketplace by incenting more orders in the book. We gave a lot of emphasis to that on this panel.

It can be done. I feel strongly about it. I am hard pressed to say if things are better in aggregate. With decimals, retail investors have been richly rewarded. Their execution costs are down. However, the last studies that I have seen say that, for the institutional community, the verdict is still out. Is it better for some? Yes. But is it better for all? I do not know.

The limit order handling rules definitely benefited the market. There is no question about it. The continuance of that is SuperMontage. The ability of people to put more orders in the book will make things better for everybody.

SOFIANOS: When looking at market quality and where we are now, given all these market structure changes, I like to distinguish between small, easy orders and large, difficult orders. For the easy orders, the answer is straightforward. We have a very competitive market, lots of alternatives, and lots of publicly available data. The SEC's 11Ac-5 data, if used correctly, can help us make informed decisions. We have competitive pressure on explicit fees, competitive pressure on spreads, and trading costs

[48] Paul Davis is Senior Managing Director at TIAA-CREF Investment Management LLC.

are much lower than they used to be. They can't get much lower on the small, easy orders. We are pretty much there. On the smaller end of the market, fragmentation also does not worry me because we have all those smart routers and electronic ways of accessing liquidity.

The difficult orders are where we still face challenges. It is still a mixed bag. Fragmentation makes it more difficult to aggregate liquidity. More fundamentally, as I have alluded to earlier, most of the liquidity remains non-displayed. I personally believe that most of the liquidity will always remain not displayed on the buy-side. The challenge, of course, is to tap this non-displayed liquidity. Another problem for the large orders is that there is little publicly available information out there to make informed choices on where to route your orders. Perhaps little that can be done about this.

I looked at the Goldman Sachs data. We found that the switch to pennies reduced trading costs across all size segments, including the large institutional size orders. But remember, this is from the sell-side. I also hear from the sell-side that they are finding it much more difficult to execute now because there is much less displayed liquidity. However, from our point of view, trading costs have gone down. Even after I back out the explicit commissions that Goldman has been charging on Nasdaq trades since January 2nd, trading costs are lower now, across almost all size segments, than they were before pennies.

SMALL: The quality of the markets has deteriorated, but for good reason. We are in a transition period. We are absorbing the changes. The future is very, very bright for the markets to come out of this in a more centralized, aggregated fashion. In the future, the markets will be much more efficient. But we are feeling the pain now.

The pain is in conjunction with the bear market that we are experiencing at the same time. The bear market has put added pressure on everyone. Nevertheless, as tough as it is to execute size, ultimately we will be OK. The SEC is going to do the right thing by letting the markets decide how they will develop. I am as encouraged as I have been in the last few years about being able to get the job done.

MADOFF: I do not mean to contradict your opening statement, Bob, but I think the quality of our markets has never been better. We have seen an increased number of players. We can see some of the competitive spirit here in this room, between myself, the exchanges, the ECNs, and the ATSs. That is a tremendous positive. Execution costs have gone down dramatically. ECN fees have gone down dramatically. We are getting faster executions. Each year, average execution speed goes down. The effective spreads in stocks are constantly declining. Combining the 11Ac1-5 data with better evaluative tools will enable everybody out there, who is willing to put in the time, to get a better idea of what is going on.

We need to embrace the spirit of competition. Let the ECNs, the ATSs, the regionals, the exchanges, and the market makers all compete with one another. Lets level the playing field as best we can through competition, through linking everybody together. Lets allow that competition to take place. I think we will see better and better executions over time.

KILLEEN: I am an optimist and I agree with Mark. We are headed in the right direction. We have also touched on the point that, in the current bear market environment, trading costs are very important. We are trying to save some money and improve performance in any way we can, especially from the trading desk standpoint.

The order handling rules have basically helped the market by giving the buy-side a little more control over our orders. Some fancy software has come about through competition that has allowed us to work our orders more intelligently. Even though the orders are somewhat piecemealed, we now have more hands on, which helps price discovery.

The New York Stock Exchange has a ways to go. The NYSE has started this Open Book, which can be helpful with some stocks that do not trade well. At least the NYSE is coming to the table bringing something, instead of just relaying on an agent or trying to find something short of capital to make something happen.

We are not there yet. I do not know if we will ever be there. On the buy-side, we always say we want the perfect market. We always want everyone to open up. But then, if we could see down the road, I think we would back off. We are headed in the right direction, and competition is the way to go.

BROOKS: I guess the quality of the market is better. I also think that we could do a lot better. We must continue to find ways to incent and reward people to display and to be willing to trade. This market has gone through a lot of change in the past few years. We ought to move more slowly now, because we need to digest some of the changes. Innovation comes at a cost. Innovation has been terrific. The competition that has resulted from the innovation has been terrific. But we do have fragmentation, and all of the issues that come from it. We have got to find a way to require some level playing fields. I am not sure that all of the fields are level right now. There are way too many sharp shooters out there taking advantage of order flow, causing volatility and, in general, doing things that are not as legitimate as investing ought to be. I realize that this is a very subjective statement.

We must continue to analyze the relationship between the quality of markets and intra-day volatility. The volatility that we have has, somehow, to be legitimized.

SCHWARTZ: I thank the panel for a very interesting discussion. And I thank the audience for interacting with them.

CHAPTER 4: VIEW FROM AN ECN

Joel Steinmetz[49]

An old couple is having trouble remembering things, so they visit a doctor. The doctor tells them, 'It is really nothing, everything is OK, but maybe you ought to write things down so you will be sure to remember them.' The couple goes home. Sitting later in their den watching TV, the wife gets up to go to the kitchen. She says to her husband, 'Can I get you anything?' He says, 'I'd like some ice cream with whipped cream on top.' She says, 'No problem.' He says, 'Let's try what the doctor suggested and write it down.' She says, 'No, no. Ice cream and whipped cream. I got it. Don't worry about it.' She gets closer to the doorway. He says, 'You know what? I would like some ice cream with whipped cream and hot fudge, but I think you ought to write it down like the doctor said.' She says, 'Don't worry about it. Ice cream, whipped cream and hot fudge, a classic. I got it, don't worry.' She goes into the kitchen and comes out a few minutes later with a toasted English muffin. He says, 'A toasted English muffin? What? We ran out of bagels?' (laughter).

I'll come back to that joke later. But let me start by saying that the media and industry usually describe Instinet as an electronic communications network. We typically describe ourselves as a global electronic agency broker. The word 'electronic' is dominant in both descriptions. We believe in electronic solutions. But, interestingly, the electronic solutions providers such as ECNs, ATSs, liquidity consolidators and smart order routers, have taken their eye off the ball. The last great era of growth for the electronic solutions providers was in the mid- to late 90's. It was five to seven years ago when you had the explosion of all these types of players. During that time, there were problems in the market that we were trying to solve. What

[49] At the time of the conference, Mr. Steinmetz was Senior Vice President for Equities, Instinet Corporation.

was needed was an aggregation of information, a consolidation of all the information that was in the marketplace. The innovators came up with consolidated order books. Smart order routing came out of that. New ways were developed to manage your lists more easily in an environment where execution was fragmented.

The electronic solutions providers as a group stepped in and did the job. They came up with ways to access multiple pools of liquidity at once. They came up with smart order routers, with intelligent algorithms to figure out where the best place to trade was. Consolidated order books were developed that gave you great information.

All of these things were good for the marketplace. They provided value. If you were either a retail customer or an institutional investor, you now had something a little better in the marketplace. You could get liquidity better, you could get information better. You could use some intelligent order routing to get to the best place to trade. These were important improvements in the market.

The discussion on the previous panel was a microcosm of the issue. I will cover some of the same topics as the last panel but from a different angle. If you noticed, the previous panel started off with the buy-side dominating the conversation. The reason was that we were talking about trading large orders. Doing things that would provide value to investors. As we went on, we took our eye off the ball. We forgot, like the joke about the old couple, that we wanted the ice cream. We started talking about things like getting to the inside quote, narrowing spreads, and SuperMontage. And then finally we came back to the issue: what to do about the large orders?

What has basically happened is that all of the electronic solutions providers came up with these things in the mid to late 90's. Those solutions either created other problems, or there were so many things that had to be solved at that point that the new electronic solutions could not fill the gap. So we came up with ways to reduce fragmentation, and to consolidate information, and to route our orders intelligently. We started coming up with things like reserve quantity, discretionary pricing, and sophisticated algorithms. We started branching out into other things. Whether due to market conditions, or perhaps just pressure from competition, brokerage commissions started getting driven down lower and lower. Innovations and more efficient processes resulted in cost savings. We were looking to solve cost issues, instead of providing value. We were playing the game of solving the cost, of getting faster and cheaper, cheaper and faster.

But we forgot about providing value. We have to refocus. I will give you an example. It is an Instinet example. Around the mid 90's, we had something that we called an order management system. At that time, our order management system focused on the ability to trade lists or baskets of stock. We went out to the brokerage community in the mid-90's to offer that. Since it was focused on lists and baskets, the natural place for us to put it was at program desks, index arbitrage desks, and the small but growing model-driven trading shops. We presented this tool to that group of customers. At the time, there was hardly any list or basket trading in over-the-counter securities. There was just no way to do it. The over-the-counter structure at the time was such that, if you wanted to trade a basket, either you went to one market maker with the entire basket, or you didn't trade it. Unless someone wanted to give their entire basket to one particular player (which was the norm when people are bidding for them), they really had no way to trade a list of over-the-counter stocks.

We brought in a system that allowed you to manage your orders and to trade those stocks efficiently in multiple liquidity pools whether it was ours, NASDAQ's or other pools of liquidity. Our system did not just divide up the same piece of the pie. It didn't make us go after liquidity that already existed in the market. Our system created a whole new way of trading for a group of customers. They were able to put money in the market in a different way than they had ever done before. Once you do that, you are not going after the same piece of the pie. Rather, you are making a larger pie.

In the beginning, we had a disproportionate percentage of that larger piece of the pie. Once it got out there, it grew to be something that people expected. Then competition started coming in, and people started playing, and then we had a bigger pie for everyone to divide. By focusing on providing value, we enabled people to use their money in different ways, to provide extra liquidity to the market so that all market participants could benefit.

Currently, the main focus is on 'how can I get to the 200 shares that are offered quicker and cheaper?' It is the same 200 shares that are out there. It doesn't really provide me with what I need, but I have to know how I get there quicker and cheaper. I do not mean to trivialize the importance of that, and we are going after that as well. Enabling people to get to the current market faster and cheaper is definitely a need, it is a value that can be provided.

But we have lost what we have to do to provide value to get to the next level of the market. As was stated before, we must provide something that will get those limit orders out in the marketplace. The people who use limit orders must feel comfortable with the way these orders are handled in the marketplace. An investor should be able to put out a large order and feel comfortable that it will get traded.

My view differs somewhat from the previous panel. I am not sure that the best way to solve our problems is through market structure or market quality issues. The best way might be for players who innovate to come up with the solutions. It is players like the electronic solutions providers who in the past have generated much of the innovation. These players must refocus their energies and look at delivering value, rather than concentrating myopically on cost or current market conditions. They must go to underlying needs and provide value so that, overall, the market will grow.

Here are some possible solutions. Right now, everyone is talking about how important it is to get all the market data in one place. It is important. But, take a look at NASDAQ's model. Anywhere from 30% to 50% of NASDAQ trades happen on ECNs. The majority of that kind of order flow is not in the public display. According to some studies, that order flow accounts for over 70% of the volume handled by ECNs. It is what is called undisclosed orders. SuperSOES also came up with a reserve feature, and SuperMontage has a reserve feature as well. When you think about it, the vast majority of the data that you need to make your trading decisions is not available to be viewed.

There must be some other way to come up with the data people need to make efficient trading decisions. Maybe it is data, maybe it is trends, maybe it is some way of understanding what happens in the first half-hour of trading. We talked about the first half-hour of trading this morning. Is it that people are putting their orders in there? Is it because people are putting in at one price and are actually willing to trade at another price? Is it because we saw 10,000 shares when actually there were 10,000,000 shares available?

Much information and data can be aggregated and delivered in a very generic form to the marketplace. That creates value. Based on our conversations with buy-side customers, I know that would be something the buy-side customers could use. That kind of information, and those kind of electronic solutions, are the things that we need to focus on to provide value.

A second example is one we have spoken about today. It is the big topic lately. It is trading in size. On the NYSE, consistently over the last few years, about 50% of all shares are traded in blocks. On NASDAQ, block trading had accounted for about a third of all trading, and now it is at about a quarter of all volume. So the decline is not just because of the bear market conditions. It is down as a proportion of all market trading activity. Regardless, there are a huge number of shares that are traded as blocks. Yet no one feels comfortable actually trading blocks in the traditional way. That does not mean that there is no need for the traditional way as well, as stated earlier. There definitely, at times, is a need for intermediaries. But there must be a better way to get to the other side, which is the goal of the buy-side.

What is the underlying need? I am not sure that the underlying need is necessarily to get to the other side and knock off 500,000 shares all at once.

Of course, if you could get 500,000 shares in the same amount of time that it would take you to call up your broker, and have him match up the 500,000 shares, and have the impact on the market be even less, everyone would be pleased. The underlying need is not necessarily to trade a block as a single large trade, which would be nice, but rather to trade a large block effectively, even if it is done in smaller pieces.

A refocusing of the electronic solutions providers on these kinds of issues will provide value to the ultimate investor. The investor could be the retail investor. But generally the bulk of the market is represented by retail investors going into the institutional community, whether that's through pension funds or mutual funds and other institutional investors. For the sake of the retail customer, we must provide solutions to that institutional community. The electronic solutions providers must refocus their energies. That is not to forget about the idea of trading that 200 shares at the inside cheaper and faster, and not to stop thinking about five levels of depth which SuperMontage will get to, as all the ECNs get to today, and as the liquidity consolidators have been able to do for a couple of years as well. But once we can do cheaper and faster executions for smaller orders, we also need to examine the brokerage side of the business. We need to provide solutions that will enhance performance and allow larger trades to be executed more efficiently.

This is not to say that people do not focus on this, and that there aren't any solutions out there. But a key element is missing. It seems that we either have people who are providing solutions who do not concentrate on the commoditized offering of the 200 shares, or people who are only concentrating on the commoditized offering of the 200 shares. What we need is a way to integrate the two. We are all rowing together. That's the analogy. As an electronic solutions provider, you are taking the right approach if you can offer technological, value-added services for trading complex orders that simultaneously interact with all the liquidity in the market.

How will we do that? We have been in a NASDAQ-centric world. The panel before was typical of the way these conferences and discussions usually go. They start out in the general sense about order flow, and maybe they are even global in nature. But, eventually, they go right back down to what is going on in Microsoft. That seems to be how everyone tends to focus. The electronic solutions that can be provided span across all markets, across all geographies, and possibly all instruments. If you can provide a solution that says I will be able to trade large size in my Microsoft order, I assume I will be able to trade large size in IBM. If you are looking for a way to get to the buy-side, or to get to ultimate liquidity, it is not necessarily a market structure issue. It could happen by providing a solution one step above the market level.

Once you do that, you can do it in the NASDAQ market, in the NYSE market, in global markets, and in other instruments. There has been an attempt to go into options trading as well. Single stock futures are on the horizon. Solutions can really be provided in that way.

I want to end with three things that need to be done to get there. There are three players who have to act. First, the regulators have to create an environment that is open for competition, an environment that will allow all these players to create, to innovate, to provide valuable solutions to the marketplace. Once the regulators step in, they should realize that they are doing so to help competition, not to hinder it. The SEC has come a long way in getting there. The commission is totally focused on issues like this, and it is a good environment for this to happen now.

The second player that we need is the buy-side. The buy-side must continue to pressure the solution providers to give value. They must let us know what the value is. They must pressure the entire industry to make sure that value is provided, not just cost solutions. Not that they shouldn't pressure for cost solutions to make sure that we get faster and cheaper executions. However, there has to be constant pressure to make sure that value also continues to be provided.

Finally, the electronic solutions providers must at least take one foot out of the game of 'how am I going to trade 200 shares quicker?' They must get back into the realm of providing trading solutions that will deliver value to the ultimate end user.

That is what I have to say. If there are any questions, I will be happy to take them.

UNIDENTIFIED SPEAKER [From the Floor]: It seems to me that the one guarantee is that commissions are only going one way. They are going down. Island, Archipelago, and NeoNet, internationally, have made the push to drop commissions in all markets. Is it in Instinet's future to change from being an agency brokerage? It seems that a new model for Instinet could incorporate traditional services with the current agency brokerage that you provide.

STEINMETZ: As far as the commission question goes, you are right. They are only going down. It is incumbent upon the solution providers to adjust their cost structure accordingly and to make sure that they can continue to compete. As far as where Instinet's future lies, we will adjust to whatever the market throws at us. Whether it is market structure issues or new competitive threats, ultimately what we and everybody in our space needs to do is to make sure that we continue to provide solutions. If that means changing our model, we will look at doing so as we move down the road.

PAUL DAVIS[50] [From the Floor]: I am intrigued by the search for a value proposition and what people can bring to the table. As markets have evolved, a number of institutions have tried to level the playing field. In fact, I am against leveling the playing field. I am for tilting the field in favor of me. I say that somewhat facetiously, but in some respects that has happened in the past. Instinet's first value proposition was to bring to the table a system that was tilted to the advantage of the institutions. Over time, even if it is nothing more than the price advantage that they give to the broker dealers, the system has now tilted in favor of the broker dealers. Posit brought to the table a crossing network that was tilted in favor of the institutions. But, over time it also tilted over to the broker dealers, if for no other reason than the way they structure their pricing. It would be great if someone could take the initiative and, once again, come up with a system that is not a level playing field, but that is tilted towards me. And they should keep it that way.

STEINMETZ: Firstly, if everyone else will cover his or her ears, we will tilt it totally in favor of CREF (laughter). Secondly, I think there is a two-front war that needs to be fought. We have to recognize that the northern terrain is a lot different than the southern terrain. The northern terrain is a pricing war, and it is providing fast, cheap access to current markets. The southern terrain is a value war. Ultimately, what we need to do, in essence, is to tilt the scale towards the specific customer segment that we are targeting. We would like to tilt the scale towards the institutions for the institutions' needs, which are different than the sell-side needs. We also would like to tilt the scale towards the brokers for their needs. We actually have the possibility of doing both. The player who can do both (this is in a sense what you said, Paul) is pricing in one way and adding some value in another.

The player who does both will win. That does not mean that there cannot be multiple winners. But those who win put up a tremendous barrier to entry to others. The player who needs price can also get access to fantastic quality liquidity. The players to whom you have delivered value, quality, functionality and product, will also find the ultimate liquidity that they need. If you can marry these two things, price and quality, you will tilt the scale.

Lets go back to my ice cream analogy. The problem is, you had your eye on the ice cream and the next thing you know someone walked in and said here is NASDAQ's model and we started thinking about the bagel. We

[50] Paul Davis is Senior Managing Director at TIAA-CREF Investment Management.

forgot to say, 'let's keep our eye on the ice cream.' We have got to get back to value, which means tilting the scale towards the buy-side.

CHAPTER 5: PERSPECTIVE OF THE MARKET ARCHITECTS

Moderator – William Freund, *Director, Freund Center for the Study of Equity Markets, Pace University*
Michael Cormack, *President, Archipelago Holdings*
Sanjiv Gupta, *Director of Research and Strategy, Bloomberg Tradebook*
John Malitzis, *Senior Vice President and Associate General Counsel, Citigroup Global Markets*[51]
Seth Merrin, *Chief Executive Officer, Liquidnet*
Brett Redfearn, *Senior Vice President, American Stock Exchange*
Richard Schenkman, *Managing Partner, Elm Tree Group*[52]

WILLIAM FREUND: Bob, you covered so much in your panel, you did not leave much new for us to discuss. But then again, there is that old joke about the Dean who calls in the Professor of Economics and says, 'You have given the same exam for 25 years. We have been receiving complaints about that.' And the Professor replies, 'Don't you know Dean, that in economics the questions are always the same? It is only the answers that change' (laughter).

I would like to emphasize the future in our discussion. Let's start with each of the panelists taking a minute or two to say how you envisage market structure changing over the next three to five years. Then we will come back to the points and elaborate. Mike, let's start with you.

MICHAEL CORMACK: I was talking to some friends at lunch about what they think might happen in the marketplace in the next three years. The central theme, from my perspective, is that market structure will become less confusing for participants. The past five years have seen the order

[51] At the time of the conference, John Malitzis was Vice President in the Transaction Services Department at the Nasdaq Stock Market.

[52] At the time of the conference, Richard Schenkman was Chief Executive Officer of Brut.

handling rules, the expansion of ECNs, new entrants in the exchange space, decimalization, and a lot of different alternative trading systems that have been directed at institutional clients. Things are bound to become less confusing.

We have seen some consolidation in the ECN space. In general, in the near future, we will see more consolidation in liquidity pools, whether it is Nasdaq or New York Stock Exchange pools, or a combination of Nasdaq and an ECN, or some other pools. ECNs, such as Archipelago, are merging.[53] I see that trend continuing. I see the liquidity pools consolidating into two or three.

There were comments earlier about competition. I am a big supporter of competition. It helps the investment community. I like the competition between the panelists who, on all other days, are trying to kill each other giving better service to their clients. It would be a sad day if it turns out that only one player is a winner. I think Alan Greenspan said that markets evolve into natural monopolies. That is not such a positive outcome. The competition helps you, and you have to balance that with the fragmentary aspects.

SANJIV GUPTA: I see it a little differently. I will take a U.S. focus, but will present it from a European perspective. That is because I have just returned from a trip visiting some of the major desks in Europe.

It is amazing how unanimous the disdain is in Europe for the U.S. market structure. I was struck by the kind of bad-mouthing I heard for the New York Stock Exchange's system, and for the complexities of Nasdaq's system. They point to their own CLOBs as the obvious place where the U.S. will go. In their opinion, it is only a matter of how long it will take us to get there.

Many of the European marketplaces have simple, transparent systems. They basically have a marketplace that is transparent, that looks very clean. It makes it look like retail investors have been protected. However, the 30%, 40%, or 50% of the market that resides upstairs cannot trade very effectively in that market because their order sizes are very large. The broker dealers like it because the 30%, 40% or 50% that sits upstairs can be worked for their benefit. They get to cross it and to work it over the phone. It is a two-tiered marketplace.

In the U.S., we have strived over the years to create marketplaces that allow for the interaction of all types of order flow. This is a messy business. The institutional buy-side has a different set of needs from the retail

[53] In May 2002, Archipelago purchased RediBook and by the following September the integration was completed.

investor. The sell-side has a different set of needs. The quantitative traders and the program traders, all have a different set of needs.

There may be times when you see some consolidation, when two or three players get together. We have also seen the emergence of new players like Liquidnet and Harborside+, and some other new systems. Because the special needs of the institutional investor are always there, there will be different innovative solutions in the future. From a regulatory perspective and from a buy-side perspective, we must recognize that this is very beneficial. If we were to call for centralization, we would stifle this.

JOHN MALITZIS: One thing is for certain. It is impossible to predict the future. If you had asked me three years ago what our markets would look like in 2002, I could not have answered that question correctly. And neither could anyone else on this panel.

FREUND: Will Rogers once said, 'It is too difficult to predict, especially about the future' (laughter).

MALITZIS: One thing that I can say for sure is that competition will increase, and you will see the markets responding. Things will continue to move faster as technology improves. The focus will be much more international. I know that Nasdaq has been talking about internationalization for years, so has the New York Stock Exchange. I imagine that we will see some synergy occur between markets both in Europe and the U.S.

On a pure micro level in Nasdaq, the movement to an order driven market will continue, particularly with the advent of riskless principle and agency trading. I can see that developing in Nasdaq. Many questions have been raised over the past year about how market makers can move from an implicit fee to an explicit fee model. I see a lot more movement on the regulatory front in that area. SuperMontage ties into that nicely.

FREUND: We will get back to SuperMontage.

SETH MERRIN: I can only talk from an institutional perspective. We are seeing more recognition of the different needs of retail and institutional participants. The problem has gotten so bad, it is quantifiable – by people like Wayne Wagner – and it is no longer possible to ignore. In an environment where the market is going up 30% per year, you can push these things under the rug. But now they are in the open, right in front of you.

These costs are so large that we must do something about them. I foresee a separation of the marketplaces between retail and wholesale. People have said, on the previous panel and already on this one, that the exchanges today are perfectly fine for retail order flow. It is great when a retail player can go into a marketplace and spend ten dollars for an instant execution that has no market impact. But when you have an inverse relationship[54] with the wholesaler and the institution pays a premium for size, there is a problem.

This is how it works: 'the larger he is, the more he pays.' Right? Hopefully the securities market will recognize that every other industry caters differently to retail and wholesale customers. One does not go to a corner Gap and buy 30 dozen red shirts. The problem in our marketplace is that everyone has to go to the same store. I do not believe that one store can handle the needs of both constituencies.

FREUND: We will get back to the issues we have raised so far – consolidation versus fragmentation, retail versus wholesale, and some of the new technologies that are developing. First, let's continue with opening comments from the panel.

BRETT REDFEARN: I would like to echo what Seth said. When we look at trading on the exchange, we are looking at the evolution of a bifurcated market. In the exchange markets you are going to see more of an inside retail market with more automatic execution for smaller orders. But you will also be seeing more of an institutional market. For example, in our Nasdaq program (which we will be talking about later), we will be publishing a secondary outside size quote. This quote will be specifically for institutions so that they can see where 'quantity price discovery' happens. We want to bring size back into the price discovery process. So I anticipate that we will see a natural bifurcation between retail and institutional pricing.

Another consideration is how exchanges compete. There is the competition for trades – the competition for order flow – and the competition for listings. I anticipate that where a company lists will become less of an issue, and that competition will intensify more around where a company's shares trade. For example, the New York Stock Exchange is now trading ETFs and Nasdaq, as was mentioned earlier, will soon be trading some of the listed stocks.[55] We at the American Stock Exchange will be trading Nasdaq stocks. Who is trading what, and exactly where, is going to be the key competitive issue, and the listing issue will become less and less important.

Third, I would like to point out a theme that I thought would come up on the previous panel. There is an increasing integration of equities and options

[54] Seth Merrin notes that the retail investor generally pays more in stock trading than a wholesaler. The opposite leads to an inverse relationship.

[55] An Exchange Traded Fund, or ETF, is a type of investment company whose investment objective is to achieve the same return as a specific market index. An ETF will invest in either all of the securities or a representative sample of the securities included in the index. Examples include SPDRs and QQQs.

and different types of products and trading strategies. When you think about different ways of providing liquidity, you should think about the linkage between the ability to trade an equity and an option on that equity, or even a single stock future. These linkages will become increasingly important. The ability to do centralized risk management between product types will be important in terms of new ways of providing liquidity in an increasingly difficult trading environment.

The last theme that I will discuss is what I refer to as 'regulatory harmonization.' Right now, what we have is the listed market with one set of rules, Nasdaq with a different set of rules and trying to become an exchange, and the ECNs that have a completely different set of rules that they have to abide by. Each one of these venues – if not already – will eventually be trading the exact same securities. Eventually, we will have to have some regulatory harmonization so that all of the different markets will, increasingly, be playing by the same set of rules.

RICHARD SCHENKMAN: I agree with Mike Cormack that the markets will simplify. I just won't predict when. The other panelists' comments lead us to believe that a highly competitive and complex structure will get us to the point where a bunch of unbundled choices will drive structural change. Right now, we have a high degree of focus on the ability of the investor to access all markets and instruments directly. This should force the agents who provide services to those markets to unbundle their services more rapidly. This will produce a whole set of choices in a Darwinian evolution. In fact, this is what we are seeing now.

The next issue for us to focus on is repackaging. This involves bringing together the diverse execution solutions that are there to satisfy individual needs. We must bring the services back together much like you would put a mall together – with independent providers linked together – rather than a single department store supplying all things under the one roof. We must provide a customized set of solutions to the investor, whether it is an execution of equities or an execution of other instruments. Doing this will be the next challenging trend. It will end up simplifying the markets. But getting there will be complicated. We will have a very complex market structure for a while. That structure will be driven by a bunch of choices available to both individual and institutional investors.

FREUND: Thank you. Let's now get to an issue that has been raised several times here – consolidation and fragmentation. I heard mention this morning that Nasdaq will trade NYSE stocks, perhaps even this year, on its systems. Brett, you said that the Amex would trade Nasdaq stocks. How imminent are these changes? Will we see more fragmentation of trading?

I also heard the opinion that some of these centers will consolidate, and that we will have more centralization. Can it be both? Can we get more centralization and more fragmentation? John, how do you see that issue?

MALITZIS: Nasdaq trading NYSE securities? We currently trade them through our Inter Market system, through the ITS/CAES system. I think what you are referring to is trading those listed securities through SuperMontage. That is not imminent.

FREUND: Trading Big Board stocks on SuperMontage is not imminent?

MALITZIS: Right. In part, because we would probably need to go through plan amendments. The ITS plan governs how Nasdaq and the regional exchanges trade New York Stock Exchange listed securities. At this point, we have not determined to amend the plan to trade those securities. Our focus is on getting SuperMontage up and ready for Nasdaq. But long-term, who knows? If the demand is there and the environment appropriate, we would seek that path out.

We think that competition is good to the extent that it forces markets to compete for order flow, to compete on price and on services. We welcome competition from the Amex. However, we are also concerned about fragmentation because we would like to serve our customers in the best and most efficient way. We think SuperMontage will help reduce fragmentation, but the future remains to be seen.

FREUND: Brett, what about your plans?

REDFEARN: Our intention is certainly not to fragment the Nasdaq market any more than it currently is. One of the things that came up in the last panel was the ability to access markets and to see displayed prices. If you can access the markets properly, then you really do not have the same fragmentation situation. With the tools that are out there today to access markets, fragmentation should not be a problem. At the Amex, we have gone out of our way to make sure that anybody who wants to access our markets can do so. In fact, we even have some materials on the table over there if anybody wants to know how. The bottom line is, there is nothing about fragmentation that we see as an issue.

FREUND: Your point is that, as long as there is complete and free access, there is no fragmentation, but there is competition.

REDFEARN: Fragmentation today is an interesting debate because there are so many different types of market centers offering so many different types of products. It definitely is not the same as it used to be. Neither is it the same on the NYSE where there is such a large concentration of order flow. When you look at the Nasdaq environment, the key is the ability to access those markets.

FREUND: What do some of you other panelists think? Do you see more of a trend toward fragmentation, do you see more of a trend toward consolidation, or do you see a trend toward competition with a centralization of information?

CORMACK: There are two forces at play. First, there are structural changes in the financial services business. In another year, there will be fewer brokers than there were two years ago. As exchanges that provide services to the broker dealer and buy-side communities, we are essentially utilities. It is only natural that we will experience pricing pressure.[56] The industry consolidation is also part of that force at work.

The next factor is the explosion of alternative trading systems. The pace of change over the past five years is unsustainable. We will see incremental changes; we will roll out new order types. But I do not think we will continue to see the same number of ECN players coming into the business. The same phenomena occurred in the dotcom space in which a phenomenal growth in the number of new players was followed by a sudden reduction. The trading industry will not continue to make the necessary investment to support more products. There is more care and thought involved in the investments. All of this will lead inevitably to more consolidation in the ECN and ATS space.

FREUND: So, you see consolidation, but also increased competition?

CORMACK: What we will see is consolidation and probably stronger competitors. That is because the survivors will be stronger financially, and their business models will be proven. This will give us more stability.

GUPTA: You have to separate the discussion between listed and Nasdaq because we do not have competition in listed.

FREUND: Yes, we don't. May I ask you how come? I have seen some of the statistics that have been referred to here before. Namely, that the ECNs do some 30%, 40%, or perhaps even 50% of the Nasdaq business. But they do only a negligible amount of big board business. Please explain.

GUPTA: In my opinion, it is a simple fact of regulatory market structure. ECNs and ATSs offer a different style of execution that appeals to many types of clientele. The listed world has something called ITS that makes it virtually impossible to offer those different styles of execution. You have to reroute your orders to the New York Stock Exchange or to the other listed exchanges, and then wait 30, 40, 50 seconds for a response. At the same time, your own business is offering instant executions. I believe

[56] There was a price war among the ECNs and various market centers throughout 2002. The Cincinnati Stock Exchange, for example, competing for Nasdaq order flow, offered rebates to ECNs that reported their trades on the exchange. On another front, ECNs were lowering fees to capture market share. Island, for example, started executing shares for 0.10 cents and offered 0.11 cents per shares for liquidity. It became so competitive that analysts say the Island pricing package was ultimately responsible for convincing Instinet to purchase its former rival.

that the ADF proposal,[57] which is in front of the regulators, allows for alternative systems to choose between competing in the listed space as ITS partners, or as non-ITS participants.[58]

That is the key to listed competition in the next couple of years. With the integration of the quotes, etc., there will be a transition phase. Then you can allow other entities to offer business models that provide different execution styles. Everybody will be welcome to take the style that appeals to him or her.

Traders are doing listed business. But a lot of it is interacting with the primary limited pools of liquidity.[59] Some of it is after-hours and in the pre-market hours. The listed market is not that competitive. I speak to institutional investors all the time. There is a constant yearning from the buy-side. Buy-side traders, who have seen the innovations in the Nasdaq marketplace over the last few years, would love to have some of those technologies and tools to trade with in the listed market. These tools include reserve, pegging and discretion features, which gives traders more ways to handle large orders.

The listed market, as long as the regulators go along with it, will see tremendous competition. The New York Stock Exchange and the other exchanges are formidable forces, so it will not be an easy fight. But we will definitely see more competition.

In Nasdaq, we have had an incredibly competitive environment over the past five years. Now, suddenly, we have Nasdaq, soon to be a for-profit organization, calling for centralization. They want to be the central gatekeeper and toll collector of the marketplace. I am not sure that this is a good step. Nasdaq may be successful in centralizing some part of the marketplace in its SuperMontage, but it is not a foregone conclusion. Unless all participants are forced into it by legal action, it is unlikely that a simple

57 Alternative Display Facility, or ADF, is a facility operated by NASD, to collect and disseminate quotations, compare trades, as well as collect and disseminate trade reports. It was introduced as an alternative system for ECNs and other participants that want to trade OTC stocks away from Nasdaq's SuperMontage.

58 The NASD, as of early January 2003, was still seeking permission to allow participants to trade listed stocks on the ADF, in addition in OTC stocks, which do trade on the ADF. A ruling was expected in the second quarter. Under the plan for listed trading, which was earlier rejected by the ITS operating committee, ADF participants could trade inside or outside the ITS but would have access to ITS members.

59 There is relatively limited trading in listed stocks on ECNs, while the volume of listed stock trading done away from the NYSE is around 20% of the overall volume. Most of the volume in listed trading, around 80%, occurs directly on the NYSE, the primary market.

attempt to centralize a marketplace will be successful. The central issue is that clients need different solutions. A central marketplace won't cater to all of those needs.

It could be that the make up of the marketplace will change over the next two or three years. I suspect that we will have just about as many players, but the players will be different. Some of the current players will merge, and that will create room for slightly different offerings. The Nasdaq market will stay competitive with about the same number of players. Where you will see the greatest change in the next two to three years, if the regulators will allow it, is the listed market.

FREUND: I was intrigued reading recently that Island intends to send its quotes to SuperMontage, but it prints its trades on the Cincinnati Stock Exchange. That is a slightly different model. Do you see a model developing that will fragment the printing of trades?

GUPTA: Those are just marketplaces competing for the business of printing. If the marginal revenue to an organization is $1 higher over there, it is going to appeal to them to go there. We are in a world of predatory pricing.

FREUND: Predatory pricing?

GUPTA: I think so. In some cases it is virtually predatory, where business models are predicated on doing something in the future. They are not predicated on making a whole lot of money right now, which means a desire to extract every incremental dollar. If it means printing trades somewhere else, they will do that.

SCHENKMAN: Listed trading is on a tipping point. There are things that are aligned now, more than ever, that will change the structure of listed trading. It is not driven by us, the agents. It is driven by the investors themselves and by either their satisfaction or their lack of satisfaction with the current environment.

You could go to a conference like this three years ago, and only hear complaints about Nasdaq trading. Today at these conferences you hear a lot of complaints about trading on the listed stock exchanges. Block size is obviously a major part of this: The ability to execute large blocks of stock has been frustrated more on the NYSE than on Nasdaq since the introduction of decimals and penny increments. Nasdaq has done a much better job than the NYSE in allowing direct and unintermediated access for the institutional trader.

These, as well as other changes, are putting pressure on the current listed trading structure. Sector trading is another change. A few years ago a trader either traded listed – that is, NYSE or Amex stocks – or Nasdaq stocks. Today, at dealing desks, the same trader is trading AMD and Intel, or IBM and Dell, where the stocks he handles are based on a specific industry or sector, rather than on the exchange or market center the stock is traded on. Having the same trader trade stocks in both markets will cause trading to harmonize in the two major market centers.

Other factors are putting pressure on listed trading. The focus on decentralization of markets since the tragic events of September 11. In this sense, fragmentation is good from a risk perspective. Nasdaq market makers that are exploring making markets in NYSE listed trading is another issue. So all of these things combined are leading, now more than ever, to some significant changes in the listed environment.

Liquidnet is an example of the changes that we will see. As decimalization came in, the need to trade blocks attracted a solution like Liquidnet, particularly for listed trading. The competition for QQQ order flow is another example. More volume trades outside of the listed environment in the Qs than in the central market.

REDFEARN: First, I would like to say something about printing Nasdaq stocks on the Cincinnati Stock Exchange. One of the interesting things that happened when Nasdaq decided to become an exchange, was that it opened up the question, 'what is an exchange'? It used to be that, with an exchange, executions take place inside the facilities of the given exchange market. Historically, Nasdaq was essentially an association. Hence, it could be both a market center and a printing facility. That is, it could print – not execute – all of the ECN trades, as well as the trades of Knight and the other wholesalers that were executing in their own systems.

As Nasdaq moved to become an exchange, the question then arose, 'Can you be both an exchange and a printing facility,[60] more or less?' Nasdaq has been going down that road. Now the other exchanges also have to answer the same question. If you can be an exchange and a printing facility at the same time, we would want to get into the printing facility business as well. The Cincinnati Exchange made the first step by going to Island and saying, 'we can be a printing facility,' and we will share the revenue. Cincinnati shares something like 80% of its tape revenue with Island in this particular situation.

But this raises real issues with exchanges. Exchanges use tape revenue to fund much of their regulatory programs. If tape revenue is siphoned away by non-listing markets through tape sharing deals, how will primary markets fund their regulatory programs? How do exchanges operate? If you are an SRO and have to do all of the things that SROs have to do, can you do them if this game is being played with printing facilities?

[60] Printing Facility means that there is an option to print the ECN trades in the market systems.

FREUND: What is your answer to that?

REDFEARN: I do not know how this one will play out. If it turns out that you can be an exchange and a printing facility, then Island could play all of the exchanges off against each other until they have virtually 100% of the tape revenue. This is because all of the exchanges will also sign up to be printing facilities because of the economic value inherent in printing trades. At that point, if Island has not become an exchange, it might as well forget about its filing for exchange status. Island will have received all of the benefits of being an exchange, without having to go through the trouble of actually becoming (or being) an exchange.

If it turns out that you can't be both an exchange and a printing facility, Nasdaq may want to think about its desire to become an exchange. It will lose an awful lot of tape revenue if it can't be a printing facility for all of the executions that take place outside of its exchange marketplace, which would probably be limited to SuperMontage. This gets back to something I mentioned earlier about regulatory harmonization. You really have to ask, what is an exchange? What are the rules that exchanges abide by, and what is it that ECNs can do to play in that space? Should Island be able to get all of the benefits of tape revenue without having a regulatory program and without actually being an exchange just because they have cut a good tape sharing deal or deals?

The second point I would like to make here is in response to the assertion that the QQQs or ETFs can be used as an example that suggests that listed flow will migrate to ECNs as it has in the Nasdaq world. It is true that a substantial amount of QQQ volume trades in Island. The question is, 'Is this an indicator of what's to come for listed equities or something particular to ETFs?' I believe it is the latter. In particular, ETFs are quite distinct from equities in how they are priced. Exchange Traded Funds are priced based on futures and based upon NAVs[61] of underlying baskets. Consequently, the price discovery function is fundamentally different from equities. So the suggestion that the Island QQQ story is an indicator of what's to come with your typical listed stock is flawed. Island has tried to make some inroads into the listed market where it ignores the ITS rules, yet it has no success gaining substantial market share in listed equities.

FREUND: We will address the regulatory issue. First, let me ask you this question. You are about to start a new facility for trading Nasdaq stocks. But there is a catch 22 problem in the securities markets business. The market that has the order flow is the best market, and institutional investors have a fiduciary obligation to send their order flow to the best

[61] NAV is the acronym for Net Asset Value.

market. And, as long as they send that order flow to the best market, it remains the best market. So, how can order flow be attracted into the new facility?

REDFEARN: We have a very different approach to what we are offering in the Nasdaq world. In effect, our model is in recognition of the fact (and this came up in the earlier discussion) that there is presently a problem discovering the price for the size order.

We have deeply capitalized specialist firms on the Amex. This is different from what we are seeing at some of the regional stock exchanges. We are talking about Bear Wagner specialists, Performance specialists, and other large firms who will be involved in trading Nasdaq stocks on our floor. What they intend to do is to step up and say, 'here is where you can price 25,000 shares or, depending on the stock, maybe 50,000 shares.' This is where the size price is. It embeds size back into price while at the same time widening the spread a bit. But if an institution wants to come in and hit size at one price in an agency environment, it will be able to do that in our market.

Specialists who are involved in this program are also involved in our options business and our derivatives business. So trading strategies once utilized will link trading of some of the most liquid stocks in Nasdaq to the Q, or to the Q future, or to a related HOLDR product.[62] Those are the sorts of strategies that we think will improve the ability to offer size, and to provide deeper liquidity.

SCHENKMAN: Bill, your question has a fundamental assumption that it is all about price. It may indeed be mostly about price. But, as Brett said, best execution is about more than just price. It is about price/size and price speed. It is a very personal thing for the investor. You ask any institution that needs to buy a block of stock immediately what it is more sensitive to – speed, size, price – or where it will trade. Different institutions will trade in different venues. They will go to capital which may cost them more money to execute, but will get them an execution within the parameters of the trading strategy that they consider best execution, in this case speed.

To divorce the trading strategy from best execution is bad. It is not realistic. Once you come to that conclusion, then the destination for trading becomes clearer. If you are going for a size execution, and have the luxury of time, you may choose a crossing network. If you are extremely time sensitive, you may use a broker's capital. Or if you are going for something in between, you may use an ENC, or an alternative trading facility.

[62] HOLDRS were created by Merrill Lynch and trade on the American Stock Exchange. HOLDRS allow investors to own the common stock or ADRs of specific companies in a certain industry.

FREUND: That is a good point. Best execution has many dimensions. This will be dealt with further this afternoon by Ananth Madhavan's panel.

MALITZIS: One objective is to actually access the quotes that you see on the public quote screen. But what is the price you pay to access them? Do you actually get to execute against the quote, at the price and in the size that is out there? This is a complicated matter. It is something that is buzzing around in the industry right now. What happens when all of the other exchanges start trading? What happens if and when ITS stops trading and there is no inter-market trading system?

This issue is coming to a head. Just because there are routing systems to get to the quotes today, doesn't mean that the practitioners are happy. They have to pay to join these services at a time when everyone is cost conscience. People look at the issue of fragmentation, the issue of best execution, and the prices they have to pay to access these quotes. As they do, they gravitate to the most liquid, most efficient markets.

FREUND: Do you think that SuperMontage will be that market?

MALITZIS: Yes.

FREUND: Before we get to the audience (and I will allow enough time for that), let me explore another aspect of what we have been talking about – the harmonization of regulation. The term rolls off the tongue, but I do not quite know what it means. Could you clarify what kind of harmonization you want? It is sometimes called a level playing field. What is that?

REDFEARN: Absolutely. We are in an environment now where, if you look at the rules on the listed markets, the rules on the Nasdaq market, and at the rules for ECNs, you see three different sets. There are three different competitive playing fields. For example, in the listed markets, we have ITS rules that the exchanges and Archipelago must abide by. There is a trade-through rule[63] in the listed markets. You cannot trade-through a better price in another market. If you do, you are going to get a call, and you will have to make good on the better price. The trade-through rule really drives the dynamics of how different markets trade and interact with one another. The rule does not exist in the Nasdaq market.

Increasingly, it is being questioned whether there should even be a trade-through rule in an era when you have institutional size business that might not care about what the penny wide, hundred shares or even thousand shares up market is. Maybe somebody wants to pay a few cents more (or receive a few cents less) to get 25,000 shares done. In Nasdaq, you can do this. In the listed world, it is different. You have to run 'walk the book' before executing against a size price. With respect to the ECNs, Island does not

[63] The Trade-Through Disclosure Rule (Rule 11Ac1-7) would eliminate the requirement that a broker-dealer disclose to its customer when a trade-through has occurred.

abide by the trade-through rule, and does not participate in ITS. The big dispute that we have had with Island is that Island is an ECN that is operating in our ETF business but is ignoring the rules that we have to abide by.

Somebody commented earlier that people will gravitate to that model because you get an instant execution. Well, if the Amex could in effect give an instant execution and ignore all the quotes and all of the other markets' prices, then we could be a hell of a lot faster. But we have to say, 'OK, Archipelago's quote is such and such,' so we have to outbound route through ITS and see if we can get a fill on ITS, or we might have to go to the Chicago Stock Exchange. Obviously there is delay involved with this set of rules.

A lot of this speed issue is not so much about execution systems. In fact, we have automatic execution capabilities now that we could put in place. But as long as we are in an ITS environment and have to abide by the trade-through rule, inevitably it is a completely different structure. It is a different playing field.

FREUND: I saw Sanjiv shake his head.

GUPTA: We all know that, when you send your order to a listed exchange, it takes a bit more than a second or two to hear back. To say that it is just to look at what Archipelago's quote is, etc., does not explain the 30 seconds of specialist intermediation. This is the fundamental problem that the alternative systems are trying to solve for the institutions and anybody else who wishes to trade with them. The whole dispute with Island *is* over the ITS rules which, in my completely personal opinion, are absurd in this marketplace. I suspect that within a year they will be gone,[64] or else there will be a choice of whether you want to participate or not.

I am not sure that the abolition of ITS would be particularly good for the exchanges. I stand by my earlier comment that ITS makes the marketplace far less competitive. I am not sure that the exchanges would get that many benefits out of the elimination of ITS.

FREUND: Sanjiv, I keep hearing you say that it takes 30 seconds. I think it takes more like 15 seconds. But let us say 15 to 30 seconds. Do you think that an institution that wants to buy 750,000 shares, as we heard this morning, cares whether it takes 15 or 30 seconds more when they are trying to buy a big block?

CORMACK: Yes (laughter).

[64] The rules of the ITS were still in place in early 2003. However, the SEC in late 2002, granted a temporary 'de minimus' exemption from the trade-through rule restrictions for the QQQs and other ETFs, provided the trades occurred within 3 cents of the National Best Bid or Offer, or NBBO.

GUPTA: When you do not know what has happened to your order, that spells trouble. Here's an example: You look up at the screen and see a 50,000 share offer, so you route your buy order, and try to lift the offer. Then, in the auction, the specialist interacts with the crowd, and you haven't heard back; and still later you haven't heard back. After 30 seconds, you see the quote move, and suddenly the specialist's bid is a penny above your limit price. And you still haven't got an execution. This is the penny jumping phenomena. You want to lift an offer but instead people in the crowd have lifted it in front of you. The bid is higher than your limit order and you've been shut out. In that 30-second process, you didn't know who you were in competition with. If you had heard immediately that you were not going to get this 50,000-share trade done, you'd have been able to do something positive about it. Maybe you could have paid a penny higher.

These are the problems. If you heard immediately, even if it was a rejection, that immediate turnaround would allow you to take advantage of other pools of liquidity. That is what people want to do now. They want to try something and, if it doesn't work, they want to re-route.

But price improvement does not make sense to a lot of investors. It made sense in a teenie and eighth world, but the concept of price improvement in this penny environment does not. A lot of institutions would give up price improvement for immediacy. We now have a system on New York called Direct Plus, which gives up price improvement and allows you to access the quote in two seconds. The technology exists. Unfortunately, the NYSE limited that technology to 1,099 shares, with only one order allowed every 30 seconds.

CORMACK: Every unexecuted order has an option value associated with it. The larger the order, and the longer it is out there, the higher the option value. If I send a 100,000-share order to a system, and if it hangs there for 30 seconds and I will not be able to get out, I will have given up a lot of value. If I can hit Island in a sub-second time frame, the opportunity cost for exposing that order is very low.

FREUND: You meant to say Archipelago.

CORMACK: I am trying to be neutral (laughter). If I was to hit Island or Archipelago, and I could execute that sub-second, that is a much better fill. You know, as a former trader, I am much more comfortable with that speed, and there is value there.

REDFEARN: I encourage everybody to go to one of the websites where you can look at the Rule 11Ac1-5 execution quality data and the QQQ product. Look at the data by order size, and look at the speeds going up by order size. For a lot of orders under 500 shares, or under 1000 shares, you will see speed. In all the other markets, the execution speeds are going to go up. Certainly for the small orders, because we are handling both institutional and retail business, our speeds are generally slower for the smallest order sizes. When you get to about 2,000 shares, execution speed numbers flatten out. I can tell you that the effective spreads and the executions you get are better on the Amex. If you compare the effective spreads here versus what you see on Island, it is almost egregious how far outside of the NBBO quote the executions are on Island.

This gets back to who the participants are. Does a retail investor want to give up ten seconds and pay a penny and a half or two cents more per share? I am not so sure the retail investor does. It might make sense for certain program traders or certain professionals who are hedging and want to get off the hedge right away. But this trade off does not make sense for many institutional traders as well. For larger orders, even in those particular statistics, the time differentials are not quite as big as those seen in the data for small orders, if at all.

CORMACK: It is about choice. However, because of the trade-through rule, people do not have that choice. We have to abide by those trade-through rules because we are an ITS participant. No matter how much that day trading client of ours wants to pay up two cents to buy those 3000 shares out there, we cannot do it. I have to send it somewhere else. In Nasdaq, you have that choice. You can trade-through for speed, the customer has that choice. No one is forcing anyone to do it. Let them make the decision.

FREUND: Have you heard any agitation to remove that rule?

CORMACK: Yes.

FREUND: Do you expect that it will happen?

CORMACK: It is a very controversial rule. I can see both sides. If I could buy, for example, a million shares of AOL up two cents through the entire million shares offered on the floor of the New York Stock Exchange, I would do it 100 times out of 100. I have exposed too many large orders on the floor of the NYSE, and too many weird things have happened. Pay up two cents to get the job done in a sub-second? I would do that 100 times out of 100. But you cannot do that today with the trade-through rule.

REDFEARN: For our Nasdaq strategy, we want no trade-through rule. It makes it easier to do size. You do not have to pay so much attention to a 500 share, one cent wide spread. Institutions do not care about that. A one-cent spread is not the price for 50,000 shares.

Imagine a scenario without any trade-through rule whatsoever. Let's say, hypothetically, the Amex opened its own ECN, Chicago puts in an ECN, and then you have an Island ECN. Let's say that there is no linkage, or not real integration because everybody could ignore the other markets. What would the price be then? How would that affect price discovery? I mean you could have different prices in different markets locking and crossing all day long. That would create another set of issues. Getting past the trade-through rule in this environment may not be as easy as one might think. In my view, efficient electronic linkages and arbitrage will reduce the negative consequences of fragmentation.

CORMACK: Except for the retail investor, I do not think that would be a problem. Arbitrage would take care of those issues. That is what has happened with Nasdaq. But it comes back to the point about our bifurcated regulatory structure. Most rules are designed to protect the small individual, the 100-share investor, Aunt Tilley or Uncle Ned with their orders in the marketplace. The rules do not protect the institutions. The institutions generally drive these problems, and they come back to roost for the retail customer. That is what happens when markets that are regulated for retail are, at the same time, supplying institutional size investors.

At this point, technology has offered institutions a significant amount of control over their executions. But the 15 seconds that they are leaving their orders and waiting, is a loss of control. The wait leaves them with less choice, with less of an opportunity to take advantage of a different market situation. This brings us back again to the bifurcated regulatory structure. This time, the split is between the individual investor and the institutional investor.

FREUND: When I asked for your perspectives on the future of market structure, one of you said that you expect a separation of retail and wholesale trading. Can you speak to that?

MERRIN: Sure. Wayne, in your latest survey, I think you said that it costs the institutions on average 46 cents per share?

WAYNE WAGNER: The number you want is 46 cents a share for the search costs.

MERRIN: Right. That is above and beyond what they pay for commissions, correct? I believe that in your updated iceberg the ratio of hidden costs to explicit costs is now about 9 to 1. In other words, for every dollar that the institutions pay in commissions, they are paying about 9 dollars in other hidden transaction costs. Right? When we first started Liquidnet, it was a 7 to 1 ratio. Hidden costs, which have increased, were 36 cents above and beyond what you were paying in commissions two years ago.

If you add it all up (this is something that I am not going to attribute to Wayne), you are talking about over $100 billion a year that goes out of the returns of these institutions, and into the hands of somebody else. The way that our markets are structured today, going out and searching for liquidity means giving up information.

As far as I can see, two major factors move market prices against the institutions. Number one is information dissemination. A broker gets an order and tries to find the natural other side. This should be good for an institution because presumably there would be less market impact. So the broker calls up other institutions, advertises on AutoEx, and/or sends out FIX indications of interest. These are nice gadgets. The problem, according to New York Stock Exchange statistics, is that the process I've just described works only about 30% of the time. That 30% is when the order is crossed upstairs. The other 70% of the time, the procedure works to the disadvantage of the institution. It only serves to inform everybody else. It gives the rest of the market the information that there is a large buyer or seller out there.

Information dissemination is the first major market mover. Information starts the time clock ticking against the institution. Compared to five years ago, there are now tens of thousands of day traders who make their livings off of this information. There has been an explosion of hedge funds. Not all hedge funds are bad, but some hedge funds are, and they too make their living off of this information.

The other major market mover is size disparity. The average *order size* for institutions is now well over 250,000 shares. At the same time, average *execution size* is 1,100 shares for New York, 800 shares for Nasdaq, and 300 shares for the ECNs. Whenever you have that kind of size disparity, there will be market movement. There is no way to fill that square hole with that round peg. That is the only way to get orders done in our current market structure. Our current market structure is no longer working for institutional participants. Period.

The amount of money that these guys are losing every day, every year, is too much. View it this way. $100 million a year is approximately what the Bush tax incentive was (at one time). This dollar sum flows out of institutions every single year. Ultimately it comes out of the little guy. If you can fix that gaping hole, you can tell Bush to relax.

The only way to fix that gaping hole is to go outside of the current market structure and establish a market that works for institutions. I can guarantee you the following. If you talk to institutional participants and say, OK, you have a blank sheet of paper, go and design a marketplace, I guarantee you that they will not design a marketplace with a bunch of people running around on a trading floor.

Once again, what we have might be perfectly fine for retail. But it is not working for institutions. The NYSE is saying that there is a different marketplace for institutions, that they are going to give institutions a different quote.[65] Perhaps the market makers are going to put up capital every time the institutions want to trade. Perhaps that is good. Regardless,

[65] Merrin was referring to various NYSE systems for offering institutions quote information distinct from what is offered to retail customers.

the market makers are also saying that retail has to be separated from wholesale.

FREUND: Do you see any reason to believe that separation is going to happen any time soon?

MALITZIS: Didn't the SEC address this in the order handling rules? In essence, they took a bifurcated market (I would argue that there was a wholesale market and a retail market) and merged them into one. That was my perception of what the order handling rules did: I could be wrong.

MERRIN: Yes, that is correct, but my argument is that this is the wrong approach. Retail and institutions need two completely different structures. Retail needs price transparency and it needs to know what's going on out there. Retail wants to look at a quote system and to enter an order and execute at the bid or the offer. Institutions don't want transparency. They are not going to agree to put their bid and offer out there for everyone to see. Their trades are so large that the information could move the market. What the SEC did was favor the retail investor by creating greater transparency and merging retail and institutional in the order handing rules. Consequently, the brokers could not protect the institutions anymore.

MALITZIS: Yes, the order handling rules forced the quotes of all market participants – large market participants, ECNs, Nasdaq market makers, etc. – into the public quote stream.

MERRIN: A big hidden reserve is the problem. Nobody can regulate it. No one is going to tell all the institutions that they have to show their entire hand. We must realize that there will never be perfect information.

The whole random walk theory contemplates perfect information. An exchange is supposed to be a perfect capitalist environment, right? For every buyer there is a seller. The problem is that because institutions hold their orders so close to the vest, the supply and demand of the institutions is not represented on the exchanges. Only retail supply and demand is represented. This leads to a tremendous amount of volatility because, ultimately, the institutional demand goes against the retail supply. You are bumping two different sizes together. There has to be volatility. And it is this volatility that leads to a 47 cents cost per share, on average, every time these big guys go into the market. Ultimately, it is going to flow back. When the institution is done, price goes back to reflecting the retail supply and demand. Price finds its natural value based on the set of retail orders.

REDFEARN: Given the general principles of supply and demand, some market impact is inevitable. This may be a bit sacrilegious but, if there are more buyers than sellers or more sellers than buyers, prices are bound to move if you try to get 100,000 or 500,000 shares done. If there is a natural buyer on the other side you will get filled. If there is not, where do you go for liquidity? In this context, many of the institutional services that are provided on the floor of the exchange make a lot of sense. People can come down to the floor, have a floor broker hold or work the order, and feed that information to the market in a gradual, controlled way. This process reduces market impact.

I would like to also get into the game of throwing out Plexus figures (laughter). We have done some work in the past with Plexus. We have looked at the pre-trade costs and the overall market impact costs, both in the auction market and in the dealer market. Wayne, tell me if I am wrong here. All of the studies that we have looked at have shown that pre-trade costs and market impact overall on the Nasdaq market has been higher because search costs are higher in that marketplace. Nobody will put all of his orders in a limit order book.

In an environment where there is institutional order flow, there must be a way to control information release. A controlled release of information helps to serve the institutional community. It reduces their market impact to a certain extent.

MALITZIS: This is a great ad for why you should to put your orders in SuperMontage (laughter).

I want to touch again on another point – regulatory harmonization. To an extent, there will always be regulatory differences between the exchanges, the ECNs, the over the counter market, and so forth. The Amex can argue about the trade-through rule, and we can note that there is no short sell rule for Nasdaq securities. The debates never end. The SEC's role here is to look out for the investor, to ensure that there is a baseline level of regulation. At the end of the day, markets must compete on quality. If an investor has had a bad experience with a particular market, if he has received a print significantly outside of the inside quotes, or if his order is treated poorly and a bad execution has been realized, the statistics show that the investor will walk away from that market. That is what we believe at Nasdaq.

We invest a lot in our regulatory infrastructure. We would have a different definition of print facility.[66] If you put your quote up on Nasdaq, you should have to pay for that regulation. At the end of the day, competition, with regard to both speed of execution and regulation, is going to win.

[66] At the time of the conference, Island was quoting its trades on Nasdaq but printing them on the Cincinnati Stock Exchange. Nasdaq obviously was not pleased for business reasons but it cited another concern. 'Our view is that there should be a nexus between the place you quote and report trades, in part because we incur regulatory obligations when a market participant quotes here and uses our facilities,' Malitzis explained in a note after the conference. The market participant in question, who Malitzis did not identify by name, committed what 'looked to us like regulatory arbitrage.'

FREUND: Questions from the audience?

ROBERT WOOD[67] [From the Floor]: Fragmentation is a synonym for competition. Because the regionals were small back in the old days, they could not give price competition to New York. But a lot of technical innovation came from the regionals. For instance, SCOREX[68] preceded DOT.

We know the behavior of monopolists. They never want things to change. They are not into innovation. They are not into adopting new technology, and so forth. The very fact that the ECNs came into existence is a reflection of how inefficient Nasdaq had to have been. Order flow attracts order flow, and if the Nasdaq marketplace had been efficient, those ECNs would not have had a chance. But the innovations provided by the ECNs have been important. My concern is, if SuperMontage becomes really successful, how can the ECNs survive in a world of best execution?

GUPTA: First of all, you have to realize that SuperMontage basically is an ECN. It takes the elements that the competitive forces of the marketplace have created over the last four or five years. Nasdaq has created a super ECN with regulatory approval that can sort of fashion a marketplace that is a virtual monopoly. I talked about the ADF before. The ADF is the alternative structure that people could choose. But the ADF is having growing pains. It can't succeed overnight. To launch a whole new marketplace and a whole new regulation is a tricky business.

Once you have that whole new marketplace, as you pointed out, there tends to be inertia. But so long as the choice remains, so long as everyone does not have to be a complete flag-waving member of SuperMontage, competitive forces in the marketplace will create new solutions. I do not think that a centralized marketplace like SuperMontage offers all of the choice that institutional investors need. Take down the barriers to competition, and you will see what you get. It is as simple as that.

FREUND: On the other hand, isn't it true that the New York Stock Exchange has spent huge sums of money, like $400 million a year, on automation? Isn't it true that the problem is not the electronic systems in place, but the regulations and the rules?

GUPTA: The New York Stock Exchange has its version, as I said earlier, of institutional trades in the crowd versus more retail type trades in the book, but they want to limit any other types of choices. They choose

67 Robert Wood is Distinguished Professor of Finance at The University of Memphis.

68 SCOREX was the acronym for Securities Communication Order Routing and Execution System, which was introduced by the Pacific Stock Exchange. It was active in the early 90s. Specialists used early systems like this to execute orders from member firm, to update their markets and to transmit and accept quotes from SIAC.

what works in the best interests of their business model. Even European exchanges have iceberg trading similar to reserve order trading. Nothing like that exists in the New York Stock Exchange market where, for example, you could post 49,000 shares on the exchange and only show 1,000. You reserve the other 49,000. On the New York the specialist would see all of that order. We have not seen a whole lot of innovation. We have seen small amounts of responses to criticisms from pennying and other areas.

CORMACK: The question is, can New York survive with incremental changes over the next couple of years? Is the business model of having a floor unsustainable? What has happened to spread compression with the influx of ECNs and Nasdaq over the past five years, is only beginning to happen in the listed markets.

By rolling out an ECN or an electronic exchange, you in essence lower the barriers of entry to market making. That makes everyone better off. It compresses spreads. The guys on the floor in New York have to compete with tighter spreads. Great, if they can do so. If not, somebody else wins. But the bigger question is whether those business models operated by the specialists are sustainable. We all have our opinions about that.

MALITZIS: It is important to note that, prior to SuperMontage, we had proposed to establish a book. As early as 1990, we had a book in SOES. It was not fully integrated. My point is that we were not just pushed towards creating SuperMontage by the competition and the innovation that the ECNs brought to the market. Prior to that, we had been looking to create book-like functionality in Nasdaq. This is the nature of Nasdaq's open architecture. That is why ECNs exist in our market. We invited them in. We wanted them in our market.

RUSSELL MONAHAN[69] [From the Floor]: You mentioned that ITS is a major barrier for the ECNs to come into the listed markets. But Island does not abide by ITS rules. So, how come they are not a player in trading IBM?

GUPTA: That is the debate that rages. Obviously, the American Stock Exchange is showing considerable concern that Island is not abiding by the ITS rules. However, we have now reached a problem that the regulators are not addressing. It is that people are reading different things into the fact that Island is not being told to stop. We do not know whether or not there will be new regulation that makes them effectively in compliance. Suddenly, we now have a new market center that is not complying, and that market center has a huge market share in a very important security (the Qs).

[69] Russell Monahan is Director of Strategic Research at the American Stock Exchange.

We are going to see something. In the current state, we have regulations on the books that are not necessarily working or being abided by. But an attempt was made to take action, and the regulators said, 'Don't take action, we are aware of the situation and are working on it.' This suggests that we probably will see something soon.

CORMACK: Island submitted an exchange application in mid-1999 and nothing has thus far happened with it. We went through the process of getting the exchange application submitted. Part of the battle is getting through the issues in DC. I can tell you that there is a lot of pain to be had on ITS committees, UTP committees, etc.

John mentioned getting SuperMontage up for listed securities and having an ITS amendment for that. That is not easy. Basically, any regional exchange can veto any change. How progressive is that? That is the environment we live in. We may all choose to go down different paths on how we are going to trade listed securities, or any securities for that matter. But it is not easy to get into the ITS club.

SCHENKMAN: Fix the governance structure, and you can fix a lot of the problems in ITS. But we all make choices. We choose to participate in ITS or not. Some of us choose to go the exchange route. Some of us choose not to go down the exchange route and therefore trade within ITS or outside of ITS. Our choice is based on our customers' needs and what they want to see from us, on the services that we provide. The issue is more one for the exchanges – how do they get out of the ITS regulation?

REDFEARN: I would put a slightly different spin on this. What happened with the ETFs gets back to the way that ETFs are priced. ETF price discovery is based upon futures, based upon NAVs, based upon baskets, of underlying stocks. People who are trading in programs or other markets can price these without being on the floor, so it is easier to take them off the floor. In our equities and the rest of the equities on the Amex, we still have somewhere around an 80% market share in our equity volume. This is similar to what you see on the New York Stock Exchange. The ITS argument doesn't hold up so much as the key barrier to ECNs getting into the listed market, given that it is not enforced. It is not abided by at all by Island. It is not a relevant rule right now. I would say that as long as you have a degree of concentration of order flow of that magnitude (80%), and as long as you have other typical equities where pricing is based upon supply and demand (and where the buying interest and the selling interest are concentrated on the floor), so long as you have all of the above, that there still is a gravity that pulls orders down to the floor. The existing concentration has itself helped to keep the order flow there. There never was this same sort of concentration in the dealer market, simply because of the way the dealer market is structured.

NATAN TIEFENBRUN[70] [From the Floor]: I have heard a lot of anecdotal evidence that the New York Stock Exchange itself does not really abide by ITS. One reason why the ECNs that participate in ITS have failed to get very far is that, as a buy-side client, you might post your quote, go best bid in a stock, and then see it printing in New York straight through your quote. Would anyone want to comment on that?

SCHENKMAN: Our ECN participates on ITS. We see anywhere from 1200 to 1800 trade- throughs a day from New York.

MERRIN: We all keep talking about why it is not necessary to change the rules. But nobody seems to like the rules. The exchanges are not going to be hurt by the competition. Just allow it.

SCHENKMAN: If it is not going to be enforced, get rid of it. Or enforce it and let's deal with it. We have spent enough on technology resources to comply with the trade-through rule. It should be either enforced or removed.

BARRY SMALL[71] [From the Floor]: Seth, are your customers concerned with information leakage? Also, is their behavior modified as a result of seeing information in your system, by being able to trade away from that information, by not being obligated to trade, and by the invitation of hedge funds into your system?

MERRIN: I think that you just about hit on all of them (laughter). Some people have the perception that they are giving up information by simply being in the system. I say it is a perception because I do not believe it. I guess if perception is reality, we have to deal with it. But in our system, what we tell people is that you have two contras with orders in Liquidnet. This is in contrast with what goes on every single day with every single order on your desk.

This is the way the market structure works. You pick up the phone and call a broker. You hang up the phone and have lost all control over where that information goes. The broker is obviously incented to try and find the other side. The broker makes phone calls and sends stuff to AutoEx. He might also send FIX indications of interest to pretty much anybody who would accept them. As a result, with most of the orders that you give to traditional brokers, a lot of information runs away from you.

In Liquidnet, by contrast, if there is one buyer and one seller, there are only two people in the entire world who know that there is something to be done. And you are one of them. Further, the information that is being

[70] Natan Tiefenbrun is Senior Vice President at Instinet Corporation.

[71] Barry Small is Chief Executive Officer at Weeden & Company.

disseminated is limited. Regarding the counter party, you have no idea what his size is, or who he is. You ask (and we have done our data analysis on this one) whether orders in our system move any markets. Of course, the answer is no – because they are our studies (laugher). Kidding aside, we found that there is no market movement.

Regarding hedge funds, we have been very selective about which hedge funds we have let into the system. Because of that, we have probably excluded 95% of the hedge funds from participating. The major reason for an exclusion is whether they are involved in any day trading whatsoever. If the traders have any discretion over what symbols they trade, they cannot come onto the system.[72] In addition, every participant in Liquidnet that so desires has the ability to exclude trading with a hedge fund. I think we have ten hedge funds to begin with, and they are actually excellent members.

FREUND: We have just a couple of minutes left. I would like to pull a fast one on all of you. Can you identify just one major change in the architecture of the securities markets that you expect will occur over the next year or two?

SCHENKMAN: The fundamental change that will occur is the morphing of roles of all of the players that provide a liquidity function to the market. This will force the industry as well as the regulators to differentiate the players by their function rather than by designation such as exchange, broker and ATS.

The core competency and primary function of dealers in the marketplace is the creation of liquidity through the use of their capital. The core competency of an exchange is the aggregation of liquidity and the dissemination of information about that liquidity on the tape. The core competency of an agency broker or an ATS is the search for liquidity. The fundamental change that I foresee as the morphing continues is that there will be less regulation by designation, and more regulation by function. This will free the players, brokers, dealers, exchanges, and ATSs to produce a more robust set of choices.

REDFEARN: I see a gradual evolution towards a much more integrated marketplace. An integration that includes equities, options, derivatives trading, and single stock futures. When single stock futures start trading, a

[72] Liquidnet said it does not admit customers whose traders make the decisions to buy or sell stock for a portfolio because that could invite traders who 'fish around.' In this environment these traders could, for example, put in orders to find out what interest is available, then use that sensitive information to force a stock price down or up on an ECN. 'Our members are people who have a serious problem: filling orders that the portfolio managers give us,' Merrin said after the conference. 'All of our members would be greatly disadvantaged by having these day trading firms allowed on our system.'

whole new item will be introduced in the markets. The SEC has already allowed the same specialist firm to trade the equity in one market and the option on that equity in another market. I foresee the evolution continuing in that direction – especially in Nasdaq, where it has become more difficult for people to find ways to provide liquidity. Complex trading strategies, centralized risk management, and the ability to hedge will all be instrumental in bringing more liquidity to the table.

FREUND: And when that happens, it will be to the great advantage of the Amex.

REDFEARN: And fortunately, we have an options, ETFs and equities business already on the floor of the exchange (laughter).

MERRIN: I do not see any major regulatory changes coming any time soon. What interests me is what ECNs have shown to be the portability of order flow. Until five years ago, if you had a Nasdaq order you went to Nasdaq, if you had a New York order you went to New York. Now the ECNs have shown that order flow can be transacted anywhere. We have not yet seen this so much on the listed end, but the trend is the interesting part here. You do not necessarily have to deal with an exchange. You have to deal with what may be construed as best execution, wherever that is.

MALITZIS: This is sort of esoteric, but I think the following. You are going to see the SEC looking at tape revenue and tape revenue sharing among exchanges. In connection with that you will see the SEC looking at the question of inter-market linkages. I cannot tell you what they are going to do, but that is a front burner issue for them.

GUPTA: Hopefully, some time this year, you will see approval of the ADF.[73] Then, as I pointed out earlier, I think they are going to allow for non-ITS participation, which is an easy way to kill ITS. You do not even have to put it to sleep. It will automatically go to sleep when the choice to participate becomes voluntary. At that point, you will see a changing landscape in the listed marketplace. I would suspect that, once you allow competitive forces in, you will see appropriate market share gains by the people who offer innovative solutions, whomever they may be.

CORMACK: The monopoly on listed trading will be broken (laughter).

[73] As noted, the ADF is approved for trading in OTC stocks. Regulatory approval for trading in listed stocks was still pending as of early 2003.

FREUND: Well, I am sure we could use another hour. I also know that the same questions will be covered in the next panel. But, of course, they will change the answers. Thank you very much.

CHAPTER 6: DOES BEST EXECUTION MAKE SENSE?

Moderator – Ananth Madhavan, *Global Head of Trading Research, Barclays Global Investors*[74]
Theodore Aronson, *Managing Principal, Aronson+Johnson+Ortiz*
Minder Cheng, *Global Head of Equity and Currency Trading, Barclays Global Investors*
Natan Tiefenbrun, *Senior Vice President, Instinet Corporation*
Wayne Wagner, *Chairman, Plexus Group*

ANANTH MADHAVAN: This panel, the last of the day, is on 'best execution.' The topic is important, it is charged, and it is highly controversial.

Let me begin by putting it in perspective. The topic is now at the center of debates on market structure. Anthony Neuberger, in his remarks this morning, mentioned one of the factors that is driving this interest in best execution on his side of the Atlantic – the Myners report. The Myners report has shaken up the U. K securities industry and raised awareness of best execution. It has emphasized the importance of non-commissioned costs, which is something that Wayne Wagner has been talking about for a long time.

Wayne is the person who popularized the concept of the 'iceberg of costs.'[75] That notion has now gained widespread acceptance. The Myners

[74] At the time of the conference, Ananth was Managing Director of Research at ITG, Inc.

[75] According to Wayne Wagner, 'Trading costs are like an iceberg. The real danger comes from the portion that cannot be seen. Commissions are easily observed but represent only the tip of an iceberg. The remaining costs are far more significant, but cannot easily be observed.'

report spends a lot of time talking about the non-commissioned cost elements of trading.

On our side of the Atlantic, best execution has most recently been driven by the Association for Investment Management and Research (AIMR) initiatives and by the Securities and Exchange Commission.[76] The AIMR has issued its trade management guidelines. Ted Aronson, is the chairman of the committee on trade management guidelines (otherwise known as the AIMR Best Execution Committee). These are voluntary guidelines, but they will lead how we think about best execution in this country in the future.

It would be useful to set the stage for our discussion by giving you a sense of what the AIMR thinks best execution is. As we all know, it is very difficult to define best execution, but let me read from the AIMR report. It defines best execution as follows:

In summary, best execution refers to well-informed trade execution decisions, made with the intention of maximizing the value of client portfolios under the particular circumstances at the time. This definition recognizes that best execution is, intrinsically tied to the portfolio decision value and cannot be evaluated independently, is a prospective, statistical concept that cannot be known with certainty ex ante, has aspects that may be measured and analyzed over time on an ex post basis, is integrally woven into complicated and repetitive practices and relationships.

The bottom line is, the AIMR guidelines do not prescribe a universal standard for how firms should measure best execution. Instead, they focus on the procedures in which firms check that client portfolios are properly handled. It is not a trade-by-trade process. The proposed guidelines, as originally unveiled by the AIMR, seek to establish more than 20 best practices in trading in three broad areas: trade practices and policies, disclosure and record keeping. The AIMR is looking for managers, traders, and brokers to put into place a set of processes that will ensure that considerations involving trading are carefully looked at during day-to-day operations.

The AIMR report is one element that is driving interest in the topic. A second element is equally important. Many more companies' investment managers, along with brokers at large trading desks, on their own, are now looking at trade measurement in a systematic and fundamental way. They are doing it in a way that looks a lot like what the AIMR report describes.

[76] On November 16, 2001, the Best Execution Committee of the Association for Investment Management and Research released proposed 'Trade Management Guidelines,' calling on investment firms to execute trades and manage the trading function in a way that is always in the best interest of clients.

Part of this is driven by a growing awareness that implicit trading costs are much larger than commission costs. This awareness has taken a while to seep in, but people are now looking at the trading room and traders as if they are of some value, as if they do help to control execution costs.

People recognize that trading costs, especially the market impact costs and opportunity costs, are very large relative to net alpha.[77] This is especially true in the post bubble environment that we are currently in. Today, net alphas are lower, and transaction costs are a significant portion of them. Consequently, good control over transaction costs can add meaningful value to the portfolio manager and to the trading desk.

Now let's turn to the panel for further discussion. We will begin with Minder Cheng.

MINDER CHENG: Thanks, Ananth. The essence of best execution is our trading strategy and we must be sure that we design that in the best way possible. We must make sure that the way that we allocate trades is in line with the minimization of our transaction costs. On the buy-side, we have a natural incentive to achieve this goal. The sell-side's interest to do so is not as clear, although there has been quite a lot of discussion. At the end of the day, if a broker dealer cannot fulfill his responsibility for best execution, who will suffer? The broker dealer's clients. However, the sell-side basically can just pass any impact on to the clients. I have the impression that it could be self-motivated on the sell-side, but they may also need some help from the regulators.

The buy-side should be financially aligned with our obligations to achieve best execution, since failing to do so impacts our investment performance directly. I think for stock exchanges, some of the things that we heard earlier, say Boston having a better quote than the NYSE, what do you do? Per the Intermarket Trading System (ITS), the NYSE specialist has to route the order to another market which has a better price. This principle does not apply so much to the sell-side, and certainly not apply to the buy-side, because we tend to trade with the brokers not with the stock exchanges directly. We don't have control over where the orders are going to be routed. Having said that, it would be helpful to go through the methodology that we have been using. It is similar to what some other buy-side firms may be doing to control their transaction costs.

[77] Net Alpha was introduced by Ananth Madhavan to signify the difference between the expected Alpha – which is a measure of performance over an established benchmark – and what is actually realized. Net Alpha, in this context, is calculated by subtracting trading costs from the expected Alpha. The term was also used by Minder Cheng, who stressed however in a later review of his remarks, that he used it interchangeably with the term, Alpha.

I will highlight one number that is important to a firm like Barclays Global Investors (BGI). BGI trades with more than 100 parties globally. The question is, even if you want me to use a random number generator when I have a list of orders to trade, from out of the 100 brokers, whom am I going to pick for this trade? This highlights the need for us to have in place a methodology to quantify how we allocate our trades and to make it consistent with our performance objective, which is lower transaction costs.

There are two questions that I will not try to answer now. I will leave them to the panel. One is, do I think that broker allocation should somehow be tied into best execution and, if so, how? The answer depends on whom you talk to. It could be something that you can quantify. It could be that I just went out for a nice dinner with a broker, so tomorrow I am going to allocate some trades to the broker. It will not always be one way or the other; most of the buy-side firms are probably some where in between.

This brings me to the second question – can execution quality be quantified? I am sure that, if I turn to Wayne Wagner, he will say 'yes.' I also believe that the answer is 'yes.' But that answer applies only to the portion of execution quality that can be captured in price. There are other factors that impact trading quality. As we heard on previous panels, speed matters. Suppose you can get the same price, but that there are two different ways of trading – one is slower and one is faster. How are we going to capture that?

Something else that is often talked about among buy-side players is infrastructure. For example, suppose I want to process a large basket order involving, say, 40 countries. I could place that huge basket with a single counterparty, or maybe a few. How efficient can these counterparties be in getting the fills back to us? Should I instead hit a button and send an order to a broker, and then have to wait for hours or days to get everything cleaned up? My choice between these two alternatives makes a difference. But the quality of the result, again, cannot be captured by prices alone. Nevertheless, it feeds into our considerations. If you do not get your fills back in time, then you cannot re-optimize your position for the next trade. So, while it is not price related, it does feed into overall trading quality.

Exhibit 23 presents an equation for a broker score that we assign to all of the counter parties whom we trade with.

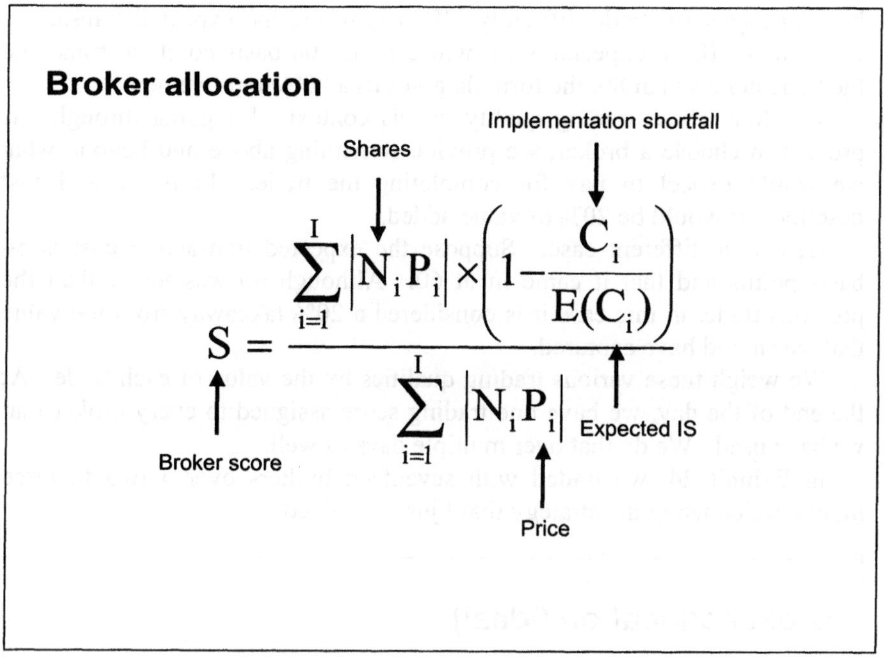

$$S = \frac{\sum_{i=1}^{I} |N_i P_i| \times \left(1 - \frac{C_i}{E(C_i)}\right)}{\sum_{i=1}^{I} |N_i P_i|}$$

Exhibit 23

The score is a value-weighted measure. In this particular score, there is a total of (capital) I trades included in the analysis. The first term in the numerator on the right hand side is, $N_i P_i$ the total value of a trade. It is also the weight associated with the trading quality that we are trying to quantify. The second term in the numerator, 1-C_i, divided by the expectation of C_i, can tell you a lot. It is a large part of the iceberg and quantitatively describes the quality of the trade. We call C_i either total transaction costs, or implementation shortfall. It is what we think, from the time we decide to trade (from the moment that we cut the list) to the time the entire order gets completed. It could be one day or multiple days. Wayne Wagner could undoubtedly provide more color on this. We have our own in-house methodology to capture this for our own trading strategies.

On the bottom of the fraction, $E(C_i)$ is expected transaction costs. It is not enough to measure the actual transaction cost of every individual trade. We also have to keep in mind that there are easy trades, and there are difficult trades. It is not fair to compare a trade that cost us 10 basis points with a trade that cost us 100 basis points, and conclude that the broker that gave us the 100 basis points trade failed. To make the comparison fair, we have to adjust for trade difficulty. That is where the expected transaction costs enter. If, on expectation, it will cost us 100 basis points to trade and the trade comes in at 80, the formula gives us a 20% improvement.

We think about trading quality in this context. By going through this process to choose a broker, we provide something above and beyond what we would expect to pay for completing the trade. In the case I just described, it would be 20% of value added.

Here is a different case. Suppose the expected transaction cost is 50 basis points and that it came in at 60. Although 60 was lower than the previous trade, in this case it is considered a 20% takeaway from the value that we should have captured.

We weigh these various trading qualities by the value of each trade. At the end of the day, we have one trading score assigned to every broker that we have used. We do that over multiple days as well.

In Exhibit 24, we traded with seventeen brokers over a two to three month period using the strategy that I just explained.

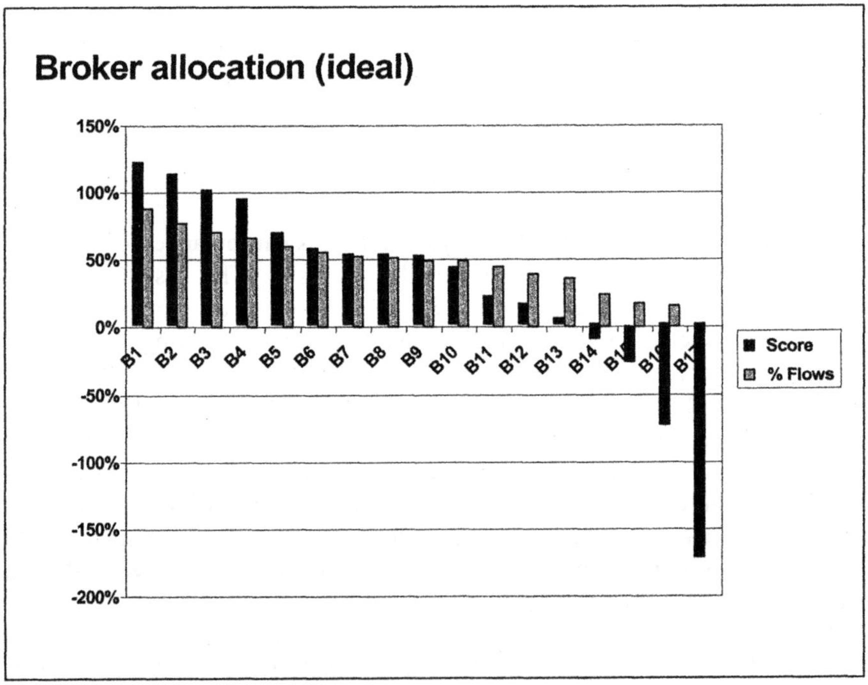

Exhibit 24

The black bar is the execution score. You can see that, in this case, thirteen of the brokers were able to trade and provide value above and beyond what we had expected to pay. There were four brokers, especially number seventeen, who were way below our expectation. Ideally, you want to see that the gray bar, – which is the allocation of the trade flow among the brokers – roughly matches the black bar which represents each broker's execution score. In other words, more trades go to the top performers and fewer trades go to the bottom performers. That is what you want to see. Ananth, by the way, the gray bar has been scaled if you are wondering why the numbers do not add up to a hundred percent. I want to make it easier visually to compare the two bars. More trades go to the top performers and fewer trades go to the bottom performers.

This highlights the difficulty of quantifying best execution. I do not think that I can recall a single time (unless maybe by chance) that I have gotten what I showed you on the Exhibit 24. Instead what I often see is represented in Exhibit 25.

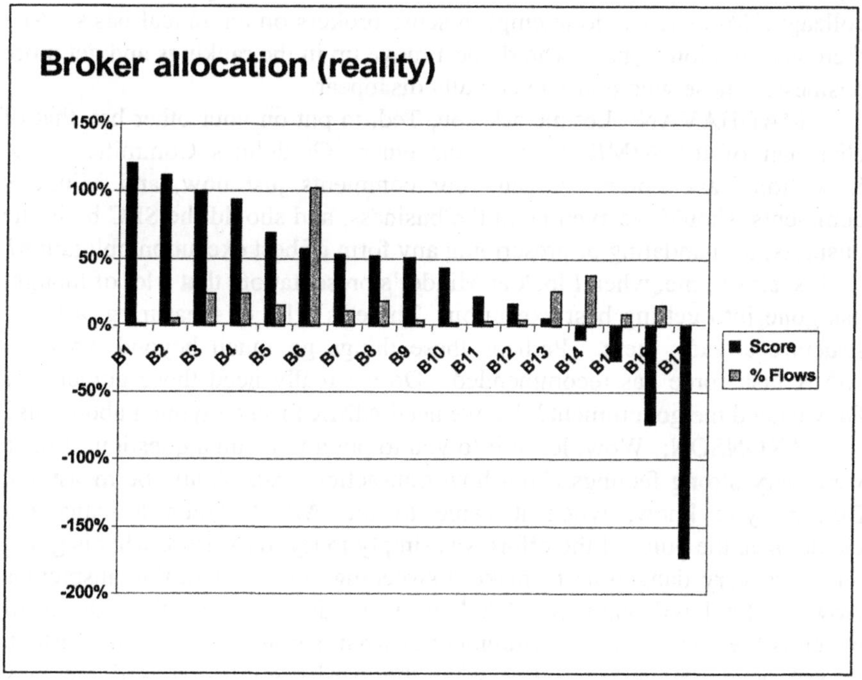

Exhibit 25

This is the same slide with the black bar, exactly as we had before, but look at the distribution. You may ask, if broker 1 did such a good job, why didn't we allocate more trades to broker number 1? Why did broker number 6 get so much more? The question comes down to the fact that one size does not fit all. Especially given the trades that we do. There are large sized trades. There are small sized trades. There are listed trades, and OTC trades. There are liquid names and illiquid names. Further, some of the brokers are not actually brokers – they are ECNs. There are trades that we tend to, given the economic design of the trades and how they design their trading system, we just tend to send to them. For instance, B6 could be one of those, or B1 could be one of those – it is an ECN trade. But we are not able to allocate more, given the nature of that trade and the reason we want to trade it. We might be more patient and go through the upstairs market. This is one reason why it is so hard to line these two up.

On that note, I will stop and hand the mike back to Ananth.

MADHAVAN: Thank you, Minder. I will turn to our next buy-side panelist, Ted Aronson. Ted, do you use the same formula (laughter)?

THEODORE ARONSON: Yes, but I have it memorized so I don't need any slides (laughter). Actually, we do use something similar. Like my colleague Minder, we do attempt to score brokers on an annual basis. And there is a rotation. Those who do best move up in the rankings and get more business. Those who don't, eventually disappear.

MADHAVAN: Let me ask you, Ted, to put on your other hat, that of chairman of the AIMR Trade Management Guidelines Committee, Best Execution Task Force. Given your comments just now, and Minder's comments, should we even be in the business, and should the SEC be in the business, of mandating or prescribing any form of best execution obligation?

It seems to me, when I look at Minder's presentation, that a lot of thought has gone into getting best execution. There is a lot of measuring, a lot of structure already there. Perhaps these things go much beyond what the AIMR task force has recommended. Do we really need those guidelines? Do we need the government? Do we need AIMR to say anything about this?

ARONSON: Wow, leave it to you to put a twist on a question. I have very, very strong feelings about how transaction costs should be measured. But, as you know, when it came to the AIMR Trade Management Guidelines, the point of the effort was simply to try to measure what is going on. It is very dangerous to make a sweeping statement in this auspicious crowd. But I will anyway. I believe in modern finance, the essence of which is the quantitative measurement of what is going on. It is not perfect. It will never be perfect. But what the AIMR guidelines and the new standards indicate is that there *must* be an effort to quantify the process. Why? Because the process seems to be taking a lot off the table for a lot of investors.

The guidelines do not specify how to measure transaction costs or how to quantify best execution. But, at least according to our sources at the SEC, they underscore that an effort had better be made.

MADHAVAN: I want to follow-up quickly on that and then move on. Can you clarify for us. just where the SEC stands given the AIMR task force recommendations? Will the Commission's recommendations be different? Will they second what has been done by the AIMR? Where do we stand on that?

ARONSON: It is my sense, and I suspect that most members of the task force would agree, that this is a major focus of the SEC. Indeed, in the last meeting of the task force, one of our members was undergoing an SEC examination when we were meeting. He was on the phone from his office. He could relate right from the front that notions and details of best execution were one of the first lines of questioning that the SEC led with.

MADHAVAN: Thanks, Ted.

Natan, there seems to be a presumption among the panel (I will speak for Wayne, I know him well) that best execution is something we can certainly get a handle on measuring. How do you come down on that? Can we really measure best execution, given the subtleties of the marketplace? Specifically, how do you measure best execution for stocks traded on the NYSE, given some of the debate that we have just had? What about the role of the specialists? I know how the other three guys feel. How do you come down on this issue?

NATAN TIEFENBRUN: We looked at the AIMR guidelines at Instinet, and felt quite comfortable with them. We have a broad mix of clients at our firm – institutional, hedge fund, broker dealer, direct access, and retail. They all have different needs. We track their needs on five different dimensions. The first is obviously price (and there is a great deal of emphasis on it). The second one is, as Minder mentioned, time (the need for speed). The third is liquidity (the need for size). The fourth is efficiency in the sense of information leakage. If you are going to take a long time to trade, you want a means of trading where you are guaranteed to leak as little information as possible. The fifth is operational efficiency. This one appeals to the big institutional clients. Every investor has a different mix of these five dimensions.

To answer your question, I do not think that it is possible to measure best execution. I do think it is possible to measure transaction costs and implementation shortfall, and that there is no excuse for not doing so.

There is a lot of fluff around. People try to avoid measuring transaction costs and implementation shortfall by using benchmarks that are inappropriate. Most of the smarter institutions (certainly the quantitatively biased ones) are doing it the right way. But it is important to distinguish between measuring execution costs and implementation shortfall, and measuring best execution. Best execution is not a number, it is a process.

How do you go about achieving best execution? You look at the motivation for the trade, you evaluate your needs in the five dimensions that I spoke about, and you choose the appropriate trading strategy and trading avenue. It is through the process of the trade, how you monitor what is going on, your response to the feedback that you are getting (if indeed you have chosen a means of trading that gives you feedback), and your ability to respond. After the trade, it also matters how you measure the actual cost, both in absolute terms and also relative to the costs that you anticipated beforehand. There is more. Subsequently, you must evaluate your own strategy selection and your own internal processes. Also, you must evaluate the performance of the different fiduciaries who have been involved in the trade with you.

We have defined best execution as a very holistic term. This is all part of the best execution obligation. I think that is right. It should be a holistic term. This is what we should be very focused on – how to get a money manager to look at the entire process, from end to end. How do we minimize all of the frictions that exist between the portfolio manager and the trading desk, and between the trading desk and a broker? How do we mitigate the conflicts of interest that exist?

The U.K. government felt that money managers spend their plan sponsors' assets too freely. That, in fact, was the underlying motivation behind the Myners report. Money managers were just spending their plan sponsor's assets for soft commissions, research, etc. Traditional broker dealers might be incented to turn a quick buck, rather than to deliver the best economic price to their clients.

So best execution to me is about the holistic process, and about how we get firms to adopt it. This involves educating the end clients (the plan sponsors). Unfortunately, we have end clients who are poorly educated. In many markets, less so in the U.S., they are volunteers.[78] They are not doing this professionally. Further, there is a real kind of 'cover your ass' mentality, where they give all of the responsibility over to a consultant. If the consultants were better educated, that would not be such a bad idea (laughter). But most of them are not.

MADHAVAN: So, if I could paraphrase, transaction costs can be measured with a high degree of precision. Transaction costs are an element of best execution, but obviously there is a whole process. And it is that process that we need to focus on.

[78] Most officials on pension boards in Europe, for example, are essentially unpaid volunteers. These posts are not fulltime salaried jobs.

You didn't quite say this, but let me take a leap. Given your comments about the educational level of the parties involved – plan sponsors, consultants, and so on – can I presume that it is an argument for regulation? Can I say that you are in favor of government regulation and the AIMR trade guidelines? Do you believe that things like this move the industry forward? Or perhaps you think that they will naturally occur.

TIEFENBRUN: They are occurring naturally because people are getting a better understanding of what their fiduciary obligations entail. It is not so much regulation, as it is court cases that are advancing it. For example, in the U.K., Mercury Asset Management was sued for not having the appropriate controls. As a consequence, it will be many years before we see an event like that again in the U.K. market.

Through experience, things are always evolving. The danger of regulation is that the regulators come in with a one-dimensional approach. They say that you must minimize cost, or that we must have a market structure that will protect the retail investor (as has happened here in the U.S.). In my mind, the regulators have often missed the boat. I am encouraged by the remark that the SEC is looking at the world in a similar way to the AIMR. But I also think back to the order handling rules. These rules were a good thing for the retail investor. But I do not think that the SEC put serious thought into how the rules would affect the institutional community. So I am a free-market kind of guy (laughter).

MADHAVAN: Now to Wayne. This is a natural set up for him. Your fellow panelists, Wayne, seem to believe that there are no issues in measuring transaction costs that it is pretty straightforward to do. But anybody who has actually gone out there and talked about transaction costs may have a different impression. You sometimes get blank looks and comments like, well, we trade with market on close orders, and they do it for zero commission, so we have zero trading costs.

Trading costs are an element of the best execution process. Is it so easy to measure them? What benchmarks do you use? People use different benchmarks. VWAP, opening prices, closing prices, mid-points, all kinds of things and, as they do, they come up with very different numbers. I am sure that with the Plexus data, you have run the numbers a bunch of different ways and have gotten very different answers based upon the benchmark that you pick. If we cannot pick benchmarks for measuring trading costs, how can we regulate a process like best execution in any sort of a meaningful way? Start there (laughter).

WAYNE WAGNER: The place where I would like to start is a bit different. There was a lot of confusion on the AIMR committee about whose behavior we were actually prescribing standards for. My view was that the regulations that we have governing the 33 Act[79] companies (the exchanges and the broker dealers) pretty much define what best execution is for that part of the universe. But we did not have a decent standard for a money manager, or for a trader for a money manager. What standards apply to the behavior of these people? How can they tell whether they are doing their part toward best execution or not? We ended up with the following rather soft sounding statement. We said that, in effect, the objective of trading is to capture the value of the process that is underlying those decisions.

But it gets complicated. These decision processes are all very different. Consequently, what represents best execution for a hedge fund that wants immediate execution, may not apply to Minder who is mostly running index funds and therefore is interested in achieving lowest possible costs. It is also different for a momentum manager who simply has to get the shares that his portfolio manager has decided on into the portfolio, no matter what the cost.

You cannot make a decision about what is best execution, until you have considered what the decision process is that is driving that execution. You really have to assess trading costs in the context of the values of the portfolio decisions that are being made. Then you can make rather simple mathematical (actually arithmetic) computations to determine whether your trading process is adding value to your client portfolios, or is taking value away from your client portfolios.

That brings up a couple of other issues. Here is the first. You can accurately describe whether the flip of a coin was a head or a tail by observing the coin after the fact. But that observation does not describe the process of coin flipping. The process of flipping a fair coin is described by the probabilities, 50% heads, 50% tails. You cannot tell from one trade, overlaid with the kind of noise that Bob was talking about (both noise in the fundamental process and noise induced by the trading process), whether it was heads or tails, a good execution or a bad execution.

The second thing is, you need a benchmark that makes sense. Let the measurement be an 'x minus y' kind of statement. That is, if you have x

[79] The Securities Act of 1933 mandated disclosure of information about new corporate securities, required that all new corporate securities be registered with the Federal Trade Commission (later the SEC), demanded that financial information in a registration statement be certified by an independent accountant, and stipulated antifraud provisions. The Securities Act of 1934 established the SEC and empowered the SEC to approve commission rate changes proposed by the exchanges and to request commission rate changes, empowered the SEC to prohibit stock manipulation, established regulation of the business conduct of broker/dealer members of an exchange, left disciplinary power over its members to the exchanges, and empowered the Federal Reserve Board to set minimum margin requirements.

dollars when you start the trade and you have y dollars of value after you are through with the trade, then, in some sense, x minus y is what it must have cost you to get that decision into the portfolio. But that is not enough. 'x minus y' does not say whether or not it was a good trade.

What you need is a difficulty-adjusted measurement. For instance, if you do a trade equal to two days volume under momentum conditions that are strongly adverse to the trading situation in a small cap stock, you must have a high benchmark. That is, high relative to what you would apply to a 1000 share order that got sliced and diced and dumped into the NYSE's DOT system. We have been working hard on the equations that would help us here. And we have our r^2s (unlike the Madhavan r^2s which are around . 05 or . 06).

MADHAVAN: This is Plexus data I might add (laughter).

WAGNER: Yeah, well, it took U.S. a long time to get past that. But we have them up to around 15.

MADHAVAN: Meaning that you are leaving 85% of the variation unexplained (laughter)?

WAGNER: Yes, but we have big samples (laughter).

In some of the overseas markets, we have r^2s going up to around . 3, which is about as good as betas. But we do have a lot of independent samples. On Minder's desk, tens of thousands of trades are handled every quarter. This is a good sample size. You can see what the process is generating in terms of whether or not it is bringing the value of the ideas to the portfolios.

MADHAVAN: Minder, ultimately, these are statistical constructs. Do you ever think about execution on a trade-by-trade basis, or is it purely statistical aggregates?

CHENG: The building block is trade-by-trade, but we do not decide trade-by-trade whether a broker is doing a good job or a bad job. There will always be something better than the average, and something worse than the average. Consequently, we take the statistical view as opposed to the trade-by-trade view.

I would like to add that, although best execution cannot be fully measured, from an asset managers point of view (whether an active, index, or momentum manager, we tend to do them all), it is important to recognize that, ultimately, performance is what counts. And performance can only be captured by price. I believe that trading costs are the biggest component in best execution. But you should also consider some other things, like operating efficiency. When choosing between two brokers with similar transaction costs, this can be used as a tiebreaker.

That is, if you have two or three brokers who, from experience, give you almost identical trading quality in terms of the score, then the one that has higher operating efficiency (or perhaps the one that offers you a better dinner) would... (laughter)... I am speaking for others here (laughter). But the best way to do things is to quantify as much as possible. Other measurements such as operating efficiency can be used as a tiebreaker.

Another point that needs to be clarified is that best execution is different between the buy-side and the sell-side. That point has not yet been made. Best execution largely refers to a similar set of principles between the buy-side and the sell-side. However, there are non-trivial differences between the two sides that would make the definition of best execution differ somewhat between them. First of all, the buy-side is mandated to have its fiduciary responsibility for its ultimate clients whereas the sell-side is not. In addition, the buy-side, typically not being a member of a stock exchange, does not access the conventional exchange-centered liquidity directly – although ECNs have changed some of that – whereas the sell-side does.

What this means is that what defines best execution for the sell-side includes, among other factors, the choice of exchanges whereas the buy-side is generally not accountable for it. The analogy for the buy-side would be the choice of brokers, which obviously will not be an issue for the sell-side.

MADHAVAN: It is a very good point.

I should also clarify that the whole day we have been talking about equity markets, except for the session on options. A lot of what we are saying here carries over to other markets and to other asset classes. It carries over with one proviso, however – it is much more difficult to measure the kinds of things we are trying to measure. The data just are not there.

WAGNER: Yeah, you really need some kind of price tape before you can...

MADHAVAN: Natan, is there something that you want to add?

TIEFENBRUN: Minder, you emphasized a purely statistical process that is not able to use individual trades. We find that clients are in some sense using individual trades. We typically trade portfolios. We would not want anybody to judge us on the basis of a single portfolio of equities but, for any given portfolio trade, you can look at the distribution of the costs for the individual shares and the individual names associated with the trades. A wide distribution around the mean might indicate a lack of discipline, or that some mistakes are being made. Similarly, while the implementation shortfall[80] that was my true cost is not always a good measure in individual trades, it is possible to go to a VWAP-type benchmark. A VWAP benchmark definitely is not a measure of cost. But it can be a useful

[80] Implementation shortfall is the standard measure of realized and unrealized transaction costs.

measure of broker diligence and broker discipline in participating in the market.

So it is possible to measure some aspects of fiduciary performance with individual trades, but not to measure ultimate cost. Again, best execution is a combination of all of those things. If you give a broker an order and say, 'participate in the hour,' and if their execution price differs wildly from the average for that hour, then you can say, 'hang on a minute, there is a lack of discipline, a lack of fiduciary diligence there.' Perhaps individual trades cannot be used to measure transaction costs, but they may be used to measure some aspects of execution quality.

WAGNER: We break reports down by individual broker. If a broker does not look good, the client beats him over the head and things change. There are variables inside a brokerage firm that are under the control of a broker. If you demonstrate that this issue is important to you, you will get a response. I suppose that if you were to demonstrate a love for hockey, you would get a different response (laughter).

MADAHVAN: Which brings to mind another question for Ted. Minder makes a very good distinction between the exchanges and the buy-side and the sell-side. Should we also make a corresponding distinction between retail and institutional when we talk about best execution? Is the industry too focused on retail concepts?

ARONSON: That is a good question. I will make a prediction that will get to the answer. For the first time, our industry is really focused on the aggregate issues of trading and implementation costs. I think it is coming to a head. By the way, I have been making this same prediction for the last 27 years, ever since May Day. [81] But I do think that the forces you mentioned at the outset are coming together – the Myners report from the U.K., the SEC's focus on the costs of doing business in this regard and, one hopes, the AIMR standards (which I agree with Wayne turned out to be a bit of a camel, when we set out to design a horse (laughter).

There is something that we have avoided here. It is a dirty secret, or maybe not such a secret thanks to the likes of Jack Bogle.[82] There is the failure of money management. There is the failure in my business, in my industry, to add value. We have been through a lot in the markets. I will not belabor the point of the bubble and its subsequent deflation. But investors, both retail and institutional, are sitting up and saying that we are mad as hell and are not going to take it anymore. Think of how retail investors are

[81] On May Day (May 1, 1975), fixed stock brokerage commissions were finally abolished with the enactment of the 1975 amendments to the Securities Exchange Act of 1934.

[82] John (Jack) C. Bogle is founder and former Chairman of the Vanguard Group.

switching in droves from mutual funds into money market funds. As an industry we've failed and we haven't added value. Transaction costs are part of this issue.

MADHAVAN: We have time for questions from the audience.

MARC GRESACK[83] [From the Floor]: I have been in the institutional brokerage community for about twenty years. I talk to a lot of plan sponsors. I agree wholeheartedly with Ted (and with all the others to a degree, as they represent their cases). I see that the plan sponsors are very concerned about performance measurement. The low returns that we have been experiencing of late definitely have something to do with it.

In an industry where every manager is being measured by his ability to perform across a number of segments (and it is all extremely quantifiable), the plan sponsors are upset at trading. They wonder why trading performance cannot be measured like everything else in this industry. That feeling is really driving the present condition. All the managers go through it.

Minder, when you talk to a plan sponsor about your trading desk's performance on behalf of the sponsor, doesn't tracking error on the performance side have something to do with your story? An index manager just wants to trade at the close to get the tracking performance, because that is a good measure of index fund performance. It does not matter what the price is, just as long as he gets the close. However, is it a good performance measure? Maybe yes, maybe no, but it is the accepted benchmark.

The same thing needs to happen in trading. I am not advocating one single benchmark, but the need for a widely accepted benchmark explains why VWAP is popular in the plan sponsor community. At least it gives one number that, although arguably imperfect, they can point to. They can look at all their other managers on the basis of one single benchmark. When a manager who is more in line with what Ted does visits with the plan sponsor on a quarterly basis, he can explain to the plan sponsor why he may have out-performed the VWAP.

You take advantage of liquidity so that you may do better on a VWAP measurement. American Century, on the other hand, with their momentum funds, looks terrible. American Century may try to explain away why they did well or didn't do well, but the fact is, there is a great need for a single benchmark.

I have met with a lot of buy-side traders who talk about the importance of having a feel of the market, the sense of a buying or a selling opportunity. But if they talk to a plan sponsor about things like intuition, guts, and market

[83] Marc Gresack is Chief Executive Officer of Pipeline Trading Systems. At the time of the conference, he was a strategic consultant for Brut.

feel, the plan sponsor thinks that this trader is taking way too much risk. Face it; we are in a very risk averse environment. That is what is driving the AIMR to set standards. So, yes, the process is complicated, but so too is the investment process.

WAGNER: I can think of one example that supports what you have said. I have these numbers, and you have to interpret them for what they mean. I am not picking on you, Ananth, but if you look at the executions that you get through POSIT, they are beautiful. But you also have to consider the fact that we submitted these orders and some got filled, and some did not get filled. Was there a difference between those that got filled, and those that didn't? Is there a subtle adverse selection process at work? You cannot complete a cross without the other side. What brings the other side to the table is that they have information. Thus, you will get large fills on POSIT only when the other side has the information edge (or at least the bigger orders, which means their orders will overhang and drive the price down if a sell or up if a buy).

Oversimplification is not what we are looking for here. We are looking for something that captures as much of the essence of the process as we can.

TIEFENBRUN: I would like to add something to Wayne's point. There is a link between transaction costs and market structure, or the business model operated by a firm.[84] You know, ITG's POSIT match looks terrific in the Plexus studies. I got Plexus numbers yesterday when I returned from a trip, and Instinet comes out on top in 11 out of 12 categories in listed and 12 out of 12 categories in OTC. That is lovely, but we ask why. I would love for the audience to see where they would stick their votes here. You can pick three factors, but number one is that all of Instinet's traders are geniuses (laughter). Although that typically scores kind of low with most people (laughter).

The second factor is that you tell a CIO his performance is high because his traders are geniuses. That doesn't tend to score too high either (laughter).

The only remaining explanation, I guess, is that it is just something about our business model. Unlike the principal trading model, we don't take positions, we don't make markets, we don't trade for our own book, we

[84] Tiefenbrun used a simple analogy to illustrate his point in a follow-up interview. If a customer employs a person to purchase a specific product for him as his agent, an agent who knows he gets to keep the change from the money the customer gives him for the transaction, this agent will presumably shop around for the lowest cost product available. 'In an agency transaction you are not buying to make money for yourself. You are being judged solely on the quality of the execution you give your customer,' Tiefenbrun said. So there is a direct link between the agency business model and the quality of the execution, he notes.

protect your anonymity, and we give you control. Ultimately, if you look at all of the Plexus studies, the agency broker dealers or ATSs that have this model continuously outperform, even on a difficulty adjusted basis.

Something that surprises me is that the buy-side is not more demanding from the traditional brokers. The Plexus numbers are difficulty adjusted. It is not just the case that ECNs are doing well because they get easy trades, or that ITG does well only because it gets easy trades. ITG does well because that is all they get paid to do. Because that is the business they are in.

There are many players in the market who are in the business of trading and profiting from their own trades. They are in the primary business of leveraging the information they get from their clients. When a broker dealer leverages the information that you give him, it is always to the detriment of the buy-side.

MADHAVAN: I totally agree with that comment (laughter).

TIEFENBRUN: I thought you might (laughter).

MADHAVAN: One of the advantages of turning a spotlight on all of this is that we are going to get better practices.

I have another question that I want to throw out to the panel. Five years from now, when the AIMR guidelines are widely accepted and are not controversial anymore, when the SEC has weighed in by going along with the AIMR, when Myners has transformed the U.K. industry, and when equations such as Minder has shown us do not look so startling– five years from now, do you think that all of this will alter practices such as preferencing and soft-dollaring? Will it change those things, too?

ARONSON: It will change things significantly. For the first time in 27 years, there will be a significant, and I mean significant, decrease in the use of soft dollars, in the related sins of directed trading, and all that sort of stuff. That will be the most important result of the AIMR task force guidelines.

CHENG: I agree completely. The equation and the methodology that I put up can only work because BGI does not do soft dollars. If you do soft dollars, a large portion is not trading related. Softing makes it harder to make the performance measurements accurate. So soft dollars are a troublemaker in this case. I know it is a common practice in the U.K., as well as for a lot of asset managers here. Directed brokerage is also the same thing.

MADHAVAN: Preferencing, payment for order flow? Same thing?

CHENG: Yes, same thing.

TIEFENBRUN: I am going to disagree. I think that soft dollars can be the lesser of two evils in some respects. The real sin is that paying full service commission fees, bundled commissions, to get research and IPO access, results in your not knowing just what you are getting for your full service commission. With soft dollars, the agency broker comes along and says, 'I will bundle these services, but at least I will price them explicitly.'

The money management community has neglected to tell the plan sponsors how much softing they are doing. That is a mistake. The plan sponsor sees soft dollars, and knows it is going on, and is identifying it as the problem when they do not really understand the concept of bundled full service commission rates.[85] I think the regulators and the plans are focusing their efforts on soft dollars when they should be focused on forcing a general unbundling of brokerage commissions. As to the other stuff, I agree that directed trading and payment for order flow will go away.[86]

ROBERT SCHWARTZ[87] [From the Floor]: I would like to ask Anthony Neuberger a related question regarding the Myners report. I know from your report and the like, that it is not easy to respond with a positive solution to the problem that the Myners report has unearthed. But Anthony, one of the things that your report considered is transparency. We are now talking about being more transparent about what the costs are. How far do you think that transparency about execution costs will go towards solving the conundrum of the Myners report?

ANTHONY NEUBERGER[88] [From the Floor]: There are two aspects to transparency. One is transparency of transaction costs, which would be beneficial, although it is difficult to interpret the figures exactly. The other number that would be really interesting is much greater transparency over the commission costs. Everybody had been forecasting since May Day that you would get unbundling of transaction costs from the other services provided by brokers. I still do not really understand why this has not happened. But if the debate about transactions costs and Myners leads to a

[85] In soft-dollar arrangements the costs are calculated on an implicit basis with full service brokers and on an explicit basis with agency brokers. In other words, on the former, the total costs for the execution and other services provided to a client are not broken out. On the latter, there is an 'explicit' soft dollar cost: the cost of the execution and the costs of the other services provided as a proportion of each agency transaction.

[86] The introduction of decimal pricing in the U.S. equity trading markets caused many dealers to reexamine their payment for order flow arrangements. Some have ended the practice because of sharply reduced spreads. Decimal pricing, on the other hand, would tend to encourage directed brokerage and soft-dollar arrangements on the Nasdaq markets since large-scale agency style transactions are now popular.

[87] Robert Schwartz is Speiser Professor of Finance at the Zicklin School of Business, Baruch College, CUNY.

[88] Anthony Neuberger is Associate Dean of the Full-time Masters in Finance Programme at London Business School.

clearer demarcation of what you are getting for your commission charges, the ultimate end users will be better off.

There is a great deal of dishonesty that comes about by softing, by the fact that you are getting these bundled services. Research and information are all bundled up with transaction costs. Greater transparency here would be enormously helpful.

TIEFENBRUN: I do not think it matters what industry you are in. The reason people bundle is to protect their margins. Broker dealers bundle their services to make you pay a higher price. Instinet would love to bundle as well. It is just that we have been so transparent in the past that nobody will let us do it. But broker dealers bundle to protect their margins and to force you to pay a higher price. They force you to consume a wider array of services, whether you want to or not.

MADHAVAN: Let us take one final question.

GEORGE BODINE[89] [From the Floor]: I have two questions. The first for Ted Aronson, and the second for Minder.

Ted, you say that you assess all your brokers at the end of each year. Do your traders give 100% discretion to the brokers? Most of the traders I know on the buy-side give maybe 10% or 15% discretion to the broker, and 80% to themselves. So, when you knock a broker off the list, are you really being fair to the broker versus your own trader?

ARONSON: Great question, and it is easy to answer. We give 100% discretion to our traders–one of whom is in this room today – to choose our brokers, and our traders in turn give 100% discretion to the brokers chosen The brokers are assessed by implementation shortfall standards. We go out of our way to make sure to balance the array of trades that go to each broker, given the difficulty of the trades as measured by Plexus, ourselves, and some others. After measuring the difficulty, we actually use other dimensions to parse the trades.

When we finally let this guillotine down, we know that it is a fair assessment of each broker. If we were to gum up the works along the way, take away discretion from the traders in my shop, throw in encumbrances of any kind you want – then, the whole process falls apart. So it is pure and it is pristine. I am no choirboy (laughter), but at least at the end of the day, we know this assessment is for real.

BODINE [From the Floor]: This is my question for Minder. I struggle with it myself. A big component of your formula is the assumption that you

[89] George Bodine is Director of Trading at General Motors Investment Management Corporation.

make about execution costs. How confident are you, Minder, in your number?

CHENG: The way we do this is fairly integrated. The expected transaction cost is an all in cost, including commissions and opportunity costs, and so on and so forth. It is the whole iceberg. That is what we use in optimizing our portfolios. We use it especially for actively managed portfolios. We have a certain alpha to capture, whether it is momentum driven or earnings driven. What is the cost that we expect to pay to capture it? If the formula is wrong, we are not in the best position to capture that alpha. It will come up as a negative performance. It will have a performance drag. But it is an integrated process, and we are fairly confident about the way in which we come up with the expected transaction costs.

It also goes to the way we measure the total transaction cost. It really is trade specific. And whether VWAP is appropriate or not depends on the trade. If you are trading 40,000 shares within the next 30 minutes, and the trade is driven by an earnings announcement that will be out in the next hour or so, you want to trade now. In such a case, a VWAP benchmark is unreasonable. You may match the benchmark perfectly, but at the same time miss the point of capturing the alpha. So it has to be all in. It is not just about trading. It is about the whole investment process (which goes back to your point).

WAGNER: Two short comments. At the Plexus conference and also at the European Trader Forum, I heard U.K. traders stand up and say, the recommendations of the Myners report that research costs be paid by the managers rather than by the money owners is the right thing to do, we are going to move forward on this to a degree. Based on my experience with U.S. traders, I was surprised at their willingness to pick up the sword and say that what Myners has put forward makes sense, that we should go ahead and do that. We are going to see some pressure coming from across the Atlantic to do this all in a better way here.

Finally, I would like to go back to Anthony Neuberger's suggestion that best execution is a precursor to market quality. I would add that it is also a precursor to market design. We should have had this panel first because then we would have known what we were talking about for the rest of the day. Clearly a problem in the scheduling (laughter).

MADHAVAN: On that note of gratitude, we will conclude. Thanks to all of our distinguished panelists. It has been very informative.

CHAPTER 7: THOUGHTS FROM A FORMER REGULATOR

Laura Unger
Independent Director and Consultant

ROBERT SCHWARTZ: Laura Unger was a keynote speaker at our conference three years ago, and it is a pleasure to have her back. When Laura was here on the last occasion as a Commissioner of the SEC, she made an extremely thought-provoking speech. That speech is now presented as a chapter in the book on the conference, which we published. Welcome back, Laura. This time it will be a little different. You will not have to start with a disclaimer.

LAURA UNGER: Actually, I heard somebody else give the disclaimer for me, so I suppose that I should not worry about it. I was here three conferences ago, and left feeling that people didn't like the SEC. I see that things really haven't changed much (laughter). I know I have three strikes against me. I am a former regulator, I am the last person speaking, and I am the only thing that separates you from your cocktail hour.

Bob thought it would be interesting – for all of you – if I look back and talk about what it was like at the SEC, and discuss some of the issues that you were interested in during that period. When I was here three years ago, I talked about the regulatory process. I do not think most people really understand what it is like. As regulators, we tend to focus on the particular area that we are interested in – for example, best execution – but there is always a bigger picture into which all of this fits.

I learned three key things about regulating the markets. First, regulators cannot be ahead of the markets, ever. No matter how forward thinking we would like to believe that we are, we can only hope to keep up with the markets. Regulation is really a lagging indicator of market conditions. The commission – and I won't speak for all the regulators (that is the only disclaimer I will give) – responds to market conditions. It does not create market conditions. Sometimes there may be unintended consequences, but we are mostly responding to market conditions. I will give you a real life illustration once I complete these three points.

My second comment is that the size of the budget and economic conditions significantly impact the SEC's agenda. As you probably know, the SEC's budget is less than $500 million,[90] and the US equity markets are valued at least at $3 trillion. The SEC also has a very broad mandate in terms of regulation, including mutual funds, investment advisors, registered broker dealers, public company filings, and the markets. It is a delicate balancing act to allocate our limited resources across all of these jurisdictions. And, of course, regulating in a bull market is very different from regulating in a bear market. I will also discuss that.

My third comment is that my first two observations cause a lot of regulators to be far more myopic than we would like to be. That is a combination of the budget constraints (as I mentioned), the broad jurisdiction (as I mentioned), the changing economic environment, short-term demands and, believe it or not, political forces. They all have a significant impact on the commission.

I will give you one example that is fairly complex but interesting, and then a short example, to illustrate these points. The more complex example involves the commission's attempt to find a way to eliminate fragmentation in the marketplace that came about as a result of Regulation ATS. In Reg ATS, the commission allowed for ECNs to register as exchanges, and for existing markets and exchanges to demutualize and become public companies.[91]

There are various issues surrounding Reg ATS. One is that the strong economic conditions in 1999-2000 caused the NYSE and the NASD, at that time, to want to demutualize, conduct an IPO and become public companies. People had an insatiable appetite for IPOs at the time and, of course, with this new regulation in place, the exchanges wanted to take advantage of the opportunity.

Of course, the two market centers were fighting to be the first to demutualize. In the summer of 1999, Dick Grasso was saying that, by

[90] The Wall Street Journal reported on January 3, 2003 that Senate Republicans propose increasing the Securities and Exchange Commission's budget to approximately $650 million.

[91] Regulation ATS also requires Alternative Trading Systems that trade 5% or more of the volume in national market system securities to be linked with a registered market in order to disseminate the best priced orders. The Regulation ATS compliance date was August 23, 1999.

Thanksgiving, people would be having turkey and buying a share of the New York Stock Exchange. We know that has not happened yet.

Also, we saw competition among the marketplaces that was prompted in large part by the ECNs. These electronic markets were really giving the traditional marketplaces a run for their money. An important regulatory issue that came up as a result of this confluence of events involved the de-linking of the Self Regulatory Organization (SRO) function (in the case of the NYSE) from a public company. The NASD was initially included in the conversation about de-linking the SRO function. Then the commission felt that the NASD's new model was significantly disinterested, so it would not be that big of an issue.

But could a public company have the mandate of maximizing shareholder return, and still provide sufficient regulatory oversight? Would a public company devote the resources necessary to conduct oversight and regulation? Even if it were possible in theory, would the appearance of a conflict of interest undermine the regulatory authority of an SRO?

The demutualization issue was brought about by the NASD and the NYSE. Both markets wanted to go public. It was not something that the SEC could have raised, even with it having become a big issue at the time. So this is my example of market conditions driving both competition and the SEC's agenda.

A lot of proposals were discussed. One was to create a Super SRO. Well, why do that? It would be like a mini-SEC. And the NYSE really clung to wanting to maintain the regulatory function. The exchange believed that it was a franchise, that it provided value. The commission spent a significant amount of time looking at, and talking about this issue. In the process, it became linked with the bigger issue of market fragmentation.

While we were talking about these new structures, what were we going to do about fragmentation generally? Fragmentation was being prompted again by the same bull market economic conditions, and by the ECNs competing with the traditional marketplaces. As the ECNs captured more and more market share from the traditional marketplaces, we started asking ourselves, how are investors going to know where they will get the best possible price? What are we going to do about it?

I remember spending time talking to Arthur Levitt, our chairman at the time, and to the rest of the commission, about what we were going to do about the fragmentation issue. Probably not since 1975,[92] and certainly not

[92] The significant market structure issue in 1975 was the abolition of fixed commissions under the amendments to the Securities Exchange Act of 1934. The Securities Act Amendments of 1975 also mandated the creation of a National Market System (NMS). The creation of the NMS has been haphazard at best but it did cause change, such as the creation of the Intermarket Trading System. ITS is designed to electronically link trading

since Reg ATS, has the commission had such a significant market structure issue in place, with such potentially far-reaching consequences. The issue was obviously driven in large part by technological systems, in particular the operation of ECNs and ATSs. Finding a solution to the problem would require determining the appropriate use of technology in the trading markets. We had some Congressional hearings here in New York with the heads of five firms, the NYSE and the NASD.[93] The SEC issued a concept release, which is a document that outlines our position on the critical issues.[94] The release laid out a series of alternatives, the least of which was to provide market data – that's a word that many of you probably dislike – and the order execution quality disclosure rules. At the other end of the spectrum was a central limit order book.

One alternative was completely non-controversial and the other alternative was completely controversial. There was also a range of options in between. It was helpful to get feedback on this range of options.

Then, during the course of this development, the NYSE announced that it would no longer seek an IPO. And, to add another twist – it all happened around the same time – the NASD published its SuperMontage proposal. The NASD claimed it needed to get SEC approval for SuperMontage in order to conduct its IPO. It claimed that this would solve the central limit order book issue and reduce fragmentation.

But many other problems were raised as a result of that proposal. One is the residual market issue, which is both fascinating and far-reaching.[95] What

---

in U.S. stock exchanges. The ITS system is not popular with market participants who operate outside the listed markets. Some market participants, including the NYSE, have called for reform of the ITS.

93 Hearings were held in New York on Feb. 29, 2000. The five firms represented were Merrill Lynch, Goldman Sachs, Morgan Stanley, Charles Schwab and Credit Suisse First Boston. ECNs were not represented. The represented firms advocated the creation of a central limit order book, or CLOB. The proposal was opposed by the NYSE and the NASD.

94 The SEC concept release, which was issued during the same period, solicited opinion on whether market fragmentation was then, or would in the future, become a problem that damaged the operations of the U.S. markets. It also requested comment on six potential options. The most controversial option was the creation of a CLOB, or central limit order book (see Exchange Act Release No. 42450 (February 23, 2000) 65 FR 10577 ("Concept Release").

95 The residual market refers to the operation and regulatory approval of the NASD's Alternative Display Facility, or ADF, a precondition for the approval of Nasdaq's SuperMontage. The ADF was mandated by the SEC as a venue that would provide an alternative market – a new OTC unlisted market, in effect – for stocks that did not participate in a Nasdaq stock exchange and the SuperMontage.

happens to the Over-the-Counter market when you only have exchanges? What happens when the SEC has rules that say you must display your orders, and you have this built in potential to capture order flow? What happens when the market then shifts to a totally different model? What happens to that order flow? What happens with that need to comply with the regulation? Something needed a comprehensive fix, and a big picture approach would have provided a significant change to the market structure. What happened? The commission adopted the most incremental step possible to cure market fragmentation.[96]

SuperMontage has been approved, but the NASD is still awaiting approval on its exchange application for Nasdaq. But it is not much closer to an IPO for Nasdaq.[97] Again, this is an example of market forces and economic conditions pushing the SEC. SuperMontage – including a number of other issues – was the complete focus of the commission at the time.

Another example was market data fees. This issue is a bull market phenomenon. Its final resolution could have broad-ranging impacts. The issue is over the cost of fees for market data charged by exchanges and Nasdaq to online brokers, ATSs and other broker dealers. This group was upset that it had to pay exchanges for market data to satisfy the demand from its own customers for real-time price quote information. ATSs argued, for instance, that they added value to the transparency of trading information but they did not receive compensation in return. It became a hot topic during the height of on-line trading. A number of the firms that provided real-time market data information, real-time stock quote information to customers said, 'We can't afford to do this, the customers really want it, but it is costing us a lot of money.'[98] And they would continue, 'You, the SEC,

[96] The incremental step mentioned is Rules 11Ac1-5 and 6. Under Rule 11Ac1-5, market centers that trade national market system securities are required to make available to the public monthly electronic reports that include uniform statistical measures of execution quality. Rule 11Ac1-6 requires all broker dealers that route customer orders to disclose the identity of the market center and material aspects of their relationship with the market center.

[97] Nasdaq's plan to demutualize and become a for-profit exchange through an IPO was still in limbo as of early 2003. Laura Unger cites NASD's IPO application though some might think she has mistaken the NASD for Nasdaq. Unger, of course, is correct because the NASD was the parent of Nasdaq. As of early 2003, the NASD is still Nasdaq's parent though in practical terms Nasdaq, which is separating from the NASD, is largely independent of the NASD.

[98] An advisory panel headed by Joel Seligman, the Dean of Washington University Law School, studied the issue for several months. The panel concluded that the SEC should allow a competitive system in which entities known as "consolidators" could gather and disseminate market data. That system would replace the current model in which a "single

could not possibly have thought that this model that you have approved was OK, and that the information providers, that the exchange and the NASD should be making so much money off of market data. After all, it belongs to the market. They shouldn't be profiting.' As you know, some of the regional exchanges subsist primarily off of market data fees.

Once again, the SEC put out a concept release. It is a highly complicated issue, and something that is hard to regulate in a vacuum, particularly because the commission had a broad mandate to make the market data available on a fair, reasonable and non-discriminatory basis.

We came up with a complicated proposal, which was put out in a concept release. We did not receive that many responses (about 35), but it was enough to show that this issue was one that the commission could not solve on its own. We created a federal advisory committee, which is something the commission does not often do. Again, this was driven by market forces; the popularity of on-line trading, the desire for real-time quote information, and the rising cost of purchasing it.

It has been two years since the discussion started. There was a report provided in the Fall, but no action has taken place yet with respect to market data. It is interesting to note, however, how the market has changed in the interim. So too has the commission's focus. This underscores what I have been saying. Of course, part of it is more than market driven, it is world event driven. 9/11 took a lot of the commission's focus. We tried to be as responsive as possible, and to maintain liquidity, transparency in the marketplace, and investor confidence. Then the Enron and Andersen situations have consumed a lot of the commission's time and resources. You see a shift away from the markets, away from on-line brokerage (the investor's are turning away from that too), a shift away from 'the big-picture, market structure, market efficiency, promote competition, promote innovation.' My sense is that this is because, in a bear market, investors want more government. They want more of a protectionist feeling. They want to know that the commission is bringing enforcement cases and taking care of investors.

The shift to a corporate governance focus because of Enron and Andersen has also been event driven. It is interesting to note that the commission has shifted completely away, in my view, from the primary focus of big-picture, market structure issues (although there are many for whom it still is a primary focus, so don't get nervous) to a completely different kind of focus – raising capital, protecting investors, and

consolidator" – the Consolidated Tape Association – has control over the distribution of market data.

maintaining transparency and liquidity in a different kind of way. The mandate is the same, but the focus on how to accomplish it is different.

I will finish by saying that I hope the Commission will be able to continue to accomplish its task. As a commissioner, I found one thing kind of frustrating. It is very difficult to step aside from current market conditions, from current short-term demands, and the budget constraints that face us, and be able to really embrace big, big issues like the global marketplace, the fact that technology has made the global marketplace a reality, and that there is a huge demand for a global marketplace. Maybe not today, because people have the sense that we first have to get our domestic marketplace in order. But certainly in the back of everyone's minds is, when and how will the global marketplace happen?

I don't know what economic condition and outside forces will bring that to bear. The European community has been strident in their support of the Commission moving in their direction, toward global accounting standards and listing standards. It will be interesting to watch as the Commission gets the domestic agenda in place and moves on. I know that one of the passions of the current Chairman, Harvey Pitt, is technology. I assume that will extend to the global marketplace.

Going forward, in addition to getting investors to feel comfortable and confident about the markets, and to we need to restore people's confidence in the integrity of financial information. I think that is why you see a disconnect between the fact that the economy is doing well, but the markets aren't doing as well as they should. Investor confidence is not at the level it should be. Even if you say, OK, everything is fine, I have got my job, I have got my mortgage paid, and everything else, now is not a time when people are going to be new investors in the markets. You have people who are maintaining a presence in the markets, and thinking that now is not a good time to sell either. But we are not hearing many people say, 'wow, I really feel good about this. I want to get in there and participate. I want to buy.' However, even though bottom fishing is probably not a bad idea, I am not making any investment recommendations (laughter).

I gave you a big picture. I would be happy to answer any specific questions. I am in the transition of being a former SEC commissioner (actually I prefer to say former Acting Chairman), and I am now in a position where I can truly be independent for a little while.

SEAN MCHUGH[99] [From the Floor]: I read the comments on the concept release on market structure. One of my favorites was by an investor in Colorado who said (this is not an exact quote) that, 'trying to address

[99] Sean McHugh is Vice President at Goldman Sachs.

market structure problems with execution disclosure as a solution' (and I know it wasn't viewed as the ultimate solution) 'is a lot like, if you are having engine problems, it is OK as long as the engine light on the dash board is flashing.' This means that the car is at least disclosing to you that there is a problem with the engine (laughter).

I have the following question about fixing markets. It seems that something like SuperMontage would solve a lot of the problems on Nasdaq. Absent all the confusion in creating an ADF (that no one can really define or guess what it is going to be like), there is a sense that maybe a boat was missed. One way or the other, not necessarily because of the SEC (but in general), it seems that we did have the opportunity to have a central limit order book (or close to it) on Nasdaq. Now if we have SuperMontage and liquidity on the ADF, will it be even more of a mess than it is today?

UNGER: The notion of a central limit order book is very interesting. At first blush you think, wow, that is all we need. We just need one place to funnel in all the orders. Then you have complete transparency, connectivity and efficiency. But there are also dangers. You would also have a single point of failure. Further, a lot of the incentives to innovate and compete would be taken away. Competition is a powerful force, as you well know. But competition often results in competition to the lowest common denominator, which is not a good thing. However, it is a good thing in terms of innovation.

That is the trade off. It is a very big trade off, and many people were not prepared to let it go. The upstairs departments of many of the firms were very supportive of a central limit order book. Interesting, I thought. But many other industry participants and professionals were not. So it was not a slam-dunk. And you are right, the SuperMontage does raise many issues about competing with a regulator.[100]

STEVEN WUNSCH[101] [From the Floor]: You said earlier that the SEC is always playing catch-up, that it does not lead the markets. As I recall, in 1996 or 1997, there were a bunch of order handling rules that came out and, roughly around that time, a whole lot of ECNs were created. Which came

[100] Critics said the SuperMontage proposal would create a conflict of interest for Nasdaq and the NASD, which was Nasdaq's regulator. For one thing, NASD member firms included market maker firms and ECNs. For another, NASD still had a financial interest in Nasdaq, a stake that could grow in the event of a Nasdaq IPO. There was also a fear that executions on SuperMontage, which was sanctioned by the SEC, would become a critical factor in judging standards of best execution. SuperMontage was viewed by some critics, especially ECNs, as a super ECN that had been granted monopoly powers. That concern drove ECNs to press the SEC to mandate the NASD's ADF.

[101] Steven Wunsch is a Partner at Exchange Lab.

first, the rules or the ECNs? Which was the response to the other? Or did they just simultaneously happen to come out independently?

UNGER: I thought that the ECNs have been around for a long time.

WUNSCH [From the Floor]: Instinet is the only one that was there around that time. All of the others simultaneously came into existence with the order handling rules. I know a number of the creators of those ECNs who said that they were creating them strictly in response to the rules. I am asking this in relation to your statement that the SEC does not push the markets, but rather follows the markets.

UNGER: Then maybe I should have qualified my remarks by saying that during my tenure, that is how it was (laughter).

WUNSCH [From the Floor]: Good answer.

UNGER: Any more hostile questions (laughter)?

BRETT REDFEARN[102] [From the Floor]: The issue of regulatory harmonization came up in one of the earlier panels. We now have a situation where the Amex is looking to trade Nasdaq stocks, Nasdaq is looking to trade listed stocks, the ECNs are trading Nasdaq and listed stocks, and they are all operating with fairly different rule structures. Do you have any thoughts, going forward, about whether or not the rules that apply to Nasdaq or the listed markets, or even to ECNs, are, at some point, going to become more on a par with one another? Or will the different markets continue to operate under fairly different regulatory frameworks?

UNGER: That is a very interesting question. Probably someone is looking at the issue right now, although I could not say for sure. But I agree. The thing that was going through my mind as you were asking the question was, what then would differentiate the markets? If everybody has the same rules, then why would you go to one or the other? For liquidity, I guess? But don't the rules have some effect on liquidity?

REDFEARN [From the Floor]: There will still be differences between the technologies that are employed in the different markets. The issue that is nearest and dearest to our heart, for example, involves Island ECN and the ETF market.[103] When Island started trading ETFs, and initially Reg ATS said that after you get above a 5% threshold…

UNGER: I have been asked that a number of times.

REDFEARN [From the Floor]: So now we are in a situation where Island basically has the most volume in the product, and they are still

[102] Brett Redfearn is Senior Vice President at the American Stock Exchange.

[103] An ETF (Exchange Traded Fund) is an index product that trades like ordinary shares. Examples include, SPDRs (S & P 500) Diamonds (Dow 30), and QQQ (Nasdaq). The QQQ is sometimes referred to as "Q" and sometimes as "Triple Q."

operating under the ECN rules. Our market, for example, cannot put in the same sort of AutoEx features right now because we are an auction market. We cannot go the same route that Island is free to follow. So there is a substantial regulatory disparity. It is not necessarily a level, competitive playing field. We are wondering how this will all be resolved.

UNGER: I think that as that becomes more common, people will be looking at the situation. Situations like that are always brought to the Commission's attention by competitors in the marketplace. The competitors are not shy about coming to us and saying, 'hey, this disadvantages us.' Similarly, the ECNs were not shy about saying that the NASD had a real franchise because of its regulatory oversight authority. I suspect, if the Commission staff has not noticed it already (and I am sure that the Q issue has been raised), that you, or somebody like you, will be visiting them soon. It will have to be examined.

WAYNE WAGNER[104] [From the Floor]: Laura, another issue that came up in the conversations today involved the meshing of the institutional market and the retail market. The meshing involves complications, particularly for institutional investors. How firmly seated is that in the thinking of the SEC?

UNGER: I do not know what the complications are, not having had the benefit of hearing the earlier discussions today. I do not know the ones that you identified. Can you give me an idea?

WAGNER [From the Floor]: Basically, as Seth Merrin said, the problem is that average institutional order size is something like 250,000 shares, and average execution size is somewhere around 1000 shares. Obviously a big slicing and dicing process is necessary to break an institutional order into the bite size pieces that will fit through the funnel and get it into the exchange.

UNGER: That is a really interesting question. It relates to decimals too. One thing about a decimal market (and this is something the market needs to turn to) is that it sounds really good. Because as a retail investor you of course want the smallest possible increments. But decimalization definitely has, or appears to have had, an adverse impact on the depth, liquidity, and transparency of the markets. Decimalization can increase execution costs because of the multiple price points that it creates. That is one very real impact that is felt by institutional investors. I know that they feel strongly about it.

[104] Wayne Wagner is Chairman of Plexus Group.

In terms of leveling the marketplace, you saw Regulation FD.[105] I think that came in under a different Chairman, but it is a real indication of the belief that there should not be favoritism in the marketplace. Institutional investors have enjoyed many benefits over retail investors. Currently, the Internet has a lot to do with investors having this sense of entitlement to information because the Internet makes it possible for them to get the information. And it is cheap for the issuers and the investment community to disseminate the information. Therefore they must. I think that drives a lot of it.

THOMAS DOYLE[106] [From the Floor]: At the end of the previous panel on best execution, it was suggested that soft dollars are an impediment in the measurement process. Then another panelist retorted that you cannot talk about soft dollars without talking about bundled commission services. Could you speculate as to where you think the Commission may go in that tug-of-war debate?

UNGER: The Commission already has done a little something on 28(e).[107] But the discussion of soft dollars and best execution is a very difficult one. Soft dollars is such an entrenched practice in the industry, and it is a political hot potato. People ask, how can you possibly fulfill your best execution obligation with soft dollar payments? It seems impossible. Everybody scratches their head and answers, 'yes, but in picking your battles, this is not the one to pick.' It all goes back to our limited resources, political reality, and economic conditions.

The Commission might get there eventually, but this issue has been percolating for a long time. Some people think that the market will take care of itself as far as that goes. They think this because profit margins have gotten so narrow. They believe that, at some point, with the order execution disclosure quality rules, the decimal market, and everything else, that this is something that can eventually be removed by competitive forces. They could be right, they might be wrong. I see people nodding their heads in both directions, but that is all I know.

[105] The SEC Regulation FD (fair disclosure) went into effect October 23, 2000. The main goal of the regulation was to snuff out the selective release of material corporate information to a handful of Wall Street analysts or large institutional holders.

[106] Thomas Doyle is Institutional Sales/Trader at Nutmeg Securities.

[107] Section 28(e) of the Securities Exchange Act of 1934 generally provides that a money manager will not be deemed to breach its fiduciary duty to a client when it executes the client's trades with a broker/dealer that charges more than the lowest commission rates available, so long as the money manager determines the commissions paid are reasonable in relation to the value of the brokerage and research services provided by that broker/dealer.

Thank you.

SCHWARTZ: Thank you, Laura. What a great way to end this conference. I have one word to say, 'thanks.' Thanks to you, our panelists, our sponsors, and to all of you in the audience for being here. Now let's go outside to the drink tables and attack the liquidity pools (laughter).

CHAPTER 8: VOLATILITY IN U.S. AND EUROPEAN EQUITY MARKETS: AN ASSESSMENT OF MARKET QUALITY[108]

Deniz Ozenbas, *Assistant Professor of Finance, Montclair State University*
Robert Schwartz, *Speiser Professor of Finance, Zicklin School of Business, Baruch College, CUNY*
Robert Wood, *Distinguished Professor of Finance, The University of Memphis*

1. INTRODUCTION

Volatility is like cholesterol – there is both good volatility and bad volatility. Good volatility characterizes price adjustments that are attributable to news. Bad volatility characterizes price changes that are attributable to transaction costs. Bad volatility is manifest in accentuated price swings, the runs and reversals that occur over relatively brief trading intervals in response to the arrival of buy and sell orders in the market. We suggest that an objective of market structure is to control bad volatility. However, it should also be recognized that, to some extent, short-run volatility must be accentuated so as to appropriately compensate liquidity providers (i.e., broker-dealer intermediaries and limit order traders).

This paper examines the association between the accentuated intra-day price swings and market quality.[109] To this end, we empirically

[108] This chapter is reprinted, with permission, from D. Ozenbas, R. Schwartz, and R. Wood, "Volatility in U.S. and European Equity Markets: An Assessment of Market Quality," International Finance, Blackwell Publishers, Volume 5 Number 3, Winter 2002, pp. 437-461.

[109] For simplicity this paper has not focused on the relationship between volume and volatility.

investigate intra-day volatility over the year 2000 for five market centers: the New York Stock Exchange, Nasdaq, the London Stock Exchange, Euronext Paris, and Deutsche Börse. Consistent with previous research,[110] we find a U-shaped intra-day volatility pattern in each of these five markets. The result is striking because the five markets represent markedly different market structures – the NYSE is a floor based, primarily order driven market; Nasdaq in 2000 (the test year for our study) was organized primarily as a dealer market; and Euronext Paris, Deutsche Börse, and the London Stock Exchange primarily utilize automated (i.e., not floor-based) order-driven trading platforms.

We pay particular attention to the sharp volatility spike that occurs in the first half-hour of trading in each of the five markets. A second, less pronounced spike is also observed for the last half-hour of trading. These spikes are important, inverse indicators of market quality. As a further inverse reflection of market quality, our analysis shows that intra-day volatility is accentuated vis-à-vis the volatility of price changes measured over longer (one- and two-week) intervals.

Our analysis is consistent with that of Heiner (1983), who considers an environment where market agents have varying levels of skill with respect to their ability to evaluate information. Heiner envisions a spectrum of competence, across participants, that varies with each news event.[111] No single agent has sufficient funds to drive the market to a new equilibrium level following any news event, and agents with less competence with respect to a particular news event learn from the more competent participants who trade ahead of them. Less competent agents can introduce errors in the price discovery process by misjudging and overshooting true equilibrium values.[112] Hence price discovery is a dynamic process.

[110] There is extensive empirical literature documenting intra-day patterns in equity market volatility, including Wood, McInish,and Ord (1985), Harris (1986), Lockwood and Linn (1990), Werner and Kleidon (1996) and Hong and Wang (2000).

[111] The competency ranking of market agents may vary from news event to news event depending upon the training and experience of each market agent vis-à-vis each news event. This is in contrast to the stylized models of Kyle (1985), Glosten and Milgrom (1985) and others who posit two classes of traders, informed and uninformed (noise) traders.

[112] Heiner further enriches the analytical framework by postulating a spectrum of complexity of news events, with the more complex events requiring a greater time to reach equilibrium. This richer analytical framework rationalizes short-term autocorrelation with market efficiency without consideration of market frictions. For further discussion, see Adams, McQueen and Wood (2003).

Our volatility analysis has implications for the price discovery function of a market. When investors have divergent (non-homogeneous) expectations based on publicly available information, consensus (equilibrium) share values can be found only in the marketplace, as orders come in and are translated into trades. This implies that news cannot be translated into new consensus values until all orders based on the new information have arrived. However, in a non-frictionless trading environment, order arrival is staggered over time and, hence, the discovery of a new consensus price does not occur instantaneously with the advent of news. As we will discuss further, the process of searching for new equilibrium values after the advent of news accentuates a stock's price volatility.

We suggest that the volatility spike at a market's open exists because of the particular difficulty, after the overnight close, of discovering opening prices that are in reasonable harmony with consensus values. Accentuated volatility at the close, on the other hand, reflects the difficulty of absorbing price pressures brought about by traders attempting to complete the execution of their orders (including the closing out of positions) before the start of the overnight period. Accentuated volatility over the course of a complete trading day (i.e., the volatility of open-to-close price changes) exists when momentum trading causes prices to trend away from, and eventually revert back to, equilibrium values.

The relationship between short-term volatility and trading costs has been extensively analyzed in the microstructure literature. Schwartz and Whitcomb (1977) and Lo and MacKinlay (1988) use variance analysis to establish that short-term volatility is accentuated compared to longer-term volatility. Hasbrouck and Schwartz (1988), Stoll (2000) and Bessembinder and Rath (2002) are some of the studies that find evidence of a link between accentuated volatility and heightened transaction costs. Werner and Kleidon (1996) have analyzed intra-day volatility patterns for NYSE and London cross-listed stocks to assess the extent to which price discovery is integrated across markets. In their study of the U.S. Treasury market, Fleming and Remolina (1999) have further underscored the difficulty of achieving accurate price discovery by demonstrating that protracted surges in intra-day volatility attend the release of major macroeconomic news announcements.

The current paper extends this literature. Our primary innovation is to assess volatility for each individual half-hour period in the trading day for each of the five markets. That is, for the set of days in our sample period (all trading days in 2000), we separately consider the vector of first half-hour returns (e.g., 9:30 – 10:00 for the US markets), second-half hour returns, and so on through the last half-hour returns, and apply this methodology to two

US and three European markets. While others have looked at some of these markets individually or in pairs (e.g., Werner and Kleidon (1996) and Wood, McInish and Ord (1985)), the five-country analysis underscores the universality of our findings.[113]

Our methodology contrasts with two more traditional approaches. One, which uses the series of consecutive short-period returns (e.g., Hasbrouck and Schwartz (1988) use half-hour intervals, and Andersen, Bollerslev and Das (2001) use 5-minute intervals), focuses on the effect of differencing interval length without considering time of the day effects. The other approach, which uses 24-hour periods that start at different times of the day (e.g., Amihud and Mendelson (1987) and Gerety and Mulherin (1994)), captures time of the day effects without considering the effect of differencing interval length. Our approach seeks to achieve both objectives simultaneously. Regarding the time of the day effects, we pay particular attention to the opening and closing half-hour periods, because these are times of particular stress for the markets.

We have a further reason for our methodology. When the returns measurements are contiguous and the returns are negatively (positively) autocorrelated, short-period volatility is accentuated (dampened) relative to longer period volatility.[114] But, to the extent that negative and positive autocorrelation co-exist, the offsetting correlations tend to render each other invisible, which undermines the efficacy of variance analysis.[115] Treating

[113] Werner and Kleidon use 15 minute intervals, but for a different purpose than ours. They do not investigate intraday volatility as an inverse measure of quality, and do not focus on the opening and closing periods of a trading day as moments of particular stress.

[114] This can be shown with the use of the following variance ratio equation (for more detail see Hasbrouck and Schwartz (1988)):

$$VR(m) \equiv \frac{mVar[r_t(1)]}{Var(r_t(m))} = [1 + 2\sum_{k=1}^{m-1}(\frac{m-k}{m})\rho(k)]^{-1}$$

where the numerator on the left-hand side is the short-period variance times m, the denominator on the left-hand-side is the long-period variance, and m is the ratio of the long-period differencing interval to the short-period differencing interval. The right-hand side is the inverse of unity plus two times the summation of autocorrelation factors. The formula shows that, if the autocorrelation factors are predominantly positive (negative), short-term volatility is dampened (accentuated) relative to long-term volatility.

[115] Positive and negative correlation can co-exist for two reasons. First, in some periods (perhaps when there is little news), returns may be dominated by reversal behavior (e.g., the bid-ask bounce), while in some other periods (perhaps following the advent of new information) trending might predominate. Second, first order correlation that is positive

non-contiguous returns helps to solve this problem. With our methodology, a momentum move in one direction on one day, matched with a momentum move of opposite direction on another day, translates into accentuated volatility.[116]

An array of factors may cause the accentuation of intra-day volatility to differ across markets. These include the architectural structure of a market, patterns of news release (e.g., whether corporate and government announcements tend to be made in the over night halt or during the trading day), investor characteristics (e.g., whether the market is predominantly institutional or retail), intra-day trading patterns of institutional investors (e.g., whether or not they tend to avoid trading at the open), the cross-listing of stocks in markets with over-lapping time zones (e.g., a British company that is listed both on the London Stock Exchange and in the US market as an ADR), and the amount of after hours and pre-open trading. Our goal in the current paper is not, however, to contrast or to explain volatility differences across the five markets we have analyzed, but to establish that accentuated short-period volatility is a phenomenon that is common to all. It is also an important manifestation of market quality that can be compared across equity markets.

Volatility analysis has implications for market structure. By paying particular attention to the more challenging times of the trading day (the first and last half-hour of trading), we are able to detect imperfections in price discovery that may not be as apparent in the rest of the day. Our findings suggest that price discovery at market openings and closings needs to be improved in each of the five markets.[117] This underscores the importance of

---

can coexist with higher orders of correlation that are negative (e.g., when a trend is followed by one reversal and then a trend in the opposite direction).

116 Alternatively stated, with negative first order autocorrelation alone, short-period volatility is accentuated, and with positive first order autocorrelation alone, short-period volatility is dampened. If prices tend to run in one direction and then reverse, positive first order autocorrelation coexists along with higher orders of correlation that are negative, and the accentuation of short-period volatility is more effectively captured with non-contiguous returns.

117 Price volatility at the open is accentuated by the difficulty of finding appropriate share values after the overnight trading halt, while price volatility is accentuated in the last half-hour of trading because traders come under increasing pressure to close out their positions as the overnight halt draws near. With respect to both periods, a more efficient market mechanism would facilitate order interaction and price determination, and thus reduce volatility, at these critical times in the trading day.

making the trading systems more efficient. Our volatility metrics may also sharpen our ability to track changes in market quality over time.

The paper is structured as follows. We first consider participant attitudes toward accentuated intra-day volatility, and next set forth our analytic framework. In the two sections that follow, we describe our data and test design, and report the volatility patterns that we have observed. In our final section, we set forth a number of currently unanswered questions.

2. PARTICIPANT ATTITUDE TOWARD ACCENTUATED INTRA-DAY VOLATILITY

To the extent that accentuated intra-day volatility reflects trading costs, one might presume that participants would find elevated volatility undesirable. This is not necessarily the case. There is, of course, a net loss for the market in aggregate to the extent that high costs and high volatility discourage trading.[118] Aside from this loss, trading is a zero sum game: what one participant loses, another gains (i.e., one participant's cost is another's return).[119] Consequently, participant attitudes toward high intra-day volatility depends on how the individuals cope with the volatility, and on whether or not their revenue is increased or cost increased by it.

Generally, the passive side of the market – market makers and public traders who use limit orders – benefit from accentuated volatility. A trader can "capture" the accentuated volatility by: (1) first posting a quote or placing a limit order, (2) next buying at a relatively low price or selling at a relatively high price, and (3) then having price revert back to a previous level. In fact, intra-day volatility must be accentuated in order to compensate dealers and limit order traders for the risks they take when

[118] On the other hand, inefficient price discovery may generate excessive trading. For discussion and further references see Barber and Odean (2000).

[119] By "zero sum game," we mean that the trading costs (e.g., bid-ask spread and market impact costs) paid by one participant (generally the liquidity demander) are another participant's returns (generally the liquidity supplier). We do not mean to imply that both participants in a trade cannot mutually benefit. On the contrary, it is well established in economics that the gains of trade involve consumer surplus on the buyer side and producer surplus on the seller side. In a security transaction between a natural buyer and a natural seller, the surplus that each participant receives from a trade is attributable to the portfolio rebalancing that the participant wishes to achieve for longer run investment purposes.

setting the prices at which others can trade.[120] Further, in the opinion of one sell side participant, Henry Paulson Jr., chairman and chief executive of Goldman Sachs Group, intra-day volatility also generates a need for broker/dealer services. Paulson put it this way: "Volatility is our friend... If it wasn't for volatility, why should you need Goldman Sachs?"[121]

Technical analysis is widely used by participants on both the sell side and the buy side. While generally looked down upon in academic circles, technical analysis, in principle at least, has a valid role to play.[122] Though rarely stated this way, technical analysis can be thought of as an approach to inferring where a stock's price is relative to an unobserved consensus (equilibrium) value. Any participant who, either through technical analysis or by any other means, can properly time his or her orders in a volatile market, will have a positive attitude toward the volatility.

Not withstanding, the active side of the market – those who step forward with market orders and trigger trades – generally pay the cost implied by the accentuated volatility. They pay it in terms of the spread and market impact. They pay it in the form of the risk they incur as momentum players. And, when a temporary buy-sell imbalance pushes price up too high or down too low, traders on the "heavy" side of the market (whose orders have collectively caused the price move) bear the cost of having chased liquidity, rather than having supplied it.

High intra-day volatility is costly to the market in aggregate. It discourages trades and, for all, makes portfolio returns more uncertain. A portfolio manager who receives high scores for asset selection can see his or her returns seriously eroded by trading costs. Most PMs view trading costs as such and, with the exception primarily of some hedge funds, few count on enhancing their performance by turning trading costs into returns (except, that is, for some of the more technologically sophisticated funds who have discovered that they can earn the spread rather than pay it). Accordingly, while they should accept some accentuation of intra-day volatility as inevitable, fund managers, by and large, find it undesirable.

[120] For further discussion, see Handa and Schwartz (1996)

[121] See Weinberg (2000).

[122] Academic studies that provide theoretical justification for the use of technical analysis include Blume, Easley, and O'Hara (1994), and that provide empirical support include Lo, Mamaysky, and Wang (2000).

3. ANALYTIC FRAMEWORK

We begin by reviewing the volatility relationships that are necessary for understanding our empirical analysis. We first consider the effect that four "market process factors" – bid-ask spreads, market impact, price discovery, and momentum trading – have on short-term volatility. Next, we introduce the "news factor." We then explain why trading costs have a pronounced impact on short-term volatility (i.e., the volatility of price changes measured over short intervals), while the news factor comes to dominate when price changes are measured over sufficiently long intervals.[123]

3.1 The Market Process Factors

Accentuated short-period volatility is attributed to four well-known market process factors. We identify each in this sub-section.

The Bid-Ask Spread: Even if the quotes are constant over a period of time, transaction prices will bounce between the bid and the offer, with the staggered arrival of market sell orders that execute at the bid, and the arrival of market buy orders that execute at the offer. This effect is likely to be minimal with the current small tick sizes.

Market Impact: A large buy order pushing the transaction price above the posted offer, or a large sell order pushing the transaction price below the posted bid, means that the effective bid-ask spread is wider for larger orders, particularly when impatient traders who others think could be informed undertake the buy/sell programs. Market impact accentuates intra-day volatility in much the same way as does the spread.

Price Discovery: As noted in the introduction, the process of price discovery is the search for a stock's consensus price – the value that reflects the broad market's willingness to hold shares, given the new information and the divergent expectations of investors based on the news. During the search process, a stock's price will sometimes run up too far, while at other times it may fall too low. En route to finding its consensus value, lows and

[123] Note that, if news is public knowledge, prices may change without trading. For this reason it would be preferable to base the analysis on returns for quote midpoint rather than transactions prices. Unfortunately quote data were not available for Deutsche Börse. Thus for comparability we used transactions prices to calculate volatility for all markets studied.

highs emerge that are commonly associated with support and resistance levels.[124]

With divergent expectations, a support level may be associated with the bearish end of the expectations spectrum, and a resistance level may be associated with the bullish end. Bouncing between a support level and a resistance level has the same effect (although it is likely stronger) as bouncing between a bid and an offer quote. Both the bid-ask bounce and the high-low bounce translate into accentuated intra-day price volatility.[125]

Momentum Trading: Protracted buying or selling pressures can occur when large, institutional participants and/or informed traders, in an attempt to control market impact costs, break up their trading in a stealthy fashion for partial execution over a series of trades. Price discovery in a non-frictionless trading environment where participants have different beliefs may also result in periods of protracted buying or selling pressure. The protracted pressures lead naturally to momentum trading.

When participants buy simply because the sequence of recent price changes has been predominantly positive, a stock's price is apt to be pushed up too far. Similarly, when participants sell simply because the sequence of recent price changes has been predominantly negative, a stock's price is apt to be pushed down too far. A stock's price running up too high, and/or down too low, translates into accentuated intra-day volatility.

We have suggested that intra-day volatility is high because of spreads, market impact, errors in price discovery, and momentum trading. Bid-ask spreads and market impact are trading costs. Price discovery errors occur because, due to trading costs, accurate price discovery is not instantaneously achieved. Momentum trading occurs because momentum players believe that current prices do not reflect new consensus values, and they recognize that trades may signal new information. Thus, each of the four market factors either is a trading cost, or exists because of trading costs. Recognizing this, we can explicitly link trading costs and accentuated short-run volatility.

[124] "Support and resistance levels" is part of the terminology of technical analysis. A support (resistance) level denotes a lower (higher) reflecting barrier that price is not apt to penetrate in the absence of informational change.

[125] Most important for our analysis, the level of volatility resulting from price discovery will vary across markets (and stocks) depending upon the design and regulation of a market, as well as upon the skill of its traders.

Because the magnitude of trading costs depends in part on market design, we also have a link between intra-day volatility and market structure.

3.2 The News Factor

New information (news), whether stock specific, industry specific, or market wide, also generates price changes over the course of a trading day.[126] We can separate the "market process factors" we have just considered – spreads, market impact, dynamic price discovery, and momentum trading – from the "news factor" by relating volatility over relatively lengthy measurement intervals (e.g., the volatility of weekly or bi-weekly price changes) to that computed for very short intervals (e.g., the volatility of half-hour price changes). As we discuss below, the market process factors, being short run in nature, wash out of the longer run measurements. In contrast, the news factor generates a "permanent" price shift, and thus will be reflected in volatility no matter what the length of the measurement interval used.

3.3 The Washout

Assume an eight-hour trading day and a half-hour measurement interval. The price change over any day is the sum of sixteen price changes: one for each of the sixteen half-hour periods that comprise the day. Alternatively stated, the price change over a day is sixteen times the average half-hour price change. Is the *variance* of the one-day price change also sixteen times the average half-hour variance? It depends.[127]

What would the relationship be between half-hour price volatility and the one-day price volatility if the news factor alone causes prices to change? It is well known that share prices that reflect all information, and that therefore change only with the arrival of news, change randomly. This is because any news release, until it occurs, is by definition unknowable (whether the news is bullish or bearish is a coin flip). When share prices

[126] By "news" we are referring to *fundamental* information about share value, not to *trading* information (e.g., quotes, transaction prices, and volume).

[127] For a random walk, variance increases linearly with time and, hence, volatility (standard deviation) for a random walk increases linearly with the square root of time. When returns are serially correlated (as is the case with mean reversion), the linear relationship is perturbed. For further discussion and a mathematical derivation, see Hasbrouck and Schwartz (1988).

follow a random walk, a straightforward relationship exists between half-hour volatility and one-day volatility: the variance of the log of price changes for a one-day interval is sixteen times the average half-hour variances (just as the one-day price change is sixteen times the average half-hour price change).[128] In other words, as Schwartz and Whitcomb (1977) have shown when prices follow a random walk, variance increases proportionately with increases in the length of the interval over which the price changes are measured. Equivalently, the volatility (standard deviation) increases proportionately with the square root of the measurement interval.

What is the half-hour to one-day volatility relationship when the four market factors we have considered are also operative? To answer this, first recognize a common denominator in the impacts that each of the four market factors have on short-run price changes: each will cause the price of a stock to bounce between a lower value at one moment, and a higher value at another moment. That is, price either bounces between a bid and an offer, or between a positive market impact and a negative market impact, or between a support level and a resistance level, or between a momentum run up and a momentum run down, or between any combination of the above.

The crucial point is that, after going up, price comes down and, after going down, it reverts back up. It is reversal behavior, not random walk, which characterizes short-period price movements. At times, prices also trend in one direction or the other, either because of the path followed when adjusting to new information and/or because of momentum trading. When there is momentum trading, the trends commonly over-shoot their mark and, when they do, the trends also end with reversals.

Reversals are associated with an accentuation of the volatility of price changes measured over short trading intervals. Importantly, their effect is increasingly muted as the measurement interval is lengthened. It commonly happens that a daily high-low range is large for a stock, but that the open-to-close price change is not.[129] However, at times, over a trading day, trends can also build that accentuate volatility, and their impact may dampen out only when measurement intervals of longer than a day are used.

And so, while change introduced by news remains, with reversals, the impacts of the four market process factors tend to wash out over the longer

[128] See Schwartz and Whitcomb (1977) and Hasbrouck and Schwartz (1988). For our empirical measure of volatility, we use the standard deviation of the log of price changes, so the one-day volatility measure would be the square root of 16 times the half-hour volatility measure.

[129] For further discussion, see Schwartz and Shapiro (1992).

period. Thus, if, e.g., weekly or bi-weekly closing prices are analyzed, one might conclude that prices are relatively stable. On the other hand, if one focuses on the intra-day prices, one might alternatively conclude that they are relatively volatile. The reason is that when prices do not follow a random walk, volatility is not cumulative the way price changes are.

When intra-day reversals predominate, sixteen times the average half-hour volatility is larger than the volatility of the one-day, open-to-close price change. If trending predominates over the course of a day, the volatility of open-to-close price changes is also elevated. It is for this reason that we refer to intra-day volatility as being "accentuated." We can capture the accentuated intra-day volatility because the effect of the market factors that the volatility accentuation is attributed to tend to "wash out" when longer measurement intervals are used. We consider this further in the next sub-section.

3.4 Capturing Accentuated Volatility

Our discussion suggests two ways of capturing accentuated volatility, and we use them both in this paper.

First Approach: The first approach is to assess the intra-day pattern of volatility using a very short measurement interval. Specifically, we examine the volatility of half-hour price changes for each of the half-hour intervals that comprise the trading day, for each of the five markets that we have studied. A sharp spike in volatility for the first half-hour interval in the trading day would be attributed to the market process factors, not to the news factor.

If the news factor alone causes the price changes, the intra-day volatility pattern should reflect the intra-day pattern of news releases. If news releases are more prevalent for some half-hour intervals than for others, the half-hour volatility should be highest for those intervals that experience the most news releases. Alternatively, if news releases have no systematic intra-day pattern, then the intra-day volatility pattern, including the first half-hour interval, should be flat.

Nevertheless, would not over-night news events have relatively large price impacts at the open? They do, but the point is, this will not affect the first half-hour returns if the opening transaction prices are accurately established.[130] The reason is that the first recorded *price change* that we

[130] By a price being accurately established, we mean that the price is indeed a consensus value, given the expectations of all participants that are based on the publicly available information. However, if an overnight news event results in some participants having *private* information, we note that a consensus value based on public information can continue to

analyze does not include the over-night price change. Rather, it is the difference between the last price in the interval, and the *price at which the market opened.* Further, controllable information releases (e.g., corporate earnings announcements as distinct from floods and earthquakes) typically occur after a market has closed or before it has opened, not in the first half-hour of a trading day.

Accordingly, because of the way in which we have measured it, any accentuation of first half-hour volatility would not be attributed to news per se (either over-night or in general), but to opening prices not reflecting accurate adjustments to the news. As such, the accentuated first half-hour price volatility would be evidence of price discovery being a protracted process that extends into, and perhaps beyond, the first half-hour period. For this reason, a spike for the first half-hour would be a particularly meaningful, inverse measure of market quality.

Second Approach: The second approach we have taken to capture accentuated short-period price volatility is to normalize our volatility measures for each stock so that they can be directly contrasted for price changes measured over different returns intervals (half-hour, open-to-close, one-day, one-week, and two-week intervals). To this end, we express all of the volatilities for the different measurement intervals we have examined as rates per a half-hour interval, and divide each of them by a stock's average mid-day volatility.

As we have previously noted, as the interval over which price changes are measured is increased, the standard deviation of volatility, when expressed as a rate per a given period (i.e., per half-hour), will not change if successive price changes are uncorrelated with each other. However, if reversal behavior increases the frequency with which up ticks are followed by down ticks (or down ticks are followed by up ticks), volatility, as we have measured it, will decrease with the length of the measurement interval. Alternatively, if momentum trading increases the frequency with which up ticks are followed by up ticks (or down ticks are followed by down ticks), volatility, as we have measured it, will increase with the length of the measurement interval. It is possible for a momentum move in one direction to end and then be followed by a momentum move in the opposite direction

adjust after a market open due to the trading of the informed traders, and that volatility in first half-hour returns may be attributed, in part at least, to the news factor. However, a major reason for institutional participants to avoid trading at the open may not be that they are carefully exploiting the value of their private information, but that they are very reluctant to participate actively in price discovery. Alternatively stated, an institutional trader likes to see first how the market opens, and then to come forth with his or her orders.

(a large reversal). In such an event, volatility will increase with the length of the measurement interval for short intervals, but once the interval is lengthened sufficiently to contain the larger reversals, the observed volatility will start to decrease.

4. DATA AND TEST DESIGN

We have assessed the pattern of intra-day price volatility for two U.S. markets (The New York Stock Exchange and Nasdaq), and three European markets (Euronext Paris, Deutsche Börse, and the London Stock Exchange). We first describe the transaction price data used in the analysis for each of these markets.

4.1 The Data

We studied the transaction records for each of the five markets for the year 2000. The stocks in our sample are those that make up the major index for each of the countries: the S&P 100, the Nasdaq 100, the CAC 40, the DAX 30 and the FTSE 100. We use the TAQ database of the New York Stock Exchange, the BDM database of Euronext Paris, the Transaction Data Service database of the London Stock Exchange, and Deutsche Börse's Transactions Database.[131]

We have divided each of our five samples into two calendar periods. For each period, the sample comprises all stocks that were in the index at the end of the calendar period, and for which we have data for the entire period. A further criterion for the inclusion of a stock is that at least two trades occur for the stock in a minimum of 90 percent of the half-hour intervals in the sample period. Our final sample is 72 stocks for NYSE, 80 stocks for NASDAQ, 39 stocks for Euronext Paris, 28 stocks for Deutsche Börse, and, for the London Stock Exchange, 85 stocks for the January to May period, and 88 stocks for the June to December period.

Trading at the NYSE and Nasdaq opens at 9:30 am and closes at 4:00 pm. Euronext's trading hours at the beginning of the year 2000 were 9:00 am to 5:00 pm. On April 1st, the trading day was extended to 5:30 pm. The Euronext market opens with a call auction within the first minutes after 9:00

[131] The composition of each of the indices underwent several changes during the year 2000.

am, and closes with a second call auction that takes place about 5 minutes after the close of the continuous market.[132]

Deutsche Börse's trading hours at the beginning of 2000 were 9:00 am to 5:30 pm. The trading day in Germany was extended to 8:00 pm on June 2nd, 2000. Trading at Deutsche Börse opens with a call auction that takes place within the first few minutes after 9:00 am. Deutsche Börse also runs an intra-day auction a few minutes after 1:00 pm, and another auction about 5 minutes after the close. Before the extended trading hours, the closing call was held a few minutes after 5:40 pm. After the extended trading hours, this call has been kept as a second intra-day auction, and a fourth auction was introduced for a few minutes after 8:00 pm to close the market.

Trading hours for the London Stock Exchange are 8:00 am to 4:30 pm. Given the one-hour time difference between Great Britain and Continental Europe, the start of trading in London is synchronized with the European markets. So too are the opening and closing procedures. The London market opens with a call auction at 8:00 am and, beginning on May 30th, 2000, it also ends trading with a second auction that takes place several minutes after 4:30 pm.

The transaction data were filtered for errors. U.S. TAQ data were filtered with an algorithm developed by Robert Wood. Wood's procedure examines all trades where the absolute value of the price change is greater that 11 percent. For such price changes, the algorithm examines up to nine price changes on either side of the suspicious trade, as well as intervening quotes, to determine the likelihood that the trade was reported in error. For the current study, less than 0.01 percent of U.S. trades in our database were identified as erroneous by this method. We filtered the European data by eliminating every transaction where the absolute value of the log of consecutive prices (excluding the overnight price change) was greater than 10 percent.[133] No observations were removed with this filter for Euronext Paris and Deutsche Börse. This is not surprising because both exchanges, being fully electronic, are not as subject to pricing errors. The filter removed less than 0.6 percent of the London Stock Exchange trades.

[132] In call auction trading, orders are batched together for a multilateral trade, at a single price, at a pre-specified point in time. At the call, buy orders at the single clearing price or above execute, as do sell orders at the single clearing price or below.

[133] The European data were provided in a flat file format that cannot be error filtered in the manner applied to the U.S. data.

4.2 Test Design

For each of the five markets, each trading day is divided into the series of half-hour intervals that comprise the day for the market. For each stock in each of the samples, a price change is recorded for every half-hour trading interval in the year 2000. The first trade and the last trade in a half-hour interval determine the price change for that interval. Specifically, we measure the price change as the natural logarithm of the last price divided by the first price in an interval.[134]

The half-hour price changes are then divided into separate sets: the first half-hour of the day, the second half-hour, and so on through the final half-hour interval of the trading day. Half-hour volatility is then computed for each stock for each of the intra-day intervals, by taking the standard deviation of the series of price changes recorded for each of the intervals. Referring to London time, this gives us the 8:00-8:30 volatility, the 8:30-9:00 volatility, and so on. The first daily intervals include the opening calls in the three European markets and the NYSE.[135] Finally, the volatility for each market, for each half-hour interval in the day, is computed as the equally weighted average volatility across all of the stocks in our sample for that market and for that interval.

5. VOLATILITY PATTERNS

We first consider the pattern of volatility over the trading day (First Approach). Then we examine how volatility changes as the interval over which price changes are measured is lengthened (Second Approach).

As noted above, Euronext Paris and Deutsche Börse both extended their trading day during 2000, and the London Stock Exchange introduced a closing call auction during the year. Accordingly, for each of the markets, we have divided the year into two parts: the span of days that preceded the relevant change, and the span of days that followed. Along with being necessitated by the market structure change, replicating the analysis for the two sub-periods and somewhat differentiated samples of stocks (particularly

[134] At least two trades must occur in a half-hour interval for a price change to be recorder for the interval. If less than two trades occur in any interval, we do not ascribe a price change to it and drop that observation from the sample. However, since we select the most liquid stocks in all markets, we do not lose any observations in our US sample, and we lose less than 0.5% of the observations for each market in our European sample.

[135] The Nasdaq market does not open with a call.

for the London market) gives us further confidence that our findings are not the chance result of the particular calendar period studied. For comparability, we divided the NYSE and Nasdaq samples into two sub-periods – the first six months and the last six months of 2000.

5.1 Intra-Day Volatility

The half-hour intra-day volatility patterns for each of the five exchanges are displayed in Exhibit 26.

	NYSE		Nasdaq		London Stock Exchange		Euronext Paris		Deutsche Börse	
	First Period	Second Period	First Period	Second Period	First Period	Second Period	First Period	Second Period	First Period	Second Period
FIRST 1/2 HR	1.78**	2.04**	1.87**	1.91**	3.12**	3.11**	1.75**	1.78**	1.76**	1.96**
LAST 1/2 HR	1.18*	1.10	1.55**	1.32**	1.64**	1.53**	1.45**	1.31**	1.17*	1.15*
CLOSING CALL	NA	NA	NA	NA	NA	1.50**	1.09	1.00	0.91	0.63*
OPEN TO CLOSE	1.14	1.13	1.14	1.13	1.18*	1.20*	1.00	1.05	1.00	0.99
DAY	1.26**	1.30**	1.21*	1.24**	0.98	1.10	1.12	1.00	1.09	1.10
1 WEEK	1.14	1.29**	1.04	1.16*	0.94	0.88	0.98	0.87	0.91	0.84*
2 WEEKS	1.12	1.23*	1.06	1.05	0.84*	0.81*	0.93	0.82*	0.89	0.85*

** indicates significantly different than unity at the 1% confidence level
* indicates significantly different than unity at the 5% confidence level

Exhibit 26: Normalized Price Volatilities

Note: Price change in each half-hour segment is measured as the natural logarithm of the last price divided by the first price in the segment. The half-hour price changes are then divided into separate sets: the first half-hour of the day, the second half-hour, and so on through the final half-hour interval of the trading day. Half-hour volatility is then computed for each stock for each of the intra-day segments, by taking the standard deviation of the series of price changes recorded for each of the segments. The volatility for each market, for each half-hour segment in the day is computed as the equally weighted average volatility across all of the stocks in our sample for that market and for that interval. The reported volatilities are then normalized by dividing them by the average of the volatilities from the second half-hour segment to the second-to-the-last half hour segment. Hence, the reported volatilities are scaled by dividing them by the mean mid-day volatilities.

To further analyze the intra-day half-hour volatility pattern, we have separated the half-hour intervals into four groups: the first half-hour, the second half-hour through the second to last half-hour (not shown, but referred to as Mid-Day), the last half-hour and, where applicable, the brief period between the close of the continuous market and the closing call auction (which we label "Closing CALL"). We apply the label "MID" to the average of the set of half-hour volatilities for the second half-hour interval through the second to last half-hour interval. We use this average, MID, as a base against which to *normalize* the volatilities for each of the other groups. To illustrate, for the NYSE First Period (the first half of 2000), for the first half-hour, the value of 1.78 in the table indicates that this volatility is 78 percent higher than that of the average of the eleven mid-day half-hour volatilities.

For Deutsche Börse's second period, the formal trading hours extend to an 8:00 pm closing. However, examining volume for the 5:30 pm to 8:00 pm segment (not shown), reveals that, for all intents and purposes, the market has effectively continued to close at 5:30 pm.[136] Accordingly, we have calculated the normalized volatility for Deutsche Börse's second period by treating the 5:00 pm – 5:30 pm half-hour period as the closing half-hour of the continuous market, by considering the 5:30 pm call to be the closing call, and by taking "MID" to be the average volatility over the half-hour intervals from 8:30 am through 5:00 pm.

Table 1 also presents the volatility of the price changes from the opening trade to the closing trade. This ratio is labeled "Open-To-Close." To the extent that price swings which occur during the day have washed out by the close of trading, we expect Open-To-Close be relatively low (less than 1). To the extent that intra-day trending predominates, we expect the ratio to be relatively high (greater than 1).

The story told by Exhibit 26 is clear. The volatility spike for the first half-hour is substantial for all five markets in each of the two calendar periods. For the London Stock Exchange, volatility in the first half-hour is roughly three times the average of the other periods (excluding the opening and closing half-hour periods), while for the other European and two US exchanges it is about double.

[136] Average daily trading volume showed little increase following the lengthening of the trading day. For the January – May period, Deutsche Börse's average daily trading volume for the average stock in our sample was 1.40 million shares. For the June – December period, the comparable number is 1.37 million shares.

Volatility at the close is also accentuated, although less so than at the opening. Volatility over the last half-hour is over 50 percent greater than the mid-day volatility for the London Stock Exchange in both sub-periods, and over 30 percent greater for Euronext Paris. Volatility at the close is 17 percent more for Deutsche Börse in the first period and 15 percent more in the second sub-period. Nasdaq closing volatility is 55 and 32 percent above for periods 1 and 2, respectively, while the NYSE's closing volatility is 18 percent and 10 percent higher.

Also of interest in Exhibit 26 is the volatility between the close of the continuous market and the closing call auction (Closing CALL).[137] The relative volatility numbers presented in Exhibit 26 show that, for the three European market centers, some price volatility exists between the close of the continuous market and the closing call. The normalized volatility ranges from 1.00 to 1.09 for the continental European exchanges. Period 2 for the London exchange yields a normalized volatility of 1.50.[138] This volatility spike at London's closing call may be attributed to meaningful price discovery taking place in the closing auction. Interestingly, for the second period for Deutsche Börse, the call auction volatility is only 63 percent of the mid-day volatility at the 5:30 pm call, while it is 14 percent greater than the mid-day volatility at the 8:00 pm call.[139] Apparently, with trading activity being relatively low between 5:30 pm and 8:00 pm, meaningful price discovery does occur at the final call. This is consistent with Pagano and Schwartz's (2002) finding that the introduction of the closing call by Euronext Paris in 1996 (thinner stocks) and 1998 (extended to all stocks) did increase the quality of price determination in that market.

Exhibit 26 also shows the normalized open-to-close volatilities. The values for Open-To-Close range from 0.99 to 1.20. While the numbers are predominantly greater than unity, only the London values are significantly difference from one. Open-To-Close is highest for the London Stock Exchange, standing at 1.18 and 1.20 for the first and periods, respectively. For Euronext Paris, Open-To-Close volatility is 1.00 for the first period, and 1.05 for the second period. For Deutsche Börse, Open-To-Close is also 1.00

[137] We treated the interval from the close of the continuous market to the closing call as if it were another half-hour period. The treatment is conservative in that the actual time to the closing call is roughly five minutes.

[138] London introduced its closing call on May 30, 2000.

[139] This figure is not shown in Exhibit 26.

for the first period and .99 for the second period.[140] Open-To-Close volatilities for the two U.S. markets in both periods are tightly grouped at 1.13 and 1.14.

Because of the general lack of significance, interpreting these results as evidence of reversals may be misleading. Nevertheless, as discussed above, values of Open-To-Close of 1.00 or greater (which we have observed) does suggest that price dislocations attributable to the four market process factors (spreads, market impact, dynamic price discovery and momentum trading) may not have been totally "repaired" by price reversals that have occurred by the end of the trading day. This is because reversal behavior may not be confined to a single trading day, but could extend into next-day price behavior (and, perhaps, beyond). We assess this further in the next subsection.

5.2 Relative Short-Period and Longer-Period Volatility

The longer-period normalized volatilities displayed in Exhibit 26 are for three measurement intervals – one day, one week, and two weeks. The one-day interval, DAY (the volatility of Close-To-Close returns) captures the price change from the closing trade on one trading day to the closing trade on the following trading day. The one-week interval (1WEEK) captures the price change from the closing trade on one trading day to the closing trade five trading days later. The two-week interval (2WEEK) captures the price change from the closing trade on one trading day to the closing trade ten trading days later.

Each of these measures encompasses over-night (and over-weekend) price changes. The over-night price changes reflect the impact of overnight news releases, x-dividend price behavior, and stock splits, all of which make our recorded price changes more volatile.[141] For this reason, any diminution of volatility as we progress from the intra-day, to the one-day, to the one-week and, finally, to the two-week measurement

[140] Interestingly, when for the second period we extend the analysis to the 8:00 pm close, Open-To-Close volatility increases to 1.07.

[141] We account for splits and dividends by eliminating the extreme results that stem from such events.

interval, would be particularly strong evidence of reversal behavior in stock price changes.[142]

The first contrast of interest is between Open-To-Close and DAY. For the NYSE and Nasdaq, DAY is greater than unity with statistical significance, while Open-To-Close is statistically indistinguishable from 1 for both markets. For London, on the other hand, Open-To-Close is statistically different from 1, while Day is indistinguishable from 1. Thus, while the US markets reflect substantial volatility from the prior day's close to the subsequent open, the London market reflects substantial mean reversion during the overnight period. For Euronext Paris and Deutsche Börse, both the Day and Open-To-Close measures were indistinguishable from unity for the two study periods.

For all markets, the normalized volatility successively declines as we move from DAY, to 2WEEKS. However, this decline is more pronounced (and has higher statistical significance) for the European markets. This finding may reflect, at least in part, the diminishing influence of the bid/ask bounce and market impact as the horizon is lengthened. This could also reflect the fact that, over an extended period, errors in price discovery are largely repaired by reversals that bring prices back toward equilibrium. Note also that the levels of the DAY ratios in the US markets are higher than unity whereas those in European markets are not. These differences could reflect the relative practices of intra-day news release in the US and Europe.[143]

Across the five markets, the values for 2WEEKS are generally somewhat less than those for 1WEEK. However, the one- and two-week values are similar, and it appears that much of the reversal behavior is captured by the one-week measure.

[142] The price series could, of course, be adjusted for cash and stock dividends and for stock splits. However, the adjustment factors were not available to us for the current study.

[143] It is further interesting to note that all of the estimates of 1WEEK and 2WEEKS for the European exchanges are less than one, and that some of these deviations are statistically significant. This means that the adjusted volatility of these longer period returns is less than average mid-day volatility, and can be taken as evidence of more accentuated mid-day reversal behavior and/or more protracted trending in the European markets.

6. UNANSWERED QUESTIONS

The picture that emerges for each of the five markets we have considered is one of accentuated short-period volatility, especially at market openings. Daily opening prices are particularly volatile in the British market. We are unable to explain this result fully, but note that trading volume at the open is low for London.[144] The lower volume indicates that institutional investors in London tend to avoid trading at the open. While institutional traders in the US may also tend to avoid the open, retail trading interest in the US (and continental Europe) provides ample volume at the open and, in so doing, may lead to better price discovery. Additionally, Werner and Kleidon (1996) suggest that the extensive trading of London stocks in the US alters their trading behavior in the UK.

And so, in establishing our findings, we have not focused on the actual *levels* of volatility in the various markets we have studied. Inter-market differences in underlying volatility levels could be attributed to the different characteristics of the stocks traded in the various markets, to different inherent levels of risk and uncertainty in the various countries the shares are traded in, and possibly to other factors that we have not taken into account that have little to do with market structure per se. Rather, we have expressed our key volatility measures in *relative* terms (namely, relative to mid-day volatility). Doing so provides a cleaner picture of the volatility patterns over the course of a trading day, across measurement intervals of differing length, and across different market structures.

The five exchanges we have considered represent very different market structures. The NYSE is an order driven market that includes market makers (each of the listed companies is allocated to a single specialist). Nasdaq in the year 2000 (the test year for our study) had predominantly a dealer market structure (albeit with some characteristics traditionally associated with order-driven markets). Paris, London, and Frankfurt utilize automated (i.e., not floor-based) order-driven trading platforms.[145] Consequently, accentuated

[144] Volume data are presented in Ozenbas (2002).

[145] Frankfurt still has a trading floor, although much of the activity has migrated to its electronic platform, Xetra. Trading on the floor starts at 9:00 a.m., the same time the electronic market opens, and both venues open with a call auction. Because the call is electronic on the electronic platform but not on the floor, it is possible for the floor traders

volatility, especially at the open, cannot be simply ascribed to a specialist taking into account his or her own inventory considerations, or to order flow being fragmented in a competitive dealer market, or to the attributes of an electronic platform.

A number of questions concerning market quality/efficiency on both sides of the Atlantic could be raised in light of the magnitude of the volatility relationships. We have observed volatility spikes ranging from 76 percent to 212 percent for the first-half hour of trading, and volatility spikes at the close that range up to 64 percent. What accounts for them? At each opening, information that has been released since the previous close must be incorporated into prices. In the process, conflicting opinions held by traders have to be resolved quickly, in an orderly manner, and with a high degree of accuracy. Not surprisingly, the opens are typically periods of serious buy/sell imbalances that result in opening prices being imperfectly aligned with their consensus values.

It is not normally the case that extensive information is released at the close. We suggest that the volatility spikes at the close result, in part at least, from the price pressures caused by agents cleaning up orders that must be completed within the day, and from traders unwinding positions so as to end the day flat.

One market structure innovation that could alleviate price pressures at the close is the closing call auction that has now been incorporated into each of the three European markets. Pagano and Schwartz (2003) found that the introduction of a closing call in the Paris market resulted in more efficient price behavior, both in the closing call itself, and in the last fifteen minutes of the continuous market. They posit that availability of the closing call auction makes it safer towards the end of the continuous market for participants to be liquidity providers (i.e., to place limit orders) rather than to be liquidity demanders (i.e., to place market orders). This is because any limit orders that did not execute in the continuous market could be rolled into the call. Consequently, books became deeper and price volatility has been better controlled in the continuous market after the introduction of the closing call.

On the other hand, for the five markets that we have studied, the first half-hour volatility measures show that the three European markets that open with fully electronic calls perform no better by this metric than the two US markets that do not (the NYSE's call is not fully electronic, and Nasdaq has no formal opening procedure). However, as previously stated, we have been

---

to see the opening price on Xetra, but prices set on the floor openings are not known at the time of the Xetra call.

cautious about making cross-market comparisons. For the London market, as we have noted, the particularly sharp volatility accentuation at the open could be attributed primarily to its heavily institutional nature, and to the fact that the UK institutional investors tend to shy away from trading at the open. In any event, we anticipate that, for any given market center, proper design and implementation of an electronic call would improve market quality, especially if it is designed so as to provide the appropriate incentives for participants to use it. Further investigation of the issue would be desirable.

The research could be extended in a number of other ways. The analysis should be applied to small-cap and mid-cap stocks, in addition to the large caps that we have focused on in this study. Attention could also be given to the effect of pre-opening trading on first half-hour volatility. The trading behavior of institutional investors, and its effect on the intra-day patterns of volatility and volume, needs to be examined. The relationship between volatility and trading volume should be revisited with reference to the intra-day patterns we have observed. Of further interest would be an analysis of how the intra-day volatility metric has evolved in recent years, a period that has seen extensive change in the structure of the equity markets. Of particular importance would be an examination of the effect that the conversion to decimals in the US that was completed in 2001 had on the US markets (one might anticipate a volatility effect to the extent that institution of the penny tick has affected the liquidity suppliers). Lastly, matched samples and/or multivariate statistical techniques should be used so that meaningful cross-country comparisons can be derived from the intra-day volatility metric.

REFERENCES

Adams, Greg, Grant McQueen, and Robert Wood, "The Effects of Inflation News on High Frequency Stocks Returns," *Journal of Business*, Forthcoming 2003.

Amihud, Yakov and Haim Mendelson, 1987, "Trading Mechanisms and Stock Returns: An Empirical Investigation," *Journal of Finance* 42, 533-553.

Andersen, Torben, Tim Bollerslev and Asish Das, 2001, "Variance-ratio Statistics and High-frequency Data: Testing for Changes in Intraday Volatility Patterns," *Journal of Finance* 56, 305-327.

Barber, Brad and Terrance Odean, "Too Many Cooks Spoil the Profits: Investment Club Performance," *Financial Analyst Journal*, January/February 2000, 17-25.

Bessembinder, Hendrik and Subhrendu Rath, 2002, "Trading Costs and Return Volatility: Evidence from Exchange Listings," Working Paper.

Blume, Lawrence, David Easley, and Maureen O'Hara, "Market Statistics and Technical Analysis: The Role of Volume," *The Journal of Finance*, Vol. 49, No.1 , 153-181.

Fleming, Michael J, and Eli M. Remolina, 1999, "Price Formation and Liquidity in the US Treasury Market: The Response to Public Information," *Journal of Finance* 5, 1901-1915.

Gerety, Mason and, Harold Mulherin, 1994, "Price Formation on Stock Exchanges: The Evolution of Trading within the Day," *Review of Financial Studies* 7, 609-629.

Glosten, Lawrence and Paul Milgrom, 1985, "Bid, Ask, and Transaction Prices in a Specialist Market with Heterogeneously Informed Traders," *Journal of Financial Economics* 13, 71-100.

Handa, Puneet and Robert A. Schwartz, "Limit Order Trading," *Journal of Finance*, December 1996, 1835 - 1861.

Harris, Lawrence, 1986, "A Transaction Data Study of Weekly and Intradaily Patterns in Stock Returns," *Journal of Financial Economics* 16, 99-118.

Hasbrouck, Joel and Robert A. Schwartz, "Liquidity and Execution Costs in Equity Markets," *Journal of Portfolio Management*, Spring 1988, 10 - 16.

Heiner, Ronald, 1983, "On the Origins of Predictable Behavior," American Economic Review 73, 560-595.

Hong, Harrison and Jiang Wang, 2000, "Trading and Returns Under Periodic Market Closures," *Journal of Finance* 55, 297-354.

Kyle, Albert S, 1985, "Continuous Auctions and Insider Trading," *Econometrica* 53, 1315-1336.

Lo, Andrew, Harry Mamaysky and Jiang Wang, 2000, "Foundations of Technical Analysis: Computational Algorithms, Statistical Inference, and Empirical Implementation," *Journal of Finance*, Volume 55, 1705-1770.

Lo, Andrew and A. C. MacKinlay, 1988, "Stock Market Prices Do Not Follow Random Walks: Evidence From a Simple Specification Test," *Review of Financial Studies* 1, 41-66.

Lockwood, Larry and Scott Linn, 1990, "An Examination of Stock Market Return Volatility During Overnight and Intraday Periods," 1964-1989, *Journal of Finance* 45, 591-601.

Ozenbas, Deniz, 2002, "Intra-Day Price Volatility: A Reflection of Trading Friction," unpublished doctoral dissertation, Zicklin School of Business, Baruch College, CUNY.

Pagano, Michael S. and Robert A. Schwartz, "A Closing Call's Impact on Market Quality at Euronext Paris," *Journal of Financial Economics*, forthcoming, 2003.

Schwartz, Robert A. and James E. Shapiro, "The Challenge of Institutionalization for the Equity Markets," in *Recent Developments in Finance,* Anthony Saunders, editor, Business One Irwin, 1992, 31 - 45.

Schwartz, Robert A. and David K. Whitcomb, "The Time-Variance Relationship: Evidence on Autocorrelation in Common Stock Returns," *Journal of Finance,* March 1977, 41 - 55.

Stoll, Hans, 2000, "Friction," *Journal of Finance* 4, 1479-1515.

Weinberg, Neil, "Fear, Greed and Technology," *Forbes Magazine,* May 15, 2000.

Werner, Ingrid and Allan Kleidon, 1996, "UK and US Trading of British Cross-Listed Stocks: An Intra-Day Analysis of Market Integration," *Review of Financial Studies* 9, 619-664.

Wood, Robert A, Thomas McInish, and Keith Ord, 1985, "An Investigation of Transactions Data for NYSE Stocks," *Journal of Finance* 40, 723-741.

Participant Biographies

Theodore Aronson, (MBA, BS, Wharton), founded ARONSON+JOHNSON+ORTIZ (formerly Aronson+Partners and Aronson+Fogler) in 1984. ARONSON+JOHNSON+ORTIZ manages $7 billion for a few dozen institutional investors.

Ted joined Drexel Burnham Lambert in 1974 while still a graduate student. He was a member of the Quantitative Equities Group, which provided innovative practical applications of Modern Portfolio Theory and quantitative portfolio management. This group managed the Revere Fund, the first actively managed fund registered with the SEC to employ Modern Portfolio Theory. Prior to forming A+P, Ted founded Addison Capital Management.

Ted is a Governor (vice chairman) of the Association for Investment Management and Research (AIMR) and both a CFA charter holder and Chartered Investment Counselor. He was a Lecturer in Finance at The Wharton School and is a frequent speaker on Wall Street issues, especially innovations in trading methods to minimize transaction costs — including a session at Salomon Brothers' training program. (Salomon's training program was immortalized in Michael Lewis' *Liar's Poker.* When Ted spoke, however, he was ***not*** pelted by spitballs!).

Paul Bennett joined the New York Stock Exchange as senior vice president and chief economist in June 2001. Mr. Bennett manages the NYSE's Research division. He also supports the Exchange's business lines and Office of the Chairman by developing and supporting research into the structure of equity markets, supervising analysis within the Exchange related to its various business and public-policy activities, participating in and hosting conferences, and supporting Exchange-related research. Mr. Bennett also is responsible for the NYSE's ongoing interaction with the academic community. He holds a Ph.D. in economics from Princeton University and a B.A. in economics from the University of Chicago. He has published numerous papers on finance, economics, and securities markets.

George Bodine is currently Director of Trading for General Motors Investment Management Corporation (GMIMCo). He is responsible for worldwide equity and derivative trading relating to GMIMCo's internal investment funds. Prior to assuming his current position in September, 1996, Mr. Bodine was Vice President of Schwab Institutional overseeing equities and options trading for the small to mid-tier investment advisors. Preceding that he spent his career with Equitable/Alliance Capital starting in 1972.

Mr. Bodine received his BS in Psychology in 1972 from Syracuse University and MS in Business Management in 1979 from Central Michigan University. Mr. Bodine is currently a member of the National Organization of Investment Professionals and is a former member of both the NYSE and the AMEX Institutional Traders Advisory Committees.

Andrew Brooks is a Vice President and Head of Equity Trading for T. Rowe Price Associates. Joining the firm in 1980, Andy serves as a Vice President of the T. Rowe Price Equity Income, Value, Capital Appreciation and High Yield Funds. Andy earned a B.A. from Union College in Schenectady, New York. He is a past President of the Baltimore Security Traders Association and a past Governor of the Security Traders Association. He also has served on both the New York Stock Exchange's Institutional Traders Advisory Committee and Market Performance Committee, as well as NASDAQ's Trading Committee. Andy currently serves as a member of the Investment Company Institute's Equity Markets Task Force and is on the board of NOIP.

Thomas Cardello is a Managing Director with Morgan Stanley, and responsible for Global Electronic Derivatives Market Making within the Institutional Equity Division. He has been responsible for this business since its inception in late 1999, and has led its growth into a position of recognized national leadership.

Prior to joining Morgan Stanley in 1999, Dr. Cardello owned and managed a consultancy specializing in the structuring of large alternative asset portfolios. Before then, he was Executive Director at the hedge fund Paloma Partners responsible for investment strategy analysis and development, fund-wide risk analysis, and management of a Foreign Exchange fund. As Managing Director of the consultant firm IPS, he was responsible for development and structuring of hybrid financial derivative/insurance products. Other positions held include Principal at Timber Hill Inc.; New Product Development Manager at Bank of

America/Security Pacific; Oil Options Manager, Trading Systems Development Manager and Senior Research Analyst at Standard Chartered Bank/Mocatta; and Associate in Fixed Income Risk Management at Goldman Sachs.

Dr. Cardello, a New York native, holds Ph.D. and M.Phil. degrees in physics from Yale University, New Haven and B.Sc. degrees in mathematics and physics from The Cooper Union, New York. He is also a Director of the Kurt Forrest foundation.

Minder Cheng is Global Head of Equity and Currency Trading and Managing Director at Barclays Global Investors. Minder Cheng has overall responsibility for BGI's equity and currency trading activities worldwide, leading our trading research effort and serving as the senior owner of BGI's broker relationships globally. Prior to joining BGI in 1999, he held roles as research analyst, proprietary trader and senior strategist at Convergence Asset Management, Sumitomo Finance International and Salomon Brothers. He worked in New York, London, and Tokyo with these firms. His direct trading experience covers equity, fixed income, currency and derivatives in the U.S. and international markets. Minder also managed several projects for the research and planning division of the New York Stock Exchange. He received his Ph.D. in finance and M.B.A. from the University of California at Berkeley and his B.A. from National Taiwan University in Taipei, Taiwan.

Michael Cormack is President of Archipelago Holdings LLC, the parent company of the Archipelago Exchange and the Archipelago Electronics Communications Network (ECN). In March of 2002, trading began on the Archipelago Exchange, the nation's first totally open, all-electronic national stock exchange. At the same time, Archipelago closed on its merger with competitor REDIBook to combine the two fastest growing ECNs into one trading platform.

Mr. Cormack oversees client relation efforts including sales, trading support, and strategic initiatives. Prior to his position as president, Mr. Cormack served as National Sales Manager. He came to Archipelago from American Century Investments where he was manager of Equity Trading.

Mr. Cormack has a strong background in both trading and technology. His technical experience is exemplified by his prior position as co-head of the executive committee for the Financial Information Exchange (FIX) – an emerging electronic communications standard in the global financial marketplace. He has also participated as a member of the Nasdaq Quality of Markets Committee, a group that helps to shape Nasdaq policy. He currently serves on the TransactTools Advisory Board.

Mr. Cormack holds a bachelor's degree in economics from The Johns Hopkins University.

Viktoria Dalko is a professor, currently teaching finance at Harvard University and in the Executive Master of Science in Finance program of the Zicklin School of Business. At the age of 27, Dalko became the Chief of Staff for the Committee of Budget, Tax and Finances of the first democratic Hungarian parliament. She was a member of the advisory committee to the President of the National Bank of Hungary, at the outset of the transition to the market economy. Dalko, an outstanding teacher with 5.0/5.0 evaluations from executive students, taught extensively in the U.S., Taiwan, Hong Kong and China in M.B.A. and Executive M.B.A. and M.S.F. programs, including Thunderbird, The American Graduate School of International Business (Phoenix, Arizona) and the University of Illinois at Urbana-Champaign. She received her Ph.D. in economics from the University of Pennsylvania.

Paul Davis is a senior managing director at TIAA-CREF Investment Management LLC in New York. The TIAA-CREF group of companies, with $260 billion in assets under management, includes the premier retirement system for people employed in education and research in the U.S., serving 2.9 million participants at 15,000 institutions. The organization is widely recognized as a major voice for shareholder rights and improved corporate governance. Additionally, it offers after-tax annuities, mutual funds, insurance and trust services to the general public. TIAA-CREF Tuition Financing, Inc., a subsidiary of TIAA, manages 13 state-sponsored, '529' college savings plans, more than any other company. Davis joined TIAA-CREF in 1983 after working at Prudential Securities in New York. Before his career on Wall Street, he taught mathematics at Lehigh University, Manhattanville College and West Virginia University. Davis has an undergraduate degree from West Virginia University and a doctorate in mathematics from Carnegie Mellon University.

Fred Federspiel is CEO of Pipeline Trading Systems. Fred has more than 15 years experience developing and selling high-technology hardware and software systems. Fred earned a Ph.D. in Experimental Nuclear and Particle Physics from the University of Illinois at Champaign/Urbana. He worked for six years at Los Alamos National Laboratory as a nuclear physicist. He was the second employee hired by the BiosGroup, a complexity science-consulting firm founded by Ernst & Young. In his three years at the BiosGroup, Fred led the conceptual development and sales of several pioneering projects in electronic markets. He founded e-Xchange Advantage Corporation (eXA) (of which Pipeline Trading Systems is a wholly owned subsidiary) in 1999, and has received financial backing from BiosGroup, Nasdaq and Instinet to develop solutions to the problem of trading institutional-sized blocks electronically.

Luca Filippa is Director of Research and Development at Borsa Italiana. In this position he is involved in the definition of the Exchange's development strategy and leads the activity of statistical production and economic analysis for market support. In 1996 and 1997 he was a member of the team for the implementation of a strategy to restructure and reposition the Exchange after privatisation. In 1997 and 1998 he led the Euro project of the Exchange and was a member of the Italian Euro Committee and of the Federation of European Securities Exchanges Euro Steering Committee. In 1999 and 2000 he was the Italian member of working groups for the Stock Exchanges European Alliance. He graduated in economics. Prior to joining Borsa Italiana in 1994, he worked for five years in the Economic Research Department of CONSOB, the Italian Securities Commission, where he dealt with capital markets analysis, econometrics and taxation. An author of various articles and working papers on capital markets, he is vice-Chairman of the Economics and Statistics sub-Committee of the Federation of European Securities Exchanges and he is a lecturer of market microstructure at the Cattolica University of Milan.

William Freund served as the New York Stock Exchange's Senior Vice President and Chief Economist for 18 years (1968-1986). He was the New York Stock Exchange Professor of Economics at Pace University's Lubin School of Business from 1986 to 2001. He was Chairman of the Pace University's Graduate Department of Economics and International Business from 1986-1993. Since 1993, he has been, and remains, Director of the Pace University Center for the Study of Equity Markets (now renamed the William C. Freund Center for the Study of Securities Markets)

From 1952 to 1962, he was Economist for the Prudential Insurance Company of America. From 1962 to 1965, he was Associate Professor of Finance at NYU's Graduate School of Business. He returned to Prudential as Chief Economist and Director of Investment Research between 1965 and 1968. His Ph.D. degree is from Columbia University. For twenty years, he was an economic adviser (pro bono) to four governors of New Jersey. He has served on a number of corporate boards of directors, most recently U.S. Life Corp. where he was involved in merging that company with the American General Insurance Company. He is author of several books including Investment Fundamentals, and co-author of People and Productivity. He has written chapters for numerous other books and has authored a large number of articles.

Marc Gresack is a pioneer and successful business executive with 22 years experience in the field of global electronic agency brokerage. He has been a contributor to the profession of securities trading of such significance as to change the direction of the industry. His expert knowledge of the practices of institutional investors, plan sponsors, portfolio managers and equity traders has enabled him to translate the potential applications of new concepts to revenue throughout his career. Significant accomplishments include: he is the inventor of the industry's first 'peer to peer' institutional crossing system, The Crossing Network, at Instinet in 1985; he is a founding partner of the Marshall Plan, an innovative quantitative institutional fund manager, where he developed 'rules-based' implementation systems to enhance the value of portfolios; he was a tenured senior executive in Instinet, successfully contributing to the drive to export their still controversial electronic brokerage services in the U.S. and later the highly protectionist European markets; he participated in the development of an institutional portfolio trading group and the strategic acquisition of Lynch, Jones & Ryan, the leading provider of independent research and commission recapture services; he was President of Universal Trading Technologies, a nascent electronic trading company, and an executive consultant on the use of crossing to facilitate portfolio transitions at Chase Manhattan Global Trust unit; he was a strategic consultant at Sungard/BRUT and currently is consulting on the feasibility of acquiring a U.S. regulated securities exchange on behalf of an international group.

Sanjiv Gupta is Director of Research and Strategy for Bloomberg Tradebook LLC. Mr. Gupta is responsible for electronic trading research, development of new strategic trading solutions, transactions cost analysis, and training. The research group writes several monthly publications covering global equity trading, fixed income, energy, and foreign exchange. The group also contributes to other industry publications, and educates customers and sales personnel on Tradebook's innovative electronic trading solutions.

Mr. Gupta has been with Bloomberg since 1992. Prior to joining Bloomberg, Mr. Gupta was an Instructor of Finance at New York University's Stern School of Business. He holds a B.Sc. in Management Science from the University of Manchester in England, an M.B.A. from Lehigh University, an M.Phil. from New York University, and a Ph.D. A.B.D. in Finance from New York University.

Nari Jote's recent experience includes the following: Vice President – Business Development – Eliot & Carr Associates, Inc. (executive search firm); Management Consultant and Global Business Coordinator - Jote & Associates; Adjunct Teacher, International Business and International Marketing, Baruch College, City University of New York (CUNY); Adjunct Teacher, International Trade Operations, Zicklin School of Business, New York University. Over the past 30+years, he has held management positions with multinational corporations for Business, Marketing, IT, Joint ventures, Customer Care and high tech projects, in the U.S.A., U.K. & India. Companies he has worked for include, Matsushita Electric Corporation of America, AT&T / Bell Labs / Lucent, York (U.K.-marketing div), London, Chief Export Executive for LHS Co. Ltd. London (U.K.) and coordinated with the BOT Tatas in India for Joint Ventures, Marketing & Business Plans. He is proficient in: Global Strategic Business Development, Market and Business Research, Process Improvements, Joint ventures, and Compliance, Cost Analysis, Finance & Profitability.

Nari Jote's educational accomplishments inlcude: Fellow, Institution of Engineers (India); Member, Project Management Institute; M.B.A. in Business / International Marketing (distinction), L.I. University, New York – 1981; M.S. in Technology Management, Polytechnic University (PINY), New York, NY – 1980; D.E. in Mechanical and Electrical Engineering, India. + (Elect. Eng.- C&G Institute, London); Masters in Project Management, Washington University, Washington D.C.; Corporate Finance and Valuation, Investment Banking, Basic Corporate Finance and many other continuing study courses completed at Baruch College, City University of NY (CUNY).

Christopher Killeen is Senior Trader of Domestic Equities. He joined TIAA-CREF in 1990 after working at Lebow, Weksel & Co., a leveraged buyout firm. Prior to that he worked at Long Island Trust in the Bank Investments division. He graduated from Hofstra University with a degree in Banking and Finance and holds an M.B.A. from St. John's University in International Finance.

TIAA-CREF is a leading, national, nonprofit financial services organization serving the general public, and is also the premier pension system for people employed in education and research in the U.S. It offers high quality, low-cost mutual funds, annuities, IRA's, insurance, and trust services, and also manages several state-sponsored college financing programs. The TIAA-CREF pension system ranks as the world's largest, based on assets under management. In total, the organization manages almost $300 billion. TIAA-CREF is headquartered in New York City, with regional offices throughout the United States.

David Krell is a founder and President & CEO of the International Securities Exchange. From 1997 to 1998, he was Chairman and co-founder of K-Squared Research, LLC, a financial services consulting firm. From 1984 to 1997, Mr. Krell was Vice President, Options and Index Products, of the New York Stock Exchange where he managed marketing, systems and new product introductions for the division. From 1981 to 1984, Mr. Krell was First Vice President at the Chicago Board Options Exchange, responsible for the management and operation of the Marketing and Sales Division. Mr. Krell was also a Vice President of Merrill Lynch from 1978 to 1981 and founded its Managed Options Service.

Active in numerous industry groups, Mr. Krell was formerly a Director on the Board of the International Federation of Technical Analysts, a former president of the Market Technicians Association and a past Director on the Board of The Options Clearing Corporation.

Mr. Krell formerly was an Adjunct Professor at Rutgers University Graduate School of Management and at the Graduate School of Baruch College. He has also taught, coordinated and directed numerous seminars and workshops at the New York Institute of Finance.

Ananth Madhavan is the Global Head of Trading Research at Barclays Global Investors. He leads BGI's trading research team in San Francisco and London, with a focus on execution research and trading strategies across different asset classes worldwide. Ananth also works closely with the global trading team and BGI's alpha research and product groups to design and implement trading strategies capturing liquidity-driven market opportunities. Before joining BGI in 2003, Ananth was formerly Managing Director of Research of ITG, Inc., a leading provider of technology-based equity-trading services and transaction research to institutional investors and brokers. He was also a member of the management and executive committees of ITG, Inc. Previously, he was the Charles B. Thorton Professor of Finance at the Marshall School of Business at the University of Southern California, and Assistant Professor of Finance at the Wharton School of the University of Pennsylvania. He received his Ph.D. in Economics from Cornell University and B.A. from the University of Delhi, India.

Mark Madoff is the Director of Listed Trading at Bernard L. Madoff Investment Securities. Educational Background: BS Economics, University of Michigan, 1986. Professional Activities: President, Security Traders Association of New York (STANY); Securities Industry Association (SIA) Operations Committee; Member, Securities Traders Association (STA) Trading Committee; Member, Securities Industry Association (SIA) Telecommunications and Information Management Committee; Member, Securities Industry Association (SIA) Decimalization Committee; Director, Security Traders Association of New York (STANY); Member, Securities Industry Association (SIA) Market Data Entitlement Subcommittee; Member, Security Industry Association (SIA) NASDAQ Committee. NASDR Service: Member, National Adjudicatory Council (NAC); Chairman, NASD Regulation, Inc., District 10 Business Conduct Committee. NASD Service: Chairman, National Association of Securities Dealers, Inc. (NASD) InterMarket CAES/ITS Sub-Committee; Member, National Association of Securities Dealers, Inc. (NASD) Trading Committee; Member, National Association of Securities Dealers, Inc. (NASD) Unlisted Trading Privileges (UTP) Sub-Committee.

John Malitzis is currently a Senior Vice President and Associate General Counsel for Citigroup Global Markets, Inc. (formerly know as Solomon Smith Barney). In his current role, John provides legal counsel to senior management and trading personnel of the Equities Division in a number of areas, including: cash trading (Nasdaq and listed), equity derivatives, convertibles, program trading, connectivity, soft dollar/introducing broker, and equity capital markets.

Prior to joining Citigroup, John was Vice President, in Nasdaq's Transactions Services Department (NTS) focusing on policy and strategy. John was involved in developing regulatory policy related to NTS businesses (e.g., trading rules for Nasdaq systems, marketplace rules, and trading of Nasdaq securities by other exchanges), and worked with senior management on market structure and strategic initiatives as well as Nasdaq's corporate strategy. John also worked closely with the Data Products Business Line, on the Nasdaq UTP Plan, and related issues.

Prior to joining NTS, John worked in the Nasdaq Office of the General Counsel for approximately five years in the position of Associate Vice President and Associate General Counsel. In OGC, John focused on the areas of broker/dealer regulation, market regulation and market structure. In particular, John worked with Nasdaq senior management and industry committees (Quality of Markets, Institutional Traders Advisory Counsel, Market Operations Review Committee, etc.) to develop legal policy and trading rules for the Nasdaq and the over-the-counter markets. John worked on major market-structure initiatives, including the SuperMontage trading system; SuperSOES trading system; NASD short sale rule; trade-reporting initiatives (riskless principal trade reporting); national market system plans (CTA/CQ, ITS, and Nasdaq UTP); and Nasdaq Europe. Prior to Nasdaq OGC, John worked as a senior attorney in NASD Regulation's Office of the General Counsel, Appellate/Disciplinary Practice Group. While with NASDR OGC, John was responsible for all aspects of enforcement/disciplinary matters considered by the National Adjudicator Council and the NASDR Board. Before joining the NASD, John was a Trial Attorney with the U.S. Commodity Futures Trading Commission, Division of Enforcement, and served as a visiting law fellow at Catholic University's law school.

John is a member of the bars of Massachusetts, New York, and the District of Columbia, and a graduate of Boston College Law School where he was a member of the commercial law review.

Seth Merrin is Founder & Chief Executive Officer of Liquidnet. Seth founded Liquidnet in January 2000 and launched the service in April 2001. Liquidnet has become the fastest launching and growing ECN or ATS in history. In less than 2 ½ years Liquidnet is currently averaging over 13 million shares per day ranking Liquidnet in the top 30 institutional brokers in the U.S. Seth is known as being the pioneer of the Buy Side order management system industry. Seth founded Merrin Financial Inc. in 1985 to develop the Merrin Financial Trading Platform (MFTP) the first buy-side order management system. Merrin Financial also invented the first real-time pre-trade compliance and electronic order routing systems for the investment management industry. These components represent most of the critical infrastructure necessary to enable electronic trading in general and Liquidnet to introduce its unique design. Merrin Financial was sold to ADP in 1996. Seth's innovations have been profiled in over 100 articles in a variety of trade and business publications, including Forbes and Crain's New York Business. Mr. Merrin was also recognized by Wall Street & Technology as one of the 'Top 10 Financial Technology Innovators of the Decade' in its December 1999 issue. Seth has a BA from Tufts University

Anthony Neuberger is Associate Dean for the Full-time Masters in Finance Programme at the London Business School. His research interests include the microstructure of financial markets, and financial derivatives. He has written widely for both academic and practitioner journals, and has co-authored, with Professor Richard Brealey, a report on brokers' commissions for the U.K. Investment Management Association. Prior to joining the London Business School, he worked for the U.K. Department of Energy and for the Cabinet Office.

Deniz Ozenbas is an Assistant Professor of Finance at Montclair State University's School of Business. Her research is mainly in the field of market microstructure and has been published in journals such as Economics Letters, International Finance and the International Journal of Business and Economics. She also has been awarded the Nasdaq Dissertation Fellowship by Nasdaq for the 2001-2002 academic year, and received the Oscar Lasdon Award for best dissertation in the area of Finance from Baruch College, City University of New York for the 2002-2003 academic year. In addition, her joint work with Robert A. Schwartz and Robert A. Wood has received the Outstanding Paper award at the Global Conference on Business and Economics 2003 annual meeting. Dr. Ozenbas holds an M.B.A. and a Ph.D. from Baruch College, City University of New York, and a B.A. from Bogazici University, Turkey.

Brett Redfearn is Senior Vice President, Business Strategy and Equity Order Flow, for The American Stock Exchange (Amex). Redfearn leads the Amex's strategic development and research initiatives focused on positioning the Exchange to respond to new competition, changes in market structure, technological developments and the globalization of trading. His efforts at present are focused on leading the Amex's program to trade Nasdaq listed securities. In that capacity, he is the Amex's representative to the Nasdaq UTP Operating Committee. Overseeing the Equity Order Flow sales team, Redfearn manages customer relationships with buy-side and sell-side trading desks, helping to develop and execute strategies to bring order flow to the

Amex trading floor. Redfearn also manages the Amex's Best Execution reporting and market quality analysis. Since joining the Amex in 1995, he also served as Managing Director of Equity Research, where he led market research and business analysis. Redfearn is a regular speaker at industry conferences and is a member of the Security Traders Association of New York. When he's not working, Brett will most likely be found rock climbing, mountain biking, skiing or kayaking.

Richard Repetto is Associate Director and Sandler O'Neill & Partners. Prior to that he was a Managing Director at Putnam Lovell, heading up the firm's eFinance/eBrokerage Research team. Selected by the Wall Street Journal to its 'Best of the Street' 2003 All Star Analyst Team, Mr. Repetto was one of six analysts to be cited for stock picking in two industry categories, both Securities Brokerage and Internet. He also ranked #2 from a universe of more than 2,900 analysts in the 2002 Overall Stock Picking awards by StarMine, a leading provider of objective ratings of securities analysts. Mr. Repetto was named to the Wall Street Journal's 'Best of the Street' 2001 All Star Analyst Team. Prior to joining Putnam Lovell NBF, Mr. Repetto worked at Lehman Brothers where he established the firm's research coverage of the Internet Financial Services sector in May 1999. Prior to establishing this unit, he was part of the top ranked Institutional Investor specialty finance team at Lehman, following a 10-year career at Mobil Oil Corporation.

Mr. Repetto holds a Masters of Business Administration Degree in Finance from The Wharton School of the University of Pennsylvania and a Bachelor of Science Degree in General Engineering from the United States Military Academy. Mr. Repetto is a Chartered Financial Analyst (CFA) and a member of the New York Society of Security Analysts (NYSSA) and the Association for Investment Management and Research (AIMR).

Michael Richter is Chief Executive Officer of Lime Brokerage LLC. Prior to joining Lime, Michael was President of Citicorp Securities Services, a NYSE member firm. His career includes senior financial and operational management roles at MarketXT, Citibank, Lehman Brothers, E.F. Hutton, American Express International Bank and Arthur Andersen. Michael has an undergraduate engineering degree from Rensselaer Polytechnic Institute and a master's degree from MIT's Sloan School of Management. He is also a certified public accountant.

Sharon Salamon is currently the Director of Institutional Equities for Product Management at Thomson Financial. Prior to her employment at Thomson she was the Senior Sales and Marketing Executive at NeoNet Securities, a firm focused on direct electronic access to the global equity markets. She also worked at Bloomberg providing market data to the financial community. Sharon is a graduate of New York University's Leonard N. Stern School of Business.

Richard Schenkman is Managing Partner of Elm Tree Group LLC, a private investment firm. He has served as CEO of Brut LLC and as Chief Operating Officer and Executive Vice-President of Instinet Corporation. He is a member of the National Organization of Investment Professionals (NOIP) and has served on senior industry policy committees. He holds a BA from the University of Buffalo.

Robert Schwartz is Marvin M. Speiser Professor of Finance and University Distinguished Professor in the Zicklin School of Business, Baruch College, CUNY. Before joining the Baruch faculty in 1997, he was Professor of Finance and Economics and Yamaichi Faculty Fellow at New York University's Leonard N. Stern School of Business, where he had been a member of the faculty since 1965. Professor Schwartz received his Ph.D. in Economics from Columbia University. His research is in the area of financial economics, with a primary focus on the structure of securities markets. He has published numerous journal articles and seven books, including *Equity Markets in* Action, Wiley & Sons, 2004 and *Reshaping the Equity Markets: A Guide for the 1990s,* Harper Business, 1991 (reissued by Business One Irwin, 1993). He has served as a consultant to various market centers including the New York Stock Exchange, the American Stock Exchange, Nasdaq, the London Stock Exchange, Instinet, the Arizona Stock Exchange, Deutsche Börse, and the Bolsa Mexicana. From April 1983 to April 1988, he was an associate editor of *The Journal of Finance*, and he is currently an associate editor of the *Review of Quantitative Finance and Accounting,* the *Review of Pacific Basin Financial Markets and Policies,* and *The Journal of Entrepreneurial Finance & Business Ventures,* and is a member of the advisory board of *International Finance.* In December 1995, Professor Schwartz was named the first chairman of Nasdaq's Economic Advisory Board, and he served on the EAB until Spring 1999.

Barry Small is Chief Executive Officer of Weeden & Company. He graduated with a Bachelors of Arts in economics from Colgate University in 1976. After college Mr. Small played professional soccer for two years in the North American Soccer League and the American Soccer League. In 1986 he was one of the founding partners of Weeden & Co., an institutional broker dealer where he served as head trader until 1995 when he became President and Chief Executive Officer. Mr. holds various securities licenses.

George Sofianos joined Goldman Sachs in January 2001 and he is leading the firm's trading costs and market structure research effort for equities. Prior to joining Goldman Sachs, he was Vice President and Head of Research at the New York Stock Exchange. In that capacity, he oversaw the development and maintenance of databases, the production of trading statistics, reports and research papers.

Before joining the NYSE, he worked at the Federal Reserve Bank of New York, in the Financial Studies department and at the Open Markets Desk. Prior to that, he spent three years teaching economics and finance at the Stern Graduate School of Business, New York University.

Mr. Sofianos has published research on trading costs, the cross listing and trading of non-U.S. stocks, the NYSE specialist trading behavior, stock price behavior on expirations, the impact of program trading on intraday stock price volatility, index arbitrage, margin requirements, and monetary policy. He holds B.Sc. and M.Sc. degrees from the London School of Economics and received his Ph.D. in economics from Harvard University.

Holly Stark is Principal and Director of Trading at Kern Capital Management. Holly manages Kern Capital Management's trading desk and is responsible for developing execution strategies designed to maximize returns while minimizing transaction costs. Prior to joining Kern Capital Management in 2000, Holly was with Dalton, Greiner, Hartman, Maher & Co. (DGHM) for ten years where she was responsible for all trading activities. For eight years prior to DGHM, Holly was with Dillon, Read Capital, Inc., the predecessor firm to DGHM. Through her current and past participation on advisory committees at the NASD, New York Stock Exchange and The Investment Company Institute, Holly is actively involved with the changing structure of today's capital markets. Holly earned her Bachelor of Arts from Rutgers College in 1978.

Joel Steinmetz is currently Senior Vice President for Equities and Head of Strategy for the Americas for Instinet Corporation. In his role as head of the U.S. Business Strategy Team, Mr. Steinmetz supports the Chief Operating Officer and the members of the U.S. Equity Operating Committee in developing and implementing U.S. business strategy. He also works closely with the business segment leaders and regional business managers to formulate Instinet's global trading product strategy.

Mr. Steinmetz joined Instinet in 1990, and has acted as head of the arbitrage desk, the convertible arbitrage desk, the index arbitrage desk, and the program desk. Previously, he was a member of the Commodities Exchange, trading gold and silver contracts.

Mr. Steinmetz has a B.A. in History from Queens College, the City University of New York and is a graduate of New York University Law School.

Natan Tiefenbrun is responsible for institutional brokerage products & services at Instinet Corporation. Mr. Tiefenbrun oversees the evolution and execution of the Company's business strategy in areas including Client-Site Trading, Client & Market Connectivity, Execution Management technology, Portfolio Trading, Rules-Based Trading, Transaction Cost Estimation &

Measurement, Equity & Foreign-Exchange Crossing, and International Equity Trading.

Mr. Tiefenbrun joined Instinet in 1993 in London and relocated with his wife to New York in March 2000. Mr. Tiefenbrun graduated from the University of Edinburgh with a B.Sc. in Computing Science with honors.

Bruce Turner joined CIBC World Markets, the U.S. investment-banking subsidiary of the Canadian Imperial Bank of Commerce (NYSE:BCM), as a Managing Director and Head of U.S. Equity Trading in April, 2002. Turner is responsible for all day-to-day U.S. equity trading floor activity. Turner joined CIBC World Markets from the Nasdaq Stock Market, where, as executive vice president of Transaction Services, he led the effort to develop the SuperMontage trading system.

Before he joined Nasdaq in July of 2001, Turner spent nine years at Salomon Smith Barney. He was head of equity trading for Nasdaq stocks from 1998-2001. Prior to his service at Salomon Smith Barney, Turner worked as a position trader for Oppenheimer – now CIBC World Markets. He also served on several Nasdaq advisory committees, including the Quality of Markets Committee, before joining Nasdaq.

Turner holds a B.A. in Economics from Connecticut College and currently serves on the board of Directors for Governor Dummer Academy, the oldest preparatory school in the country.

Laura Unger served as the seventy-eighth member of the Securities and Exchange Commission, including Acting Chairman for the six months from February through August 2001. During her time as Acting Chairman, Ms. Unger tackled a number of complex and timely issues, including analyst conflicts; the impact of Regulation Fair Disclosure on information flow; and unregulated internet portals.

As Commissioner, Ms. Unger's primary focus was technology. She looked at how the SEC could optimize the benefits of technology for investors, culminating in a groundbreaking 1999 report: 'Online Brokerage: Keeping Apace of Cyberspace,' earning her an award for 'Technology Person of the Year' that year. She went on to implement many of the report's recommendations.

After resigning her Commissioner seat, Ms. Unger joined CNBC, taking on the role of Regulatory Expert. As Regulatory Expert, she provided televised commentary about business, financial and market related issues. She currently has a portfolio of company directorships and consulting and speaking engagements. Ms. Unger serves on several advisory boards, including the U.S. Institute Non Member Advisory Board, the SEC Historical Society Commissioner Advisory Board and the Wall Street Lawyer Advisory Board.

Before joining the Commission, Ms. Unger served as Securities Counsel to the United States Senate Committee on Banking, Housing and Urban Affairs. Prior to working on Capitol Hill, Ms. Unger was an attorney with the SEC's Enforcement Division. She received a B.A. in Rhetoric from the University of California at Berkeley in 1983, and a J.D. from New York Law School in 1987.

Wayne Wagner is a co-founder of Plexus Group, a Los Angeles based firm that provides implementation evaluation and advisory services to U.S. and global money managers, brokerage firms and pension plan sponsors. Mr. Wagner and Plexus Group were chosen as the 1999 Consultant of the Year by Plan Sponsor Magazine. Investment News named him one of the 'Power Elite 25' for 2001.

Plexus Group is an independent subsidiary of JPMorgan Investor Services Company, a division of JPMorgan Chase.

Mr. Wagner is author and editor of *The Complete Guide to Securities Transactions: Improving Performance and Reducing Costs,* John Wiley & Sons, 1989. His most recent publishing effort is a popular investment book written with friend Al Winnikoff entitled *MILLIONAIRE: the simplest explanation of how an index fund can turn your lunch money into a fortune;* Renaissance Books, 2001.

Mr. Wagner has written and spoken frequently on many trading and investment subjects. He has received two Graham and Dodd Awards from the Financial Analysts Journal for excellence in financial writing. Mr. Wagner served as a Regent of the Financial Analysts Seminar and served on the AIMR Blue Ribbon Task Force on Soft Dollars and the AIMR Best Execution Task Force. Mr. Wagner was a founding partner of Wilshire Associates and served as Chief Investment Officer of Wilshire Asset Management. Earlier, Mr. Wagner participated in the design and operation of the first index funds at Wells Fargo Bank.

In an earlier century Mr. Wagner earned a M.S. in Statistics from Stanford University and a B.B.A. in Management Science/Finance from the University of Wisconsin.

Avner Wolf is Chairman of the Department of Economics and Finance, which is the largest department in the Zicklin School of Business at Baruch College. Zicklin is the largest business school in the U.S. and among the best (top 20). Professor Wolf received his PH.D. from Columbia University in Finance. His research is in the derivative Financial Markets. He has published numerous papers in academic as well as in professional journals and worked with Financial Institutions world wide on a variety of projects on derivatives. He has co-authored the book entitled *The Handbook of Interest Rate Risk Management,* which is used intensively by professionals.

Robert Wood is a Distinguished Professor of Finance at the University of Memphis. Professor Wood previously taught at Penn State University for 14 years and NYU for one year. His education includes a Ph.D. in Finance from the University of Pittsburgh, a Masters in Operations Research from Stanford University, and a Bachelor in Economics from the University of Washington. He was a member of the Presidential Task Force on Market Mechanisms (The Brady Commission) that studied the market crash in 1987, and a founding member of the NASD Economic Advisory Board. Professor Wood is the founder and Executive Director of the Institute for the Study of Security Markets, a nonprofit Educational Foundation that promotes securities markets research by providing transactions data to academic institutions. He has consulted for various stock exchanges and investment firms around the world. Prior to becoming an academic, Professor Wood held various positions in industry over a fifteen-year period.

Steven Wunsch is a twenty-year veteran of Wall Street. He has written and spoken frequently on the structure and regulation of equities trading. During the 1990s, he was founder and president of the Arizona Stock Exchange, a company formed to design, build, market and operate an electronic single price auction trading system. Previously, Mr. Wunsch worked in the Financial Futures Department of Kidder, Peabody, where he was a Vice President responsible for the Department's institutional customer index futures and equity trading activities. Prior to joining Kidder, Peabody, he was a floor trader and broker on the AMEX Commodities and New York Futures Exchanges. Mr. Wunsch received a B. A. in English Literature in 1969 from Princeton University.

INDEX

9781402075100